Messiah

A Life Worth Living: C.S. Woods (1943–2007)

For Josephine

Love,
Francis

by Francis Woods

Foreword by Justin Welby,
Archbishop of Canterbury

Copyright © 2017 Francis Woods

All rights reserved.

ISBN-13: 978-1978433205

ISBN-10: 1978433204

DEDICATION

For Muther

CONTENTS

ACKNOWLEDGEMENTS

The creation of this memoir has been a team effort, with valuable contributions from a wide variety of people – there are too many to name, but I am hugely grateful to all those who have participated in one way or another. In addition to family, friends, clergy and parishioners, Jane Teal at Christ's College (NZ), and Phyllis M. Gilbert at Dartmouth College (USA), prepared extraordinary quantities of information relating to my father's time at school and at university respectively. Jane even gave me a guided tour of Christ's, divulging all sorts of fascinating trivia to keep the jetlag at bay.

I fulfilled the role of Head Chef in the family, but there were many cooks in the kitchen, chopping away sharply and adding morsels here and there. Mum, wife Emma, siblings Isabella, Madeline, Thomas and Lydia, uncle Richard and aunt Joanna: all provided remarkable levels of moral and practical support, and – along with dear friends Rev Bob Hopkins, Oliver Wright, Jonathan Stewart and Fleur Swaney – annoyingly accurate corrections and ingenious suggestions to my drafts.

Isabella was particularly generous with her time and expertise, lending her professional proofreading eye to the text with a level of minute precision hitherto reserved for quantum physics. Any remaining errors therefore only prove my cosmic levels of illiteracy. Thomas accompanied me to St Helens to conduct a number of interviews in return for a solitary pie at half-time during a Saints match at Langtree Park. Lydia contributed a poignant account of Dad's last hours, as well as a number of wonderful songs for his anniversary party. Madeline was her usual wise old self, suggesting various theological clarifications, and guffawing charitably at (some of) my jokes.

The advice of Richard and Joanna (herself a published author) was immensely valuable, particularly in helping me to clarify that this was a memoir, not a biography – suiting my rather informal style, and that of my father. Aunts Marianne and Sally provided wonderful hospitality in New Zealand as I followed in Dad's footsteps.

Emma deserves an Oscar for Best Supporting Wife, setting aside her statutory demands on my time and allowing me to take countless evenings and entire weekends away from her – and then her and our newborn son Josiah – so that I could beaver away at the book. She accompanied me to New Hampshire and New Zealand, latterly with a five-month-old baby in tow. She has been a constant source of counsel and encouragement. And she has no intention of letting me write another book ever again.

Lastly, Mum has been a true inspiration in my attempts to capture the heart and purpose of the man she married 40 years ago. Listening to her describe his life – and his death – has been momentous, and reinforced what a woman of courage and compassion she is. Someday, somebody should write a book about her life.

Francis Woods, September 2017

Edward Woods, President of the Institution of Civil Engineers (1886), Kik's great-great-grandfather

+ Ordained
++ Bishop

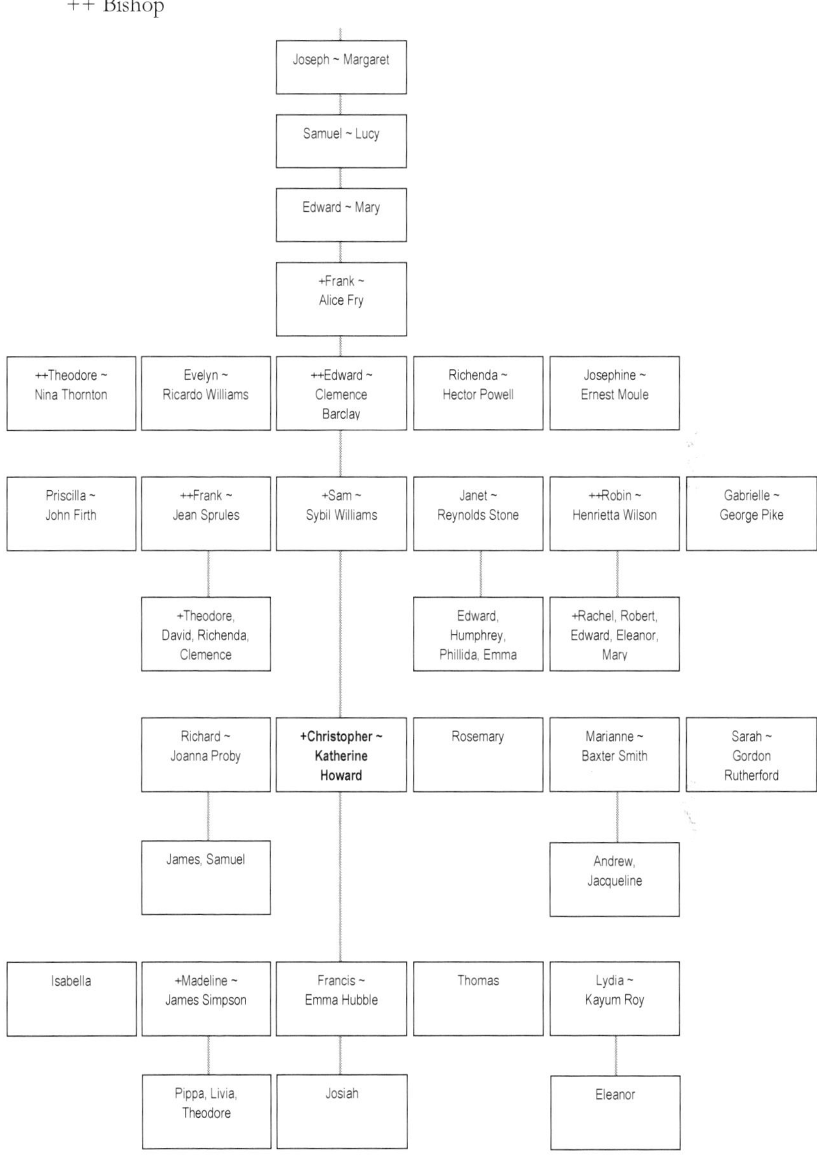

Rev Woods and Rev Welby together at St James' Vicarage, Southam, c.1996

FOREWORD

Kik is one of those people who most shaped my own life and ministry. I miss him to this day, particularly his wisdom and imagination, both spiritually driven, yet utterly earthed in reality.

In 1991, I spent four weeks on placement at Fingerpost. It changed my whole view of ministry, entirely positively. I saw clearly the need to identify and be with those in the parish; I knew it before, but saw it lived. I saw the utter realism that Kik and Kathy showed about the joys and the difficulties and their deep affection for each other, for the church and for the area. The humour and love combined in a way that I have also seen in Jean Vanier, talking about living in community.

When we moved to Liverpool in 2007 I was more than a little nervous, but we kept on saying to each other at home, "Well, we will see plenty of the Woods". It was not to be and I remember the grim day of Kik's leaving us, combined with the deep grief of the family and yet utter trust in Christ. It was the Woods all over, honest and faithful, holy and humorous.

This book is not about someone famous (although his family was), except in a relatively small corner of the Church, but it is about someone significant. Kik was prone to saying that his job was to wash Jesus' feet, yet he was remarkably good at letting Jesus wash his. The reality of that intimacy with Christ, and the obedience to the foot-washing call will make him famous in God's presence. It is worth reading for the desire it brings to love Christ, and to follow Christ, for those who follow find themselves in the place where there are no more tears and weeping, and where we live in the true light which Kik so faithfully proclaimed.

Justin Welby, Archbishop of Canterbury, October 2017

PREFACE

The decision to write this book came after an accumulation of small queries. Having read Robert Gray's brilliant obituary of my father in *The Daily Telegraph*, clergy and parishioners would ask what he was really like before his conversion and ordination, while family and friends would wonder what on earth he was up to in St Helens all those years. With Robert's magnificent template in hand, I reflected that it would be appropriate to write a more detailed account of my father's life – to commemorate the 10th anniversary of his death.

There are two things to note. Firstly, readers will observe a rather clumsy literary device: it wasn't easy to decide how to refer to my father throughout this book – I always knew him as Dad; family and family friends knew him as Kik; and yet schoolmates, parishioners and fellow clergy knew him as Chris. So, in the tradition of biblical name changes following an encounter with God (Abram to Abraham, Simon to Peter, Saul to Paul etc.), the Kik of the first half becomes Chris in the second, to symbolise his transformation. I refer to him as Dad when making personal observations.

Secondly, I must state clearly that although the book does detail how demanding it was for my parents to live and minister in St Helens, I want to honour its people in this memoir – just as Dad honoured them in life. As he once said himself, quoting 1 Corinthians 3:2, they were "written on our hearts". He and Mum were passionate about their ministry, they made many friends, and as a family we were very happy living there despite the complexities. For every burglary or belligerent parishioner, there was ten times more hospitality and humour.

***

In the preface to his biography of Bishop Edward Sydney Woods (published by Student Christian Movement (SCM) Press, 1957), Oliver Tomkins articulated a challenge and a character which is equally true for Edward's grandson, Christopher:

> *I knew that E.S.W. would be a hard figure to capture on paper. He was essentially a man of charm, and charm is never adequately described: it has to be met. But it was not merely a natural charm (though it was that): it was also compounded with grace…Edward's life is a singular example of 'the grace of our Lord Jesus Christ' working upon naturally lovable human endowments. I must be one of thousands who admired him first for his looks, his voice, his vigour, his laughter, and who then found, and quickly, that he led me beyond himself to the Lord whom he served.*

PROLOGUE

Flashbulb memories. The reason we remember those key moments in life – those JFK-9/11-Road-to-Damascus moments – is because they trigger critical levels of surprise, consequentiality and emotion. They resonate so loudly and deeply in our consciousness that clear echoes can be recalled years later, accompanied by pristine sights, sounds and smells.

A little after 6pm on Sunday 9th December 2007 I was in Juba, South Sudan, when the satellite phone started to ring. Even now I can picture the exact spot in the reception area of the office where I was standing, facing the front door, preparing for another week as Deputy Country Director for the humanitarian aid agency Medair – my last week of a long year before flying home for a Christmas break. And I can recall vividly that my heart sank through the floor.

You could argue that this was a perfectly rational response to the satellite phone going off – after all, it was the contingency phone, and generally only used in an emergency. The satellite phone ringing on a Sunday evening in South Sudan might well be cause for concern: one of our staff might have been shot, or shelled, or electrocuted, crashed a car, drowned, been bitten by a snake, stung by a scorpion, or chomped by a crocodile. Perhaps another goat had broken into the maize store in Melut and gorged itself to an explosive death. Perhaps there had been another cholera outbreak and we needed to respond. There were plenty of logical reasons to be a little unsettled by the satphone ringing, not least because the docking station it was in hadn't worked properly for weeks.

And yet, and yet…this was different. Something in that sinister little ringtone was triggering critical levels of surprise, consequentiality and emotion.

I walked into the office, picked the handset out of the docking station, extended the aerial, and made my way out of the front door. It was a typically hot and tropical Juba evening, and as I stepped outside I was enveloped by a heavy humidity emanating from the Nile nearby. Standing in the front yard, away from the mango tree, I held the phone in the air for a few seconds to allow it to connect to the satellite before answering. The generator was thudding away loudly on the other side of the yard and the voice on the other end was very quiet and distant…but no matter. Three words got my attention: "France, it's Bell."

Immediate calculation: satellite phone, Sunday evening, sister calling. Unprecedented. Someone's dead. Grandparents are already dead. Must be Mum or Dad or a sibling. Not Isabella.

"Hi Bell. What's going on?"

"France…it's Dad."

"OK..."

"He's had a stroke, a bad one. He's in intensive care on a ventilator. I'm in the car heading up there now."

"OK."

Pause. I'm staring at the large blue water pipes coiled beside the base of the mango tree. The generator continues its deafening judder.

"France, it's not looking good. He's unconscious. The doctors are recommending family to come now as we don't know how long he has left."

"OK."

Another pause. I'm looking at the dust now, beside my feet.

"France, I'm really sorry to tell you like this…you need to come home."

"No, it's fine Bell. It's fine. Thanks for calling. I'll see if I can get a flight. Keep me posted."

"Yes, I will."

"OK."

And that was that. I hung up, slid the aerial back into the handset, and stood there glaring at the ground trying to compute. Normally I would stand here on the phone to one of my team, figuring out how to get drugs to a clinic cut off by floods, or how to drill boreholes in the middle of nowhere in a country the size of Western Europe. Humanitarian aid work is mostly about finding practical solutions to complex problems in very complex environments.

And now I'm just standing there, staring at the soil, mind blank. No solutions. I stand out there for quite a while. I take in the earth around my feet, scattered with dry and dusty mango leaves; the office, with its overhanging tin roof and fading white exterior; the bamboo fence with its razor wire around the top; the brick generator house with its chimney belching out black diesel fumes; and back to those coiled blue water pipes lying on the roots of the mango tree.

But basically I'm blind to it all – blinded by the flashbulb.

I sit down against the water pipes and kind of dry-sob for a bit. It's been a while since I cried and my tear ducts are not working. I feel a pang of guilt. *Dad's dying and you can't cry! Your own father!* I reason that I am probably in shock. In the end I just sit there, on the dry dirt, reverberating inside and out.

Eventually I get up and try to get on with things. I call Klaas van Mill, the Country Director, who had passed my satphone number to Isabella. He has already arranged flights the following morning to Nairobi and onward to London. He is immensely supportive, a pillar of strength. I wander back into the office. I actually finish some emails, as well as a PowerPoint presentation of the year's achievements I was due to make at the staff Christmas conference that week.

I then drift down the corridor to my room to pack. After a few minutes, my trusty old iPod randomly selects the Aled Jones version of *You Raise Me Up* by Westlife – a cheesy version of a very cheesy song by a very, very cheesy band. The opening lyrics are as follows:

When I am down and, oh my soul, so weary;
When troubles come and my heart burdened be;
Then I am still and wait here in the silence,
Until you come and sit awhile with me.

You raise me up so I can stand on mountains;
You raise me up to walk on stormy seas;
I am strong when I am on your shoulders;
You raise me up to more than I can be.

And now my tear ducts are working. They are working very well indeed.

***

Earlier that day Dad had been taking a service at St Andrew's, Dentons Green, just up the road from his usual patch as Rector of the Parish Church in St Helens, an old coal-mining town in the north-west of England. The usual vicar had the flu. Dad was in the pulpit and about to baptise two children when suddenly he stopped, raised his hands to his head, and said, "I'm sorry, but I don't think I can continue". A doctor in the congregation helped him slowly to the vestry. There he collapsed.

He had suffered a major subarachnoid haemorrhage – a very rare form of stroke (only 5 per cent of cases) in which a blood vessel in the brain balloons and then explodes. 50 per cent of cases are fatal, and even if the patient survives they are normally severely disabled.

Lydia, then aged 18 and the last of the five children to be living at home, explains Dad's final moments:

It's worth mentioning that the day before was notable for Justin Welby's Installation as Dean of Liverpool Cathedral, to which we had been invited. Beforehand at home, the three of us were in the kitchen and Mum was peeling boiled eggs by the sink. In a brief conversation lull, Dad quietly moved over to the sink and began helping Mum do the eggs, without a word. I was taken aback as helping with the cooking wasn't like him at all! I also remember him being very relaxed and quietly content that whole day as we were celebrating in the Cathedral.

His last words to me that evening were, 'Night, Small', and a lovely big hand on my head. I woke up on Sunday morning to Dad's voice bellowing up the stairs to Mum: 'See you later, Sweet, I'm off to take a baptism at St Andrew's'. These were the last words I heard him say.

Later that morning, Mum came into the living room to tell me she'd had a call from St Andrew's saying that Dad had a headache and wasn't doing very well, so she went over there. Not long after, the phone rang. It was Mum – she sounded worried and was on the way to the hospital with Dad in an ambulance.

Mum's experience at St Andrew's had been traumatic:

When I arrived at the church, I found he had been taken to the vestry where he had collapsed in a coma. My heart sank as I could see by his eyes that he was not with us. But his body seemed to be struggling to get himself up. I prayed and prayed for healing and resurrection with a lovely Christian nurse and doctor from the congregation, but nothing happened...I had to let him go.

Back at the Rectory, a woman from the parish church congregation greeted Lydia at the door – "I'm afraid it's critical," she said, and took her straight to the hospital:

I arrived at A&E to find Mum looking horribly distressed and it hit me that it was bad. Dad was on a bed behind a curtain, totally unconscious and breathing these ugly forced breaths, caused by the life support machine, which I'll never forget. I panicked and started weeping and shouting, 'I don't want him to die'.

I went outside to make a few calls, and Dad was moved to a private room. Mum then told me that the surgeon had given us two options: they operate, and, if he survives, which would be unlikely, he would almost certainly be in a vegetative state; or we let him die. It was obvious the latter was right, and we didn't spend much time deciding. David Jennings [then Bishop of Warrington], *James Jones* [then Bishop of Liverpool] *and Justin* [Welby] *all visited during the day. They were incredibly supportive.*

At one point it was just Dad and me in the room. I sat next to him and cried, leaning on his big arm which was flat and lifeless on the bed, his big chest breathing weirdly. I just chatted to him and sort of prayed at the same time, telling him how much I loved him, and I made a little vow – now gladly fulfilled – that I would write a song for him.

Robert and Georgie Woods then arrived. He was just talking tearfully to Dad, saying things such as "You're like my brother" and recalling memories they'd shared.

Isabella, Thomas and cousin James all arrived together in the evening. I remember James kneeling beside Dad, Thomas standing next to him, and both weeping a lot and quite loudly. I remember us all standing around the bed, tears streaming down our cheeks – but then also quoting and mimicking Dad and absolutely cracking up! Later we all went into a room with a kind female doctor who told us that were Dad to be taken off life support he could either die within a couple of hours or last for several days or weeks.

We decided to take him off life support.

We called Justin and asked him to come back and pray a final farewell to Dad with us. We sang hymns, prayed and cried together. It was an intensely moving time. We then left Mum there and went home. Isabella and I slept in Mum and Dad's bed.

We got a call from Mum in the night to say that Dad had died at 2:10am, his hand in hers.

***

Back in Juba, Isabella called me first thing on Monday morning to say that Dad had died during the night. She was immensely strong and loving, a real rock for all of her siblings. She had also made the call to our sister Madeline, who was living in Vancouver with her husband James Simpson, and, like me, was due to head home for Christmas later that week after a long time away.

I was still numb. I said goodbye to my Medair colleagues in the office and boarded the UN plane to Nairobi just before lunch. I then took the overnight Kenya Airways flight to London. I would normally spend a long flight cramming in as many stupid action movies as possible – I'm 6'5" so if I try to sleep either my head will loll over the back of the chair and into the lap of the passenger behind me, or, if I shuffle down in the seat, my legs will splay outwards into the aisle like the tentacles of a giant squid, felling flight attendants and small children. But on this occasion I managed to get an exit row seat beside the window, and found I couldn't concentrate on *Rambo III.* I spent the entire flight looking out at the night sky and weeping very quietly.

At dawn on the morning of Tuesday 11th December I was collected by Rev Tom Gillum and driven up to St Helens. Tom is a man of uncommon warmth and kindness, and we spent the journey reminiscing about Dad and his boisterous ways. As we arrived at the Rectory I was greeted by Isabella, Madeline, Thomas and Lydia, and gave Mum a big hug as she came down the stairs. She sobbed quietly on my shoulder for a short while, which was the first time I'd ever seen her cry – she's not one for public displays of emotion. We passed a few moments together in silence, before being joined by my siblings in a large family embrace. Finally we were all together. All but one.

The atmosphere in those days before and after the funeral ranged from the usual rowdy chatter, crying with laughter as we remembered Dad's mannerisms and signature statements, to disbelief, sadness and tears about the unfairness of it all. Generally – in terms of the five stages of grief – the fact that we were all there to support each other meant that during this initial period we probably moved straight to Acceptance. Denial, Anger, Bargaining and Depression would come later.

Later that afternoon, we children travelled to the mortuary at Whiston Hospital to see Dad one last time; Mum couldn't bring herself to attend, dreading how he would look. The mood was solemn, but not tense. There was a great sense of peace over us as we arrived. It was Madeline who noted that Dad had died bearing a balanced ledger with all of us. As she said in her funeral tribute, "There is nothing outstanding that needs to be said, nothing lacking, nothing missing." We were joined by Tom Gillum and made our way in together, siblings embracing each other in different combinations. As we entered the small Chapel of Rest, where Dad was lying on a simple table on the left against the wall, a few quiet sobs broke out among us. He looked completely content, eyes closed, the most peaceful of smiles on his face, large hands resting on his stomach, as if he were having a snooze after a splendid lunch.

The irony was that he often looked a lot worse when having a snooze in real life – head tilted right back on the sofa, mouth agape, the occasional terrifying grunt and snort breaking the silence in the room. As children, we would approach this slumbering beast with a thrilling mix of caution and curiosity, perhaps venturing to take a closer look at his fillings, or the hair protruding from his ears. And yet, even in a deep sleep, the silverback's mere presence was enough to generate a reassuring sense of security in his troop.

With Dad's troop huddled together beside his mortuary bed, Tom performed a brief ceremonial blessing. After a short time of prayer, and a moment of quiet reflection, everyone made their way out of the room. I stayed behind to say goodbye to my father alone. I stood next to him, my lifelong hero, and felt as though I should say something momentous and meaningful, but I had no words. The flashbulbs were going off again. How do you say a final goodbye to your father? I reached out to hold his hands, and was shocked by how cold and rigid they were. And so I stood there, his hands in mine, and just enjoyed standing in his presence once again. He was reassuring even in death. After a few minutes, I placed a hand on his forehead, uttered a quiet, "Bye, Dad," and walked out of the room to join the others outside.

When uncle Richard Woods arrived from New Zealand the following morning, he and Mum agreed that they would go to the hospital together. Richard had worked in a mortuary as a young man, and was struck by how unusually serene his brother looked – far beyond the presentational skills of the hospital morticians. This was an unexpected comfort for them both, and brought an added measure of closure.

***

The funeral was a wonderful occasion. After some discussion we decided that it should take place at Liverpool Cathedral, where Dad had been a canon. In many ways it would have been more appropriate to do it in St Helens, to reflect Dad's ministry there for nearly 30 years, and he would no doubt have wanted it to be at Holy Trinity, Parr Mount, where he had taken so many funerals himself. But we weren't sure Holy Trinity or the Parish Church would be big enough; we also wanted to send him off with a bit of oomph – and you can get serious amounts of oomph in the world's longest cathedral with the UK's largest organ.

The funeral limousine was oddly comforting and familiar, given we'd had one previously as the family car (Dad had a eureka moment on the way to a crematorium and bought one from a local funeral director). En route to the Cathedral in the funeral convoy we were all overcome by a major fit of the giggles as we impersonated Dad, which must have been a little disconcerting to the pedestrians who were stopping and making the sign of the cross as we passed.

The 21st of December was a clear, freezing day and there was a small crowd waiting for us outside the main entrance to the Cathedral, at the front of which was Justin Welby, along with the funeral director and the other pall-bearers. Thomas and cousin James went at the front; cousin Edmund Howard and I went in the middle; while James Simpson and cousin George Woods brought up the rear – we were arranged in ascending order of height (George is an impressive 6'7").

Unfortunately, we hadn't realised that Dad would go in head first, which meant that the weight of his torso – and Dad was a pretty solid citizen – was borne almost entirely by Thomas and James at the front. By the time we had processed up the steps of the Great West Porch, through the Well, up another set of steps, and then all the way along the main sanctuary to the Chancel, we had walked – or rather shuffled, slowly – almost 100 metres, or over 300 feet. As we lowered the coffin carefully onto the bier, it's fair to say that Thomas and James were looking a little flustered.

Over 600 people were present at Liverpool Cathedral that day to celebrate a life well lived. It was a tremendous occasion: a wonderful turnout of friends, family and clergy; a brilliant sermon from Justin; glorious music, with choristers including aunt Diane Howard and cousin Henry Howard; a eulogy by uncle Richard; a Bible reading by Rev Bob Hopkins (curate at Holy Trinity for 14 years); prayers and a reading from *The Pilgrim's Progress* by cousins Rev Rachel Benson and Robert Woods; and a moving set of tributes from the five children. Most remarkable was Mum, who managed to say her heartfelt words of love and lament to Dad in his coffin with great courage and tenderness.

***

So this book tells the story of the life of my father, Christopher Samuel Woods. Two lives really, because his 64 years on this planet came in two quite distinct halves. As Richard said in his eulogy: "During the first half no one would have predicted the second half".

Dad himself would draw comparisons with the Parable of the Prodigal Son. His was a life of cheerful, rumbustious deviation away from the family trade of ordained ministry – sent down from the prestigious Dartmouth College in New Hampshire after five terms, jailed in Honolulu, cavalier escapades in various far-flung corners of the planet – which was halted in its tracks by an extraordinary divine epiphany on a remote New Zealand highway, galvanised by marriage to a beautiful Catholic aristocrat, and followed by a life as a cheerful, rumbustious vicar, with a clear vocation to minister in one of the toughest parishes in possibly the toughest diocese in all of England.

This is also a personal story. Dad was an immense figure in the lives of his wife and five children. We all revered him. Partly this was because of his character – by turns wise, funny, passionate, stern, irreverent, authoritative, loving, aloof, warm, strong, vulnerable. Mainly it was because of his inspirational integrity and authenticity. Throughout his life he remained true to himself and his love of people, whatever the circumstances.

When he was struggling at Dartmouth, aged 19, he wrote to his scholarship benefactor and outlined his world view:

> *Now what is important in life, Aunt Helen? Is it two numbers on a sheet of paper at the end of a term, or is it an ability, acknowledged by those in contact with you, to organise, socialise, and generally assume responsibilities of certain kinds?*

It took him a while to find out what this really meant – his true calling in life as a clergyman, a pastor to those most in need – but when he did he remained totally committed to it until the end. He was lost, and was found.

PART ONE - BEFORE CHRIST

Rt Rev Edward Woods, Bishop of Lichfield, Kik's grandfather

CHAPTER 1
The Firm

The Parish of Ross and South Westland, in New Zealand's South Island, spanned an astonishing 240 miles of the most remote wetland territory. Shimmering lakes, mangroves and lagoons, extraordinarily dense tropical forests, and magnificent snow-topped mountains – all featured along the parish's coastal expanse, from the tiny gold-rush settlement of Jackson Bay in the south, up through the glaciers of Aoraki National Park to the small village of Ross in the north. Rev Samuel Woods, with his wife Sybil, arrived in March 1941 and ministered there for 18 months.

The coastal road didn't exist back then so Sam spent days and weeks at a time travelling around his parish by single-propeller aircraft, horseback, and on one occasion by hitching a lift on a passing ship. The newly married couple were very happy in this robust, remote environment. Sybil was delighted to see that Sam's shoulders were broadening thanks to his regular wood chopping – the Vicarage at Harihari was without power or running water. Their first child, Richard, was born up the coast in Greymouth on 20th September 1941.

On 1st November 1942, Sam was due to report for duty as the new Chaplain to the Royal New Zealand Air Force (RNZAF) in the North Island city of Rotorua. The wilderness was not an easy place to leave, either emotionally or practically. As Sam and Sybil departed Harihari in early October, their old V8 station wagon struggled to make it up the vertiginous Arthur's Pass. While Sam continued to floor the accelerator, sending large chunks of the scree surface spitting in all directions, his wife – by now heavily pregnant with their second child – marched to the back of the vehicle and proceeded to push with all her might. Richard observed all of this with interest from his bassinet on the back seat. Eventually they pulled through, and after three days and nights of travel, by car, train, ship and plane, they arrived in the city of Napier on the east coast of the North Island.

It was here that Sybil's parents were based – her father, Wilfred Williams, was Superintendent of the mission to Maori in the dioceses of Waiapu (in Napier) and Wellington. While Sam would commence his duties at the barracks in Rotorua, 136 miles away, Sybil would remain with her parents to await new life in January. Where Greymouth had been a rather gloomy place to give birth, Napier was relatively fresh and charming. Much of it had been destroyed by a major earthquake in 1931, and had been rebuilt in the delightfully quirky Art Deco fashion of the day.

Sam was convinced they were expecting a girl. His father Edward, the Bishop of Lichfield, had made it clear that there were enough boys in the family already and so Sam and Sybil had taken to referring to the bump as "Gabrielle Mary". Sybil touched on this in a letter to Edward and Clemence, Sam's mother, dated 31st August 1942:

> *Now that* [Sam's sister] *Janet has had another little son I feel quite overwhelmed by the onus and responsibility of giving you a grand-daughter! I shan't know how to break the news if I dare to have another son – though I shan't mind a bit. We are hoping that it'll be a little girl – Sam says he feels it in his bones that it's*

a girl, but I'm refusing to set my heart on it as that only makes for disappointments. So please don't be too disgusted if you have a sixth grandson!

***

Christmas and New Year passed, and as the clock ticked towards the arrival of "Gabrielle Mary" in mid-January 1943, Sybil was able to spend valuable time with her parents, Wilfrid and Madeline. Sybil had only recently paused her work as General Secretary for the New Zealand Student Christian Movement (SCM), which involved travelling all over the country organising events and giving talks. She described one such occasion in the same letter to Edward and Clemence:

I was in Christchurch for four days last week, to speak at two public meetings for the Campaign for Christian Order – one in the afternoon for 'smart society' women (charming pagans!), and the other in the evening for shop and factory girls. There were about 300 at each meeting and it was most encouraging to see that the majority of them were non-Church-goers. I spoke for just over an hour on 'The World-Wide Church' – tracing the history of the Church from the Middle Ages till the present day, and bringing in the Faith and Order and Life and Work Movements, the great Missionary Conferences, and the Churches' stand today in Germany, Norway, Holland and China.

This was an impressive woman. Sybil had been Head Prefect for two years on the trot at Whanganui Girls' College, and Dux (top of her class) in her last year at school. At a time when girls' education was still fairly patchy, she had educated herself through various scholarships, from the time she entered a private kindergarten through to gaining her MA degree in Latin and French at Victoria University College, Wellington, and then a Diploma of Education at London University. When she was awarded the prestigious Johanna Lohse Scholarship during her undergraduate studies, the Bishop of Christchurch – Chairman of the Trustees – mentioned that they had never had such an easy task in making an award.

More importantly for her missionary parents, Sybil had also demonstrated a precocious thirst for spiritual development. She had represented the New Zealand University Branch of the Student Christian Movement at the Pacific Area Conference in California. While studying in England in the late 1930s she led parts of the SCM Annual Conference at Swanwick, where she met Sam's younger brother Robin (a curate, and Assistant Secretary of SCM). Sybil then attended the SCM International Conference in France, before carrying out a month's tour of addresses to various branches of SCM in North America and Canada. On her return to New Zealand, she was appointed Southern Hemisphere representative of the World Executive of the World Student Christian Foundation – before taking on the role of General Secretary of the NZSCM.

So it is fair to say that Sybil was a good match, both in mind and in soul, for Sam. She attributed this to her family's long heritage of missionary work in New Zealand. Her great-great-grandfather, Henry Williams, was the first Church Missionary Society (CMS) representative to settle permanently in New Zealand, arriving in the Bay of Islands on 6th August 1823.

Henry was a strong character. His father, Thomas, was Sheriff of Nottingham in the late 18th century. But in 1804, Thomas caught typhus and was dead within a few days. The twelve-year-old Henry longed to help his mother and to prove himself independent so that she could focus on his younger siblings. In 1805, England celebrated the news of Nelson's victory over Napoleon's French fleet at the Battle of Trafalgar – and in 1806, Henry signed on as a midshipman on HMS Barfleur. He was fourteen.

Over the next nine years, Henry saw service in several ships and took part in many engagements, first in the war with France and later against the fledgling USA. When he was only fifteen, at the second Battle of Copenhagen in 1807, he was in the heat of the action both afloat and ashore, eventually manning the land batteries as the British bombarded

Napoleon's Danish allies. And in 1815, by then a lieutenant aged 23, Henry was one of the senior crew asked to sail the captured US *President* back to England from New York. They ran into a severe storm and the captured crew took advantage of the tempest to break free and attempt to retake the ship – a sharp hand-to-hand engagement on the decks ensued, but the Americans were defeated.

The whole incident made a lasting impression on Henry, and as he returned home he began to think more seriously than ever before about the purpose and direction of his life. While visiting his mother back in Nottingham, Henry renewed his friendship with members of the Coldham family, whose father had been Mayor of Nottingham at the same time that his father Thomas had been Sheriff. The Coldhams had a daughter, Marianne. She is described at this time as having 'a very gracious personality, but under an apparent sweet gentleness there was an unbending will.' She no doubt found plenty that was romantic about the much-travelled young naval officer, and they were married in January 1818.

Five years later, with three children in tow, and with Henry having become ordained, they set sail on a CMS supply ship bound for the pioneer mission field of New Zealand and its warring tribes of indigenous Maori, piratical whalers, and increasing numbers of European settlers. They were joined soon after by Henry's younger brother, William Williams, an Oxford scholar, and his wife Jane. The legacy of the Williams family in New Zealand would become legendary.

Their primary legacy was spiritual. They lived amongst a people who, to them, could be strangely terrifying and brutal (some of whom would occasionally practise cannibalism), while trying to pastor them on the nature of Christian love and forgiveness. A letter from Thomas Williams, Henry's son, captures the context well:

> *When a little boy, some five years old, I strayed, contrary to orders, early one fine morning as far as a large pā* [fortified village] *not*

> *far from my father's house. I saw a number of warriors, who had finished their breakfast, outside the pā, all fully armed, lying prostrate on the ground praying to their god Whiro for strength to fight…*
>
> *I peeped in at the corner of the pā – I there saw three Maori lads, about ten years of age, with a kit of hot steaming potatoes between them. They had each a small pointed stick, with which they were conveying the potatoes to their mouths; but before they ate them, they pointed them with a jeer at a fresh cut-off Maori head, fully tattooed, stuck up on a stick!*
>
> *You may not quite believe all I tell you, but you may believe me when I tell you that, being myself then rather a fat little chap, I scampered home as fast as my fat little legs could carry me.*

And yet there was a surge in Maori conversions to Christianity. William even translated the Bible into the *Ngapuhi* dialect. There are many testimonies of Maori individuals choosing Christianity because of its emphasis on love and respect, and the idea of going to Heaven was certainly appealing at a time when life expectancy was so limited by war.

No doubt there was an element of expediency on the part of some chiefs, who sought to build strong links with the powerful newcomers. Others were apparently convinced merely by the strength of character shown by Henry and Marianne. On one occasion, after the mission station had been raided by a Maori party and Henry threatened to leave, Chief Tohitapu – who only weeks earlier had been on the verge of killing Henry with his spear – led the mediation and made an impassioned speech in favour of the missionaries staying. Henry's steadfastness had won him many admirers.

Economically, Henry and William – along with their children – developed increasingly successful methods of arable and pastoral farming in often harsh conditions, and established access to world markets which contributed to the sustainability of the fledgling Commonwealth nation.

Politically, it was Henry who was asked to translate the 1840 Treaty of Waitangi (although this was primarily due to the fact that his brother William, a far superior linguist, was on a mission to another part of the island). The Treaty allowed the Maori chiefs to agree a formal union with the British – the only one of its kind anywhere in the Empire – which guaranteed certain rights and lands. Henry's son Samuel was also influential in the creation of the Young Maori Party, which went on to play a vital role in the resurgence of Maoridom in the early 20th century.

Socially, Samuel was also responsible for the establishment of Te Aute College, a secondary school dedicated to the education of Maori boys.

In 1915, when someone in the House of Representatives questioned the Williams legacy (the Treaty of Waitangi had not delivered the peace and stability between Maori and colonists which had been intended), it was the respected elder, Maori MP Sir Apirana Ngata, who rose to his feet and defended the Williamses passionately:

> *No family in this country, I doubt whether any family in any country in the world, has done so much for any group of people as the Williams family has done for the Maoris.*

And so it was, as the daughter of Wilfred Williams, that Sybil had inherited such a wonderfully rich family tradition of Christian service. It was fitting that she was now in Napier, part of the Waiapu Diocese which her ancestors had established, as she prepared to add to the family tree.

***

Sam, meanwhile, was alone in the barracks at Rotorua and focusing on his new role as Chaplain to the Royal New Zealand Air Force. He was the third of six children to Edward and Clemence Woods, the others being Priscilla, Frank, Janet, Robin and Gabrielle (Edward apparently followed his own strict rules on gender diversity). Like Sybil, Sam could claim another extraordinary family lineage of Christian dedication, predominantly Quaker in origin, but more recently Church of England – his father was Bishop of Lichfield, and his uncle Theodore had been Bishop of Winchester. His older brother Frank would go on to become Archbishop of Melbourne and Primate of Australia, while his younger brother Robin would serve as Dean of Windsor and Bishop of Worcester.

The Quaker background originated with Joseph Woods (1738–1812), a prosperous wool merchant who lived at White Hart Court on Gracechurch Street, at the heart of the City of London. He was a member of the Society of Friends and played a prominent role in the anti-slavery movement. His wife, Margaret Woods, was well known among the Quakers for her writings, and excerpts from *The Journal of Margaret Woods* could be found in most Friends' Meeting House libraries.

Their son, Samuel Woods, was also an active Quaker and in 1797 married Lucy Webb, whose father was also a wealthy businessman in the City. Samuel was a man of broad tastes and interests. He built up a large library and became a Fellow of the Royal Geographical Society. Unfortunately, he devoted so much time to his literary and philanthropic interests that his business was neglected and his fortune dwindled.

A son arrived in 1814, named Edward, and due to the state of the family finances he was forced to make his own way after leaving school at the age of sixteen. He was apprenticed to an engineer in Liverpool, proved himself to be an ingenious mathematician, and eventually became one of the most distinguished civil engineers of his day, becoming President of the Institution of Civil Engineers in 1886.

Edward was an expert in gradients of inclines, the laying of wrought-iron rails on sleepers rather than on stone walls, and the types of gauge best suited to different geographical and geological localities. He was called in as a Consultant Engineer for railway projects in Spain, India, China, Peru and Australia. He was also a consultant to the Montevideo Water Works in

Uruguay and advisor to the Corporation of the City of London on the feasibility of supplying water to households by meter.

Edward lived at 45 Onslow Gardens, a five-storey house in which he installed a hydraulic lift, to the great joy and entertainment of his children and grandchildren (possibly not so joyous for his wife Mary). It was also one of the first houses to be fitted with electricity. For thirty years he attended the morning service at St Jude's Church, Kensington, walking there from his home and always tipping the sweeper at the road crossing. His grandsons, Theodore and Edward, remembered strolling with him in Kensington Gardens on Sunday afternoons. Often the talk would turn to the wonders of science and the solar system, the nature and composition of coal, or the technicalities of some new engineering discovery – this was a man who once challenged the great Isambard Kingdom Brunel in the famous 'battle of the gauges' in 1838. He would pause to draw a diagram in the dust with his walking stick to illustrate what he was describing. He was also a lover of music, and many evenings were devoted to 'home-made' music – a French marquis staying at the hotel in Asnelles, which the Woods tribe had taken over one summer, was heard to remark: *"La famille Woods est pleine de talent"*.

Frank Woods was born to Edward and Mary in November 1846 at 7 Church Street in Liverpool. He was tall, like his father, and very handsome with clear blue eyes, though he was relatively thin and not very robust. It was said of him that, "Frank's presence and looks are an ornament to any platform, whether he says anything or not".

In 1872 he married Alice Fry, whose grandmother was Elizabeth Fry, the prison reformer. Alice was a woman of warm humanity, and her lively, simple Christian faith made a profound impression on all of her children: Theodore, Evelyn, Edward, Richenda and Josephine. Every Saturday in term time, for ten years, she wrote to each of the boys and continued to do so when they went up to Cambridge.

There is no account of how Frank came to offer himself for ordination. It is possible his mother had an influence, and no doubt Alice was entirely supportive of a life committed to Christian service. Either way, in becoming the first Woods to serve the state religion, Frank unwittingly triggered a generational, genetic connection between Church and Woods which has continued unbroken to this day – his great-great-granddaughter Madeline commenced her ordination training in September 2017.

In 1876 Frank became Vicar of All Saints, Hereford, having served his curacy at Chenies, Buckinghamshire, under 'the old saint and courtly wit' Lord Wriothesley Russell, whose only vanity was to buy a new riband for his watch upon each annual visit to the Court of Queen Victoria. The parish population in Hereford was expanding rapidly, and during Frank's time as Vicar he was able to build a church for the Whitecross district as well as restore the lovely spire of the ancient All Saints Church. He became a much-loved figure as he strode about the streets of Hereford with his good looks and long stride.

After nine years, he accepted the living of St Andrew's, Nottingham, serving a large and challenging parish at the northern end of town. Here Frank spent ten busy and happy years, assisted by a succession of fine curates, one of whom, Llewellyn Gwynne, became Bishop of Egypt and the Sudan and remained a lifelong friend of the family. Years afterwards Gwynne wrote:

> *Their home was a regular training ground for spiritual effort, where love, faith and simple goodness reigned supreme – out of that rock Theodore and Edward were hewn…To parents and children religion was natural and informal. The children took to it like ducks to water and larks to the air. They passed from games to prayers, to hymns, to worship, as if they were all one…our Vicar was a real man of God and a good leader.*

Later on he added, "All I have been able to be or do, I learned from my Vicar." Another curate, F.R. Pyper, wrote:

He shrank so from sin, that sin shrank from him. I cannot tell you what a relief it was – oh, the rest it was – to go into his presence. He found room in his conversation for more faith and hope and love than most of us find room for in our prayers. In his presence every man got his due and a little more.

Tragically, at the age of 49, Frank Woods contracted a rare and horrible disease called Pemphigus, where extremely painful, watery blisters form on the skin and lining of the mouth, nose and throat. All efforts to cure him failed and his body was overwhelmed by infection from the sores. As he lay dying his children sang Christmas and Epiphany carols to him, very softly. On 15th January 1896, his last words as he died were, "God be merciful to me, a sinner." Vast crowds attended his funeral, and it was said that Nottingham's florists were working all night before the ceremony.

***

While based in New Zealand, Sam wrote many letters to his father Edward (known as "Far", and occasionally, "Ed-a-whack"). In these, his love of motorcars, trains and aeroplanes is obvious, and there is a clear respect for his brother-in-law, Maurice Williams, who was a decorated Squadron Leader with both the RAF and the RNZAF.

Sam shared this love of engineering with his father, but in many ways it was his uncle Theodore who really stirred his passion for things mechanical. Edward wrote of his brother that, "When travelling by some of the great main-line expresses, he usually found time to inspect the monster locomotive and have some chat with its driver. When he was Bishop of Peterborough he was known in the railway works there as 'the engine man's Bishop.'"

Theodore, like many a Woods before and since, also had a great passion for music. From an early age he was able to sit down and play anything by ear or by sight-reading. At Marlborough College he became an exceptional organist, helped to train the choir, and conducted glee-singing troupes.

And yet, in 1892, when he went up to Trinity College, Cambridge, his enthusiasm for music was increasingly matched by his commitment to his faith – so much so that his regular studies suffered and he secured only a Third Class degree. He then chose to study Theology at Ridley Hall, Cambridge, during which time his father Frank contracted and died of the terrible Pemphigus.

Theodore was now head of the family and this new responsibility meant that he decided to forego the missionary work he had contemplated – family friend Llewellyn Gwynne, the future Bishop of Egypt and the Sudan, was at this time just starting his overseas career as a missionary in East Africa – and instead chose to focus on working in English parishes. On 13th June 1897, Theodore was ordained deacon by Bishop Samuel Wilberforce in Chichester Cathedral, and two weeks later he was engaged to Nina Thornton of Nottingham. There followed two years as a curate at St John's, Eastbourne, and a further two years as curate at Huddersfield Parish Church. During the following twenty years he was vicar of parishes in Herne Hill, Manchester, Bishop Auckland, and Bradford.

His ministry was marked by a loving concern for all his parishioners, whom he got to know in their own homes through regular visits; glorious worship, due to his enthusiastic encouragement of organist, choir and congregation to give their best; authoritative preaching; vigorous organisation; and a vision of the responsibility of the Church to the community.

He was also known for his imposing size. On one occasion, a procession headed by Theodore was making its way through Bradford. Two workmen, repairing the street, leaned on their shovels as the procession passed, and surveyed Theodore's commanding 6'2" frame with admiration. Then one of them remarked loudly, "Eh Bill! I bet yon fellow could shift some muck!"

In June 1916, the Prime Minister, Herbert Asquith, asked Theodore to accept the Bishopric of Peterborough. This was a great tribute to him – he was only 42, he had no degree worth speaking of, and had played little part in central Church affairs. Peterborough was then one of the largest dioceses in England, covering three counties of Northamptonshire, Leicestershire and Rutland, including 600 parishes and 700 clergy. But he had shown conclusively that he had the ear of the common man, strong leadership, and a great vision of the part to be played by Christians in the life of the nation.

During the last two years of the First World War, Theodore urged not only the Church but the nation to prepare for the task of reconstruction that would follow the cessation of hostilities. His speech at the May Session of Convocation in 1917 challenged society to bring an end to the injustice between class and class, nation and nation. He saw the reconstruction of Europe and the resolving of underlying tensions between the principles of Capital and Labour as areas where Christians must take a lead. The "engine man's Bishop" was passionate about both engine and man.

Among Theodore's special gifts was his ability to present the faith in a way which appealed to the working man. His ability to act as a conciliator between employers and employees was reflected in his leadership of the 'Life and Works' ecumenical movement, which concentrated on the practical role of the Church in society, and eventually became one of the foundations for the World Council of Churches. During his time as Bishop of Peterborough and then Bishop of Winchester (from 1923), he also earned the title of "the Walking Bishop" due to his epic walks across the Diocese to conduct pastoral work. In Winchester Cathedral today, there is on display the plain oak shepherd's crook which he used as his staff on these pilgrimages. He would spend up to a month on the hoof, walking from village to village, holding services in the church or in the open air, talking to farm workers and sleeping in the home of a vicar or parishioner each evening. Villagers would accompany him along the way, and so thousands of people came to know their bishop as an approachable friend.

***

Like Theodore, Sam had spent much of his time as Vicar of Ross and South Westland on the move in remote areas of his parish. On one occasion, at Jacob's River, Sam had actually used Theodore's portable Communion set to conduct a Communion service in the house of a toothless old Maori woman called Mrs Smith.

Sam's father, Edward Woods, was also a vigorous walker, a habit formed in part from the time he had spent in Switzerland recuperating from tuberculosis. On 28th January 1907 he had been playing hockey for Ridley Hall, Cambridge, and had scored six goals, when he collapsed into a coughing attack and was despatched immediately to a German sanatorium in Davos, where it took him five years to recover. Two things were ever-present in his rucksack on his walks – the *Book of Common Prayer*, and *The Pilgrim's Progress.*

Edward had followed Theodore to Trinity College, Cambridge, in 1896. He was joyously competitive and loved sports of all kinds, particularly hockey, tennis, golf and rowing. It wasn't unheard of for the Woods family in later years to be found in the Vicarage garden playing an assertive game of hockey after the morning service.

Despite studying diligently for his Theology tripos, taking a strong Second in a year when only one man won a First, there is no record of Edward making a momentous decision to be ordained. His biographer, Rev Oliver Tomkins, noted: "Edward was a classic example of the 'once-born' Christian…his unaffected Christian discipleship flowered inevitably into a desire for ordination". Like his brother Theodore, Edward's great gift was the desire, and rare ability, to make theology and Christian faith seem simple, relevant and attractive to the common man.

His faith was fostered by regular attendance at College Chapel, and at Holy Trinity Church on Market Street. Charles Simeon had been Vicar of Holy Trinity from 1782 to 1836 and had inspired a strong evangelical and missionary zeal there – he was one of the founders of the Church Missionary Society in 1799. In the last quarter of the 19th century, some 150 undergraduates from Holy Trinity joined the CMS – including the famous Cambridge Seven, who went to China in 1885.

Edward's inner circle of six friends all had dreams of becoming missionaries. Among these was his future brother-in-law, Gurney Barclay. Together the six would attend the various conferences and camps run by the Cambridge Inter-Collegiate Christian Union (CICCU). So it wasn't a surprise when, like Theodore, Edward went on to Ridley Hall in 1899 to train for ordination – just as it wasn't a surprise when, many years later, Edward followed Theodore in becoming a bishop, in his case at Lichfield.

What was a surprise, and a very pleasant one at that, was the discovery of Gurney's sister Clemence at the Barclay family home. High Leigh, built in 1853 in a style known as 'Banker's Gothic', was the property of Robert Barclay, scion of the banking dynasty and prominent Christian layman. Robert was married to Ellen, née Buxton, daughter of the notable brewer, abolitionist and social reformer Sir Thomas Fowell Buxton. High Leigh is now a well-known Christian conference centre. It has over 40 acres of gardens, shaped by the famous Pulham landscaping family into some of Hertfordshire's most beautiful countryside – and by 1901 Edward was making the most of this by taking Clemence on long and meaningful walks.

She was tall, fair-skinned, with red-golden hair. Finally, on 13th August 1902, Edward's diary records (in Clemence's hand): "My dear Edward's new birthday – the day he told me he loved me". So began a companionship which was to last nearly fifty years. In later years, when Clemence was often painfully ill, Edward never ceased to love her devotedly and to care for her with great patience. And when she died at last on 14th October 1951, he lasted only a further three months before succumbing to death himself on 11th January 1952.

Sybil later recalled her own experience of 'Grannie' Clemence's devotion to Edward:

> *It was quite embarrassing to go on a long journey with her because she would walk into a shop to buy something in a town hundreds of miles from Lichfield and would say to the bewildered shop assistant, 'I hope you listened to the Bishop's broadcast on Sunday'. 'Which Bishop, Madam?' – a perfectly natural query – would bring a look of incredulous surprise to Grannie's face. To her mind there was only one Bishop who could possibly be worth hearing and that was her Edward.*

Mealtimes were apparently hazardous affairs in her company – in the days of rationing during the Second World War, she would seize the butter unashamedly from her guests' plates and give it to Edward. This watchful solicitude for her husband's nourishment was partly put down to his requirement in Davos to eat extra meals. And so, later in life, one brand of marmalade was known to be for Grandfar only and woe betide any grandchild who helped themselves to the special jar. Sybil learned to hide the children's rations from Grannie whenever they visited Lichfield Palace, to ensure they got their share.

It was while recuperating in the Swiss mountain air in August 1908 that Edward produced his first book: *Studies on the Parables of Christ* was published by the Student Christian Movement (SCM) Press. And in November 1910, SCM Press published his first major title: *Modern Discipleship and What it Means.* In it, Edward demonstrated the magnificent forward thrust of his faith:

> *The need of the world is pressing, the golden opportunities are slipping past. If we go about the work of God with mental timidity or qualified enthusiasm, we shall make no impression on our generation. Passionate devotion, joined with a cool and seasoned confidence – here is a two-edged sword that shall smile and win the victory.*

That brand of 'Onward, Christian Soldier' took him to the post of Chaplain at the Royal Military College at Sandhurst in

July 1915. It was a testing period for Edward, who longed to be able to join the men at the front but was barred on account of his previous poor health. He was acutely aware that the boys to whom he ministered at Sandhurst (most were still in their teens) were being called upon to sacrifice everything – most probably their lives – while he was in a sheltered position, enjoying an uninterrupted family life.

To encourage and sustain these boys, who were likely to be either maimed or dead within a few months of graduating, he wrote a little book entitled *Knights in Armour*, with a forward by the then Chief of the Imperial General Staff, General Sir William Robertson. The book was deliberately romantic and idealistic, appealing to public school boys whose favourite poetry was still that of Alfred Tennyson and Rupert Brooke. It was a short and simple rallying cry for them to hold dear the ancient virtues of Courage, Loyalty, Chivalry and Purity, while all around them was senseless suffering and slaughter.

Finally, in January 1918, he was given a permit to visit the trenches for two weeks. He was thrilled, not least because it led to his first flight in an aeroplane – an exhilarating experience. He attended a meeting in Écurie at which army chaplains met with officers and soldiers from the Yorkshire Light Infantry and East Lancashire regiments to discuss problems of social reconstruction after the War. This was a foundational moment for Edward, whose passion for the relevance of Christianity in the daily lives of working men led to his taking on the leadership of the Life and Liberty Movement. He returned to Sandhurst determined to play his part in making the Church at home supportive to the hopes and aspirations of the soldiers for a more just and equitable society than they had known before the War.

As WWI drew to a close in November 1918, Edward paid a second, longer visit to France, including a tour of the forces in Germany (he spoke fluent German after his stay in Davos), which lasted until February 1919. During this journey, he interviewed 280 would-be candidates for ordination, many of whom came from the rank-and-file soldiers, and Edward was immensely cheered to think that the 'home Church' was to receive a boost from men whose faith had been tried and tested in the crucible of war.

It was in this expectant mood that he took on his new living of Holy Trinity, Cambridge. It was a very different Cambridge, and church, to that which he had known as an undergraduate and ordinand. Many of the undergraduates were men who had come straight from the front line, and were thus contemptuous of mere academic debate – they were asking real questions about burning moral, social and political issues. A cloistered don might have quaked in his brogues when confronted with a 24-year-old ex-brigadier who had spent the last four years in the filth and tragedy of the trenches. But Edward understood their eager impatience and their thirst for a better society, and he set himself the task of meeting their needs by showing the relevance of Christianity to politics, industry, commerce, sport, family life and art.

Standing room only was the normal state of affairs at Holy Trinity when Edward was preaching, and in 1922 SCM Press published *Everyday Religion* in which he gave written expression to these topics. He soon became known as a speaker with a unique ability to express his faith with ardent but straightforward conviction, and to present Jesus Christ in such a way that it seemed to be the most natural and attractive thing in the world to want to follow Him.

Edward was much in demand, both in public and in the council of the Church, and he was elected to the National Assembly. As the demands continued, he became increasingly aware of the vital importance of tackling issues in God's strength rather than in a flush of well-meant enthusiasm.

This was never truer than when he was asked to succeed William Temple (who would go on to become Archbishop of Canterbury) as Chairman of the Life and Liberty Movement. The Movement had come directly out of the meetings with the soldiers on the front lines in France, and sought reform in the Church of England to allow the voice of the laity to be heard more effectively. And so, on 7th November 1919, Parliament passed the Enabling Act, which released from State to Church – through an elected Assembly and Parochial Church Councils (PCCs) – a greater democratic power to manage its own affairs.

Edward took great pleasure in establishing and leading the now famous Swanwick Conferences for PCC members, which he used to educate new parochial church councillors about their responsibilities. From 1923 until the year of his death in 1953, and aside from a brief hiatus during WWII, these conferences were held annually under his leadership. In doing so, thousands of Christian men and women were able to embrace what the Church wanted to say to the nation and to the world. And at the same time, they were a real means of deep spiritual and relational renewal.

At the end of 1926, Edward was asked to become Vicar of Croydon, a role which soon progressed into an offer to fill the post of Bishop of Croydon, a new suffragan bishopric in the Diocese of Canterbury. He saw his role as preacher, leader and inspirer, and pastor to the sick and bereaved – and he quickly mastered the art of delegation to his team on the administrative side of things. His preaching was by all accounts magnificent, his clear, sonorous voice charging familiar words with meaning and impetus. Sybil later commented on his magic:

I heard him preach many times and never failed to come away tremendously invigorated and strengthened in faith and encouraged to live it out more effectively...one came away from his service transported onto another level of living. And it didn't all fade away on Monday morning.

Part of his secret was that he made the listener feel that he was speaking directly to them, as if he knew their circumstances and needs. The BBC was quick to recognise his unusual powers of communication and he became perhaps their most popular religious broadcaster on the wireless. For many years before and after WWII, the BBC ran a series of five-minute breakfast-time talks known as the *Lift Up Your Hearts* series – essentially a precursor to the *Thought for the Day* slot on Radio 4's *Today* programme. Edward was so admired that he became a frequent contributor, and his talks were eventually compiled into short books published by SCM Press. One of them was entitled *A Life Worth Living*.

Just how effective and far-reaching his broadcasts were was demonstrated in the summer of 1946 – by which time Edward had been Bishop of Lichfield for nine years – when Sam and Sybil took a holiday in Dorset. As they picnicked in a field, Sam went over to help the farmer with some bales of hay, and during a break the farmer remarked that Sam's voice sounded familiar – "It's so like the Bishop of Lichfield's". The farmer was so delighted to discover that he was talking to the Bishop's son that he invited the Woods family back to his house for tea, where Sam and Sybil discovered that he owned all of Edward's books.

A few days later, Sam and Sybil were walking down the street of a small village nearby when an old woman emerged from one of the cottages and ran after them. Catching hold of Sam, she said, "Oh, do excuse me sir, but I couldn't help hearing your voice as you went past. It was just like the Bishop of Lichfield's! I just had to come and ask you if you are related to him." On learning that Sam was his son she insisted that they come back to her cottage. There, on the wall beside the fireplace, she had pinned a newspaper photo of Edward and a cutting of a review of one of his books. She explained how she never failed to listen to his broadcasts, how they strengthened her faith and gave her hope, and how it seemed as if he were sitting there in the room talking to her personally rather than addressing millions on the radio. She then gave Sam and Sybil a ginger kitten for the children, which they cautiously but happily accepted.

On 22nd September 1937 Edward had been enthroned as the 94th Bishop of Lichfield, an ancient and vast diocese comprising most of Staffordshire and Shropshire, with over 400 parishes and 700 clergy under his care. The handsome, spacious Palace, designed by Sir Christopher Wren and built in 1792, was a hub of hospitality as myriad ordinands, parish clergy, and church leaders both lay and clerical came to share meals there.

King George VI and Queen Elizabeth were visitors during the war years, and in June 1946 the Queen returned to stay at the Palace for two nights so that she could attend the celebrations marking the 750th anniversary of the founding of the Cathedral. Her presence demonstrated the strong personal links which had developed between Edward and the King and Queen ever since he had first met King George V and Queen Mary at Sandhurst. As the years passed, he became a regular visitor to Sandringham, Buckingham Palace and Windsor, where he not only preached but had long talks with George and Elizabeth about matters of the Christian faith. In 1946, the King appointed Edward Lord High Almoner, an office dating from 1103 which bears the responsibility of distributing royal alms to the poor.

Edward often sent the royals books to read, and George VI was reading one of these – *A Life of Christ* – at the time of his death in 1952. When the Queen Mother visited Australia in 1958, she met Edward's son Frank – who had just been appointed Archbishop of Melbourne – and remarked: "No-one advises me as your father did, as to what I should be reading in the way of Christian literature." One of Edward's most treasured possessions was a copy of *The Pilgrim's Progress* beautifully bound in red leather and inscribed: "To my kind purveyor of literature, the dear Bishop of Lichfield, from Elizabeth R., May 3rd 1942." As Edward lay dying, it was from this book that Sam and the others read to him.

Not everyone was thrilled with Edward's religious instruction. When the Duke of Edinburgh and Princess Elizabeth visited Lichfield after the birth of Charles in 1948, Edward dutifully took the royal couple to his study after dinner and explained which books and prayers would be most suitable for the young prince. Clemence joined them with the intent of suggesting some lighter entertainment, and Prince Philip took the opportunity to ask her whether this had been the way that she and Edward had tackled their own children's upbringing:

"Yes," said Clemence.

"And now your eldest son is Vicar of Huddersfield, your second son is Rector of Hatfield and your third son is Archdeacon of Singapore."

"Yes, that's right," Clemence replied, walking further into the trap.

"Yes, it must be a very effective method of instruction," said the Duke with a mischievous grin. "Tell me, what am I to do if, when Charles is grown up, he comes to me and says, 'I don't want to be King. I want to be a clergyman!'"

There were hoots of laughter as they finally retreated to the drawing room to play bridge. Princess Elizabeth immediately announced that bridge was "too stuffy", and so it was that the entire Woods family joined the Prince and Princess in a rollicking session of Racing Demon.

After many years of deteriorating health, Clemence passed away on 14th October 1952. Ten days later, Edward set out on a long-planned mission to visit all of the RAF stations in the Far East, which took him to airfields throughout Malaya and Hong Kong, as well as Singapore, where his son Robin was now an archdeacon. Despite his personal despair at losing his beloved wife, and enduring the tropical heat at the age of 75, Edward spoke with his usual vigour and conviction, and moved energetically around the hangars and workshops, talking with the men.

His last ever sermon was in a packed St Andrew's Cathedral in Singapore, his message and voice as clear and authoritative as ever, inciting the congregation to consider the means by which "the Spirit of Christ must enter the world of men". On a table back in his room was a slip of paper marked 'An Account of my Stewardship'. It was the title of a sermon to be delivered at Lichfield Cathedral on Sunday 11th January 1953. The sermon was never preached – he died that very day, and instead was able to give his account face to face to the One whom he had served so devotedly all his life. His funeral was presided over by the Archbishop of Canterbury, who spoke of his "transparent goodness…he was such a glorious and happy giver of himself and of all that was in him to family and friends, to Diocese and Church, to all in his care, to all whom he could reach."

It was Queen Elizabeth The Queen Mother who, later that year, commissioned Jacob Epstein to produce a large bronze bust of Edward for Lichfield Cathedral, where it has been positioned since 1958 – marvellous Woods head bowed ever so slightly, hands raised in prayer.

***

And so it was that, as Sam and Sybil prepared to welcome "Gabrielle Mary" into the family in Napier, a gene pool abundant in missional, Quaker and Church of England DNA continued to prosper. If ever there were a secret, *Da Vinci Code*-style programme of genetic meddling to produce a Protestant super race, they could surely do no better than Sam and Sybil. Williams, Woods, Fry, Barclay and Buxton were all woven into the fabric of young Richard and his new sibling.

Unfortunately, as Sam prepared to visit Napier for 24 hours to witness the birth of their daughter, "Gabrielle Mary" was demonstrating another chromosomal trait: stubbornness.

Kik, Kik's knobbly knees, Sybil, Sarah, Richard, Marianne and Sam in 1949

CHAPTER 2
There and Back Again
(1943-1960)

Sybil was certainly cut from the same robust cloth as her pioneer missionary forebears – she wasn't one to faff around, waiting for an idle child to be born. Sam had managed to get one day of leave from his position as Chaplain to the Royal New Zealand Air Force (RNZAF) in Rotorua, and had travelled down to Napier to be with his wife for the birth on the expected day. But the child was showing no sign of complying with the RNZAF schedule. So Sybil took the opportunity to give an early demonstration to her unborn offspring of who was in charge.

With Napier's coastal proximity, and with the clock ticking before Sam had to return to base in Rotorua, Sybil decided to go for a walk on the beach. This can't have been easy – the child began life, and would remain thereafter, blessed with a robust heft. But Sybil was determined. She heaved herself up and down that beach with such vigour that the baby arrived later that day: Friday 15th January 1943.

It was a baby boy. Given "Gabrielle Mary" was no longer appropriate, they named him Christopher Samuel Woods instead. And it was immediately clear that, like many second sons, he was a wonderfully straightforward, carefree little chap – where Richard was slender and cerebral, Christopher was stout and jolly. In a letter Sam wrote to Edward and Clemence on 6th October 1943, he described the boys thus:

Richard…has wooden tracks and trains which he plays with endlessly, and is terrifically keen on cars, constantly watching them out of the window or over the front wall…Christopher is a good deal heftier than Richard was and has sat up two months earlier…He and R now sleep in the same room, and have the most amusing conversations – Richard going through the list of words he knows and C replying in a series of grunts…

A little over a year later, Sybil wrote to her mother-in-law: "R is still thin and mercurial. He weighs 2 stone and 6lbs, and C weighs 2 stone and 5lbs! Of course the latter is unusually sturdy and deliciously round and dimpled and firm."

The climax of this fraternal muscular divergence came a few years later in 1948: Richard was reclining alone in the garden, no doubt pondering the meaning of life and eloquently reciting large chunks of Ecclesiastes, when Christopher charged over and leapt upon his sibling with such brute force that he broke Richard's collarbone. Interestingly, these characteristics have continued into the next generation – whereas Christopher's two sons are both rugby-playing, beer-swilling halfwits, Richard's two sons are fiendishly intelligent and witty, but puny.

***

From December 1943 to May 1946, Sam, Sybil and the boys were based at the RNZAF station at Wigram, near Christchurch in the South Island. There were ongoing discussions with the Church Board of Nominations about a return to the UK during this time. Much to Edward and Clemence's dismay, the Board (chaired by Edward's old friend,

Sam's godfather, Campbell West-Watson, then Archbishop and Primate of New Zealand) decided that Sam's ministry would be better focused in New Zealand as the Second World War raged on. Edward was clearly not thrilled about this, judging by the sensitive tone from West-Watson in a letter from March 1945:

> *I do realise your desire to get him home and I should like him to go…but his work as Air Force Chaplain is so valuable that I am very anxious for him to carry on at present. It would be very hard to get anyone to take his place…and, if we were to let him go off or ask for his release when the need is so pressing, I might be thought to be giving special favours to my godson!*

Back in Blighty, Sam's brothers Frank and Robin were also following in their father's footsteps as chaplains in the armed services, and both spent significant chunks of time abroad with the troops, Frank in North Africa and Northern Ireland, as well as participating in the miraculous retreat from Dunkirk; and Robin predominantly in Italy, where he was instrumental in establishing a chaplains' Training Centre and Moral Leadership School at Assisi.

As Bishop of Lichfield, Edward's most obvious contribution during the Second World War was his series of short breakfast-time reflections on the wireless, which brought the simple Christian messages of peace and love into the darkness of the conflict, as well as giving him a platform to condemn campaigns such as the Allied carpet-bombing of Hamburg and Dresden.

New Zealand's perspective on the War was an interesting one: while the conflict itself never actually reached New Zealand's shores (the closest it came was when the Japanese made incursions into the Solomon Islands, northern Australia and the Coral Sea), it retained a key interest in the outcome of the War given its membership of the Commonwealth. And its sons and daughters would contribute to a remarkable military effort, as they had during the First World War.

It was a Maori pilot, Sergeant B.S. Wipiti, who shot down the first Japanese plane during the battle for Singapore in 1942. Over 100 other RNZAF pilots had already fought with distinction in the Battle of Britain in 1940, forming the largest group of Commonwealth pilots in that astonishing victory. Sybil's brother, Maurice Williams, was a Squadron Leader in Europe at this time, and flew more than 50 bombing raids over Germany. Tragically, having returned to New Zealand in 1942 to conduct pilot training with the RNZAF, he was then killed in 1943 during a routine flight at Ohakea, leaving behind his pregnant English widow, Penelope, and their infant son, Anthony.

The Allied victory in May 1945 was greeted with unprecedented displays of public emotion in New Zealand – like the UK, not a population generally known for its natural exuberance. In Wellington, the trams were laid on for free and people danced and sang in the streets. In rural areas, parishioners gathered at isolated churches to give thanks. As Michael King has written in his definitive *Penguin History of New Zealand*:

> *For most New Zealanders, the war in Europe was the war. Germany had had to be defeated and Britain secured before civilisation – and New Zealand's principal market for exports and major source of imports – could be considered safe.*

In all, 194,000 men and 10,000 women had served in the country's armed forces, 140,000 of them abroad – meaning Sam was one of the 54,000 men who had served in New Zealand. Despite the relative proximity of the Pacific war with Japan, the majority of New Zealanders had been involved in 'Hitler's war' in Europe. More than 11,500 had been killed – the highest casualty rate per head of population in the Commonwealth.

***

At the end of the War, reductions in the NZ armed forces gave Sam hope that he would soon be released to return to the

UK and a parish ministry there. A good portion of his letters home to Edward and Clemence are focused on this. Edward was clearly trying to pull a few strings too – in one letter from September 1945, while suffering from "some plaguey infection of the bowel" at Wigram, Sam wrote that the arrival of some family letters had "bucked me up a lot, especially that most unexpected offer from the Bishop of Lichfield (must be a bit of a nonentity – I can't remember his name at the moment) that I should be his 'Domestic Chaplain, with special Diocesan Duties attached'. But seriously Ed-a-wack, I'm very bucked with the suggestion and feel all the more impatient to get back and be acting in that capacity". Eventually it was agreed that Sam would transfer back to the UK in the summer of 1946.

By this time, young Christopher had been anointed 'Kik' by his older brother, who had clearly inherited the family affinity for nicknames (little did Richard know how appropriate that nickname would become during the Collarbone Affair). The boys' personalities were developing in line with expectations. In a letter from Sybil to Clemence, she noted a psychologist friend's analysis:

> *'Richard is an interesting child, Kiki is a charming child'...She thinks Kiki is what she calls a 'thoroughly integrated little character' – i.e. he fits in well with people and is sort of settled in himself, but she thinks Richard feels everything intensely, is impatient of delay or hindrance etc., where Kiki plods along and is more content to take life as it comes...*

At the end of 1945, on 30th December, the two boys were joined by a baby sister named Rosemary Clemence. Sam and Sybil were thrilled to have a little girl at last. It was immediately clear, however, that all was not well – Rosemary had been born with spina bifida, a very rare condition where the spine does not form properly in the womb, leaving the baby's nervous system vulnerable to infections. Sam wrote to his parents that Rosemary was "a fine chubby baby, looking the picture of health...But directly the babe had arrived, Billy [Sybil] realised something was up and point blank asked the doctor, who of course had to tell her. She has been wonderful about it, though feeling it intensely…".

Fortunately, on 7th January 1946, Sam was able to get support from the RNZAF to fly Sybil and Rosemary down to Dunedin, where a neuro-surgical specialist by the name of Dr Falconer had agreed to help. They flew from Wigram in a 2-engined Hudson bomber – "the same type that Maurice was killed in, now, rather significantly we felt, being used to save the life of our babe". It took them 90 minutes to fly to the aerodrome 10 miles outside Dunedin, where an ambulance was waiting to take them to Dr Falconer's ward at the public hospital. Dr Falconer saw her immediately.

Sadly the diagnosis was not good. Rosemary's condition was much worse than the doctor in Christchurch had led them to believe. It was, in fact, hopeless:

> *The babe's case is considerably worse than a straightforward spina bifida…After various tests, Dr Falconer concluded that Rosemary's spinal cord was not developed in the lower regions…and after keeping her under observation for a few more days…decided that he could do nothing. He felt she might have two months to live, probably less. So we decided to come home* [to Wigram] *and have little Rosemary in the public hospital here near us* [in Christchurch]...*Today she is weaker. We are going in this afternoon. It's terribly sad seeing her pass like this, so slowly that one wishes it could be quicker…*
>
> [Break as Sam and Sybil take the boys to the playground beside the hospital.]
>
> *Mrs Williams took the boys back to Wigram in the tram, while Billy and I went to see our babe in the hospital. When we arrived, we heard that the Sister had been trying to contact us as Rosemary was very much weaker…We hadn't been with her ten minutes when with a little puff and flicker of the eyes she had gone. A wonderfully peaceful going to that house of many mansions. We felt very thankful that we had been with her when she went.*

Later that month, Sam updated the family further:

I must tell you about the two services, the baptism and funeral…We held the baptism in Billy's room the day after Rosemary was born. Rosemary looked so lovely and well, you'd never have imagined anything was wrong with her…Richard and Christopher came, and were very sweet and obviously very thrilled with the babe. One of the hardest bits of the whole business has been having to explain to them our babe not coming home…At the baptism they sat quiet as mice on the bed, with their eyes fixed on the cot. A charming touch…was the production by Richard, without a word from anybody, of some wet cardboard wrapped up in paper, for the doctor to put on the baby's sore back…

The little funeral was rather heart-rending. St Peter's [in Christchurch] *had kindly said we could have a little plot in the Churchyard, a lovely spot with the grey stone church in the middle, and big elms and other English trees all around…*

Billy and I were at the Church alone when the tiny white coffin arrived at 10 o'clock, when we put some flowers on it, and felt much helped with a quiet prayer and by the Psalm of the day (107)…After the little service in Church I carried the little coffin out to the grave, where we had the committal and all was over.

Billy and I do feel that we've been wonderfully helped both by our faith and by the friendship of our friends, and upheld in prayer. If what we have been through has done nothing else, it has certainly strengthened our faith in God's love, and our belief in that other world. We like to think that there are babies there, and that Rosemary is happy there.

Sybil then added her perspective on the death and the funeral in a letter to Clemence at the end of January:

I want too to tell you all about our lovely little Rosemary Clemence – because she was lovely, even when she got so frail towards the end…she was lying there with her soft down of dark red (your colour) hair contrasting vividly with the marble-white of her little face, and her lovely little features seemed to reveal a strange maturity of spirit – I felt strongly the timelessness of her spirit. Her big dark eyes were half open gazing fixedly in front of her but there was nothing vacant about the stare. She stayed like that scarcely breathing for several minutes, then gave a little sigh and a flicker of the eyelids and she was gone. We sat there for some time in prayer, carrying away our last earthly memory of a most lovely little daughter…

I felt so sad about Sam – he loved his little daughter so much and it was tragic walking beside him at the little funeral service as he carried her for the last time in her tiny little white casket. I had prayed often that I might give him a daughter…and please God I shall give him another daughter next year – or another comical little boy…

***

At dawn on Saturday 4th May 1946, Sam, Sybil, Richard and Kik set sail from Wellington on the *Akaroa*, bound for London. Five weeks later they arrived in England and immediately went to stay with Edward and Clemence at the Bishop's Palace in Lichfield. There they began to seek out their next parish.

Sam's brothers Frank and Robin were also demobilised after the War, and became Vicar of Huddersfield and Vicar of South Wigston, Leicester, respectively. After turning down Hoddesdon in Hertfordshire, Sam accepted the parish of Holy Trinity, Southport, in Lancashire – only twenty miles from Holy Trinity, St Helens. The church in Southport – built in 1913, now Grade II listed – is a magnificent structure, most notable for its Gothic Revivalist exterior, complete with looming 142-foot tower and, no doubt, the occasional Scouse Quasimodo swinging from the buttresses.

The family's time in Southport was notable for three reasons. Firstly, it reminded Sam that unlike his father – a naturally gifted orator with a deep and resounding Woods timbre – he really didn't like preaching. He considered it "an ef" (effort). In a letter to his parents in 1947, he wrote:

> *I've been very busy with Parish activities getting going again (good opening of my Men's Society with over 40 present) and our Missionary week starting on Sunday. This means two whole Sundays free of any preaching – joy and bliss! This Friday I speak at a Diocesan Youth Week Lunch Hour Service in Liverpool Parish Church, and that evening at a Deanery Youth Rally at Prescott. When these are over I'll be pleasantly free of sermons and talks in the immediate future.*

Sam, naturally shy and unassuming in a family of big beasts, showed great courage throughout his career in stepping up to the pulpit again and again to address the congregation.

Secondly, the family kept a goat called Bunty. In the post-war years of rationing, families were eligible for a maximum of two pints of milk per day – apparently not quite enough for the thirsty Woods boys, the constant stream of parochial visitors, and the family's two cats. So they scoured the countryside in Sam's 1938 Morris 8 looking for a goat, and found Bunty at a local farm. She roamed happily in the large garden at the Vicarage, sleeping in a shed in the corner, occasionally pursuing the boys into the geraniums, and produced a gallon of milk a day – eight glorious pints.

Thirdly, the time in Southport was notable for two additions to the family (not including Bunty). Sybil had been ill for some time with what turned out to be an overactive thyroid and after an operation to fix the problem, which was successful, she was advised not to have any more children – a real blow following the loss of Rosemary. And so, on 11th May 1948, Sam and Sybil adopted at birth a daughter, and christened her Marianne Sybil – the name they had planned to use seven years earlier if their firstborn had been a girl.

They were understandably thrilled. In October that year Sybil wrote to Edward:

> [Marianne] *is the most delicious little morsel and the apple of Sam's eye. It is truly sweet to see them together in his study after breakfast. As soon as she wakes at about 9:30am he kidnaps her*

and carries her off to his study where she lies in her cot and kicks and crows and gurgles at him until I come to claim her for her bath.

I did say two additions, and despite Bunty being transported to a billy goat in the back of the Morris 8 and producing a bouncy little kid of her own, this was not the second major addition of note – that came in the form of a totally unexpected pregnancy for Sybil, resulting in the wonderfully happy birth of a second daughter, Sarah Elizabeth, on 16th January 1949. Marianne and Sally (as Sarah became known) are therefore only eight months apart. The Woods family was now complete.

***

In June 1950, Sam accepted an offer from Lord Salisbury to become Rector of Hatfield. There had been some discussion about whether or not the family should in fact return to New Zealand. Sam had built up a strong affinity for New Zealand during his time there, and his career prospects were probably stronger there than they were in Britain. And of course Sybil's parents, having lost Maurice already, were very keen to have their one surviving child nearby.

It was a very difficult decision. In a long and emotional letter to Edward in February that year, Sybil had written:

I do hope that you don't feel I was 'unfeeling' about your longing to keep Sammy in England. I do know what it means to you and Muvie [Clemence] *to have him near and what an appalling wrench it would be if he went back to New Zealand. But, Far dear, you wouldn't let that longing stand in his way, would you?...*

As Sam says, he's not likely to get any very outstanding job in England, at any rate not for many years to come. And the longer he stays in England the weaker grows his knowledge of N.Z. and church developments there…

So you see many things have to be taken into account and the very great thing is to try to keep our minds unbiased and ready for

> *God's call. And that's not easy when parents are added to all the other calls. Parents count a lot – where would either of us be without the love (and the love of God) that we learned from you here and from mine in N.Z.? But if we regard parents' claims as prior then I feel my parents have the pull...They have no other children near them and only two grandchildren* [Maurice's English wife Penelope was still living in NZ] *whereas you and Muvie have five other children and ten other grandchildren.*

However, the lure of the living of Hatfield was clearly strong enough to keep Sam in England for now – that, plus the fact that there were no particularly interesting opportunities in New Zealand at this point. Clemence's health had also started to deteriorate and she was increasingly frail.

The family's time at Hatfield, from 1950 to 1955 (when they did return to New Zealand), was particularly happy. Sam and Sybil much enjoyed the role, with Hatfield House at one end of the parish and the De Havilland aircraft factory at the other. And Sybil's parents were in fact able to come to England and serve with them in Hatfield – Sybil's father Canon Wilfred Williams fulfilled the duties of Senior Curate, and he and Sybil's mother Madeline lived in a charming Tudor cottage next door to the Vicarage.

These were wonderful, utopian days. The boys would play cricket together in the vicarage garden and occasionally go for a ride around the village on the milkman's horse-drawn cart. The church itself, St Etheldreda's, dates from the 13th century and backs onto Hatfield House and Hatfield Park, where the family spent many glorious afternoons romping around with Rex, the dog.

The social life was also a little different to Southport. The Salisburys would often pop in for tea, and Sam would regularly go "shooting in the suburbs" with them. On one occasion, in November 1950, Sam and Sybil were invited to a tea party with Princess Margaret at Hatfield. Sybil described it in a letter to Clemence:

Sam and I were invited to tea at 5pm on Saturday. They had opened their State apartments for the occasion and Lady Salisbury met us in the Hall and took us through the magnificent old banqueting-hall with its 26 ft. long table laid for dinner and an enormous fire burning in the 17th century fireplace, and on into the State drawing room…Sam and I were presented to the Princess and then introduced all round to the party. I must say I liked the Princess at once. She has such a fine direct gaze when speaking to you, as if she's summing up your character very shrewdly.

…We were delighted to find ourselves in seats of honour. I sat on Lord Salisbury's left with the Princess on his right and Sam on her right…Sam had a terrific clack with Princess M. and I got on well with Lord S. and Lord Eldon…

After tea we went back into the drawing-room and I got drawn into a group around Lady Cranborne on a big sofa, doing The Times *crossword. Then young Duff Cooper, who seems a very likeable young man and very good-looking, brought out his guitar and sang us some really charming French songs. Then there was a request that the Princess should sing to us which she did most simply and naturally, accompanying herself on the piano. She sang a sweet little Scottish song called 'I gave my love a cherry'.*

One can only imagine what young Duff made of that.

The Woods family were then invited to Hatfield House for tea on Christmas Day a few weeks later, and Sybil again recounted the scene to Clemence:

Marianne and Sarah looked really charming in their little party frocks and behaved very well. We listened to our Church choir singing carols round the Christmas tree and then Lord and Lady S. gave really lovely presents all round (three each!). Old Viscount Cecil of Chelwood was there and Lord David Cecil and Anthony Eden and of course the Cranbornes with their three little sons.

I was sitting just in front of Viscount Cecil with the four children all round me opening their presents and I overheard a conversation between Viscount Cecil and Lord Cranborne. It was really a rather loud conversation because Viscount C. is very deaf, so I couldn't help hearing it!

Viscount C. 'Whose is this delightful family in front of me?'

Lord C. 'Oh, those are the Rector's children.'

Viscount C. 'What good-looking boys and such nice manners, and dear little girls. A charming family. Your rector is a very good man, isn't he?'

Lord C. 'An excellent man! He's extremely popular. We consider we're very lucky to have him!'

***

In terms of schooling, Richard and Kik showed themselves to be highly competent. In Southport, Richard had been top of the class in seven subjects; Kik was even in the same class thanks to his own precocious academic performance – he came fifth out of fourteen boys, when aged only six in a class with an average age of eight. Both boys were particularly capable when it came to spelling, grammar, literature and languages. Both, however – according to one school report – struggled when it came to poetry, lacking a 'variety of expression'. In hindsight, this was probably the pinnacle of their poetic achievement.

While at Hatfield, the boys attended Lochinver House School in Potter's Bar. It had only been started in 1947, in a dilapidated old house which had been used during the War by a pharmaceutical firm for storing Nivea cream. Bomb damage had accelerated an already decaying fabric of the building. Perhaps to liven the place up a bit, the founding headmaster, Harold Bayley, chose a bright pink to go with a more traditional grey for the school uniform. By the time Richard and Kik arrived in 1950, the attendance had grown from around 30 to 100 boys.

In 1953, Richard received a scholarship to study at Grenham House, a prep school in Birchington-on-Sea, Kent. The scholarship allowed him to board. Writer and broadcaster

John Suchet arrived at the same time, and although he sadly fails to comment on Richard at all, he has since written in a national newspaper about his experiences at the school. They were far from happy. He refers to Grenham House as "a monstrous place":

> *I'll never forget my first night in the dormitory. I climbed into an ice-cold bed and looked out of the window. All I could see was the grey North Sea. I went to bed crying my eyes out with the sound of a foghorn in the distance…*
>
> *My actor brother David followed me two years later and hated the place as much as I did. The headmaster, Denys Jeston, used to beat David and me with a long bamboo cane for breaking school rules. He'd move the desks out of the way so he could run right across the classroom to give extra power to the whack…*
>
> *Another ordeal the headmaster subjected us to was taking us swimming in the North Sea – no matter how cold the weather was. He'd stride in and force us all to follow. Nobody was allowed to pause…*
>
> *Jeston's deputy, Jack Lidgate, was no better than his boss. He specialised in putting his hands up the boys' short trousers and pinching their bums…*
>
> *At a function a few years ago, I met Louis de Bernières, the author of* Captain Corelli's Mandolin. *He was at the same school ten years after me…I went up to him and said, 'We have something in common. We were both at Grenham House.' His eyes bulged, his face went red and anger filled every crevice in his face. He spat out the words, 'That school was run by two b******s – a sadist and a paedophile.'*
>
> *Despite that, the one thing I will say for the school, though, and which must not be underestimated, was that academically I was given an extremely good education.*

Kik joined Richard at Grenham House in 1954. Despite the appalling abuse by staff, both boys thoroughly enjoyed their time at the school, singing in the choir together – for which they received a red ribbon on their blazers. Kik was elected a prefect of his house after just one term, and performed heroics for the unbeaten 2nd XI hockey team. And as Dormitory Captain, Richard got to dole out some corporal punishment of his own, whacking his younger brother on the hand with a slipper for insubordinate behaviour at bedtime.

***

Back in the real world, the Woods family continued to fraternise with royalty. In February 1952 King George VI had died in his sleep and his elder daughter had become Queen Elizabeth II. In April, Edward performed his duties at the Maundy Thursday service at Westminster Abbey – the first for the new Queen (and Edward's last). In May, the Queen Mother stayed at Hatfield House and Sam welcomed her to church for Matins.

In July, more royal visitors arrived in Hatfield – this time of a slightly shorter stature. At a party for small children at Lodge House, Sally was playing with the three young Cranbornes when a majestic Daimler swept up the drive and out popped Princess Anne and Prince Charles. Sybil, naturally, and with her usual frankness, reported these events to Clemence:

> *He is a very nice-looking and manly little boy. He wore a coffee-coloured linen shirt with no frills or smocking and a pair of daffodil-yellow linen shorts buttoning on to the shirt…Princess Anne wore a very pretty daffodil-yellow organdie party dress with deep smocking…She's not exactly pretty but is very attractive and bright-looking and very self-possessed and well-developed for her age…Prince Charles is two months older than Sarah. He is not as tall as Sarah but is very sturdy and straight and has a very good head with chestnut-brown hair.*
>
> *The children all played together very happily until the butler came out to say tea was ready. I must tell you that Sarah was much admired by all the aristocratic nannies. She has a great dignity and a keen sense of savoir-faire on these occasions…*

> *After tea Prince Charles walked out into the hall with Sarah, who said, 'Are you coming out to play again, Charles?' 'Yes', said P. Charles very gravely, 'but you must wash your hands first because they're sticky and so are mine.'*

***

Sadly, just as Prince Charles had lost a grandparent earlier that year, Sarah and her siblings were to lose three in a very short space of time. First Clemence died on 14th October 1952, and then Edward on 11th January 1953. Later that year, Sybil's father Wilfred died of a pulmonary embolism after a hernia operation.

With little tying them to the UK any longer, Sam and Sybil decided to look for an opportunity to return to New Zealand. And so, on 23rd November 1955, *The Times* carried the announcement of Sam's appointment as Vicar of Sydenham and Archdeacon of Christchurch. He and Sybil had responded positively to a request from Bishop Alwyn Warren to take up this post, which had become available rather suddenly, and very sadly, when the previous incumbent was jailed for sexually abusing boys in the cathedral choir.

In February 1955 Sam set sail, leaving Sybil and the children in England so that Richard and Kik could complete the boarding-school year at Grenham House. They lived at Compton, near Winchester, in a holiday house belonging to Sam's sister, Priscilla, and her husband, John 'Budge' Firth, a schoolmaster and Chaplain at Winchester College. As a schoolboy at Winchester, Budge had famously taken all ten wickets for 41 runs in a match against Eton in 1917 and was named Wisden Cricketer of the Year in 1918 – he was known for his fiendishly unplayable googly. Kik was already playing for the Grenham 1st XI in 1955, having only just turned eleven, his advanced skills no doubt aided by a few tactical and finger-twiddling tips from uncle Budge.

Finally, on 5th August 1955, Sybil, Richard, Kik, Sally, Marianne and Sybil's mother Madeline set off for New

Zealand, and a rendezvous with Sam in Christchurch. Sadly, Rex, the dog, had to stay behind and was donated to family friends.

He might well have thanked his lucky canine stars – for during the voyage there was an outbreak of polio on the ship. One woman died, and was immediately buried at sea. To Sybil's horror, both Kik and Marianne then contracted the deadly disease; one can only imagine the terrifying ordeal of trusting that the ship's medical facilities and staff were up to the task, particularly for a mother who had already lost one child. She and Madeline prayed for protection and healing constantly. In time, both children survived unharmed.

Nevertheless, the whole family was placed in quarantine for six weeks on arrival in New Zealand. This was not quite the joyous return they had expected, but the green and pleasant environs of The Garden City – including its very own Lichfield Street – soon had them back on their usual good form.

***

It had been almost a decade since the Woods family had left New Zealand and in their absence it had begun to change. Like many post-war societies, the psychological disruptions of the conflict were gradually being replaced by economic stability, suburban domesticity, and major population growth.

There was also a sequence of events which some saw as portents confirming New Zealand's position in the world as unusually blessed. Edmund Hillary's triumphant conquest of Mount Everest in 1953 was followed by a visit from Queen Elizabeth II – the first time a reigning monarch had set foot on New Zealand soil. Then, in 1956, the All Blacks defeated the feared Springboks 3–1 in a test series – nowadays, perhaps not such an oracular event, but at the time it contributed to the overall sense of a national trajectory on the up.

Some things hadn't changed: most New Zealanders still spoke of Britain as 'Home' and saw nothing wrong with the procession of decrepit British aristocrats or military men being sent over to represent the British monarchy in New Zealand. They certainly saw nothing odd in having the country's head of state live 13,000 miles away in London. Sally's tales of tea and cake with Prince Charles no doubt went down a treat with the other children in Christchurch.

Indeed, the arrival of two bona fide English maidens who had spent the past five years dabbling in royal circles generated quite a bit of excitement at the all-girls' St Margaret's College. Marianne and Sally were frequently asked by the teachers to visit different classrooms and inspire the other girls with their perfect English accents. This, of course, soon taught them to lose their accents and blend in. Sybil did not help matters when, for one birthday party, she dressed her daughters in matching white organza dresses with pink and blue sashes, and white sandals. All of the other girls were wearing shorts and t-shirts.

Sam, Sybil and the family settled into Sydenham Vicarage, a couple of miles away from Christchurch Cathedral in the centre of the city. Sam was the Vicar of Sydenham, but as one of the archdeacons Sam's role was to help administer a section of the Diocese of Christchurch for the Bishop, Alwyn Warren. Warren had taken over the position from Sam's godfather Campbell West-Watson in 1951. Rangiora and Westland, including Sam's former parish, was one of the first archdeaconries he supervised.

The archdeacons of Christchurch are some of the oldest supervisory posts within the entire Anglican province of Aotearoa, New Zealand and Polynesia, dating back to 1866. Historically, the position of archdeacon has been described as that of *oculus episcopi* – the 'bishop's eye'. So essentially it was Sam's job to oversee the day-to-day business within his division of the diocese – a challenging role which was made all the more complex given the appalling sexual indiscretions of his predecessor. No doubt Sam's integrity and warmth helped to smooth his arrival.

For Sybil, the key priority on her return was to finalise plans for Kik's schooling. Richard had already won a scholarship to attend the esteemed Christ's College, and Sybil was very keen for Kik to join him immediately after they arrived in September 1955. Unfortunately, this didn't give Kik time to sit the Entrance Scholarship exam before the start of term, so he attended The Cathedral Grammar School for one term, promptly got the scholarship, and joined his brother at Christ's for 'First Term' in January 1956.

Christ's College is one of New Zealand's oldest schools, founded in 1850 by the men of the Canterbury Association and modelled on the kinds of English public schools they had attended themselves. The position of Warden of the College is allocated to the Bishop of Christchurch, the first of whom was Henry John Chitty Harper, who had been Chaplain of Eton College until 1850. At the time of Bishop Harper's 50th wedding anniversary, which was celebrated in Christ's College Chapel in 1879 (Harper died in 1893 at the grand old age of 89), an observation was made that the choir was almost entirely comprised of his twelve grandsons. Harper's myriad progeny were among the first boys to be awarded a scholarship for their education at Christ's College – and it was this scholarship, funded by the Canterbury Association, which allowed Richard and Kik to attend as day boys.

Richard and Kik were in fact both placed in Harper House, named after the Bishop. Its motto *Semper Floreat* translates as 'May he always flourish'. And flourish Kik did. By the end of 1956, although a full year younger than the average boy in his year, he was tenth in his form of 26 – despite being described by the formidable Headmaster, H.R. Hornsby MBE, as "not a good examinee".

Kik was also flourishing on the sports field, and in June 1956, after only two terms at the College, was nominated to sit on the school Games Committee. It probably didn't hurt that Kik was built like a rhinoceros: his weight is recorded in his 1956 school report as 9 stone 5 pounds – according to US statistics, the average weight for a thirteen-year-old boy is around 7 stone. It would appear that Kik was one of those prematurely bionic boys to whom one quickly passes the ball on the rugby pitch, before standing and watching merrily as they poleaxe the poor waifs on the opposing team.

***

Kik was clearly suited to the robust, down-to-earth environs at Christ's. The entire College was given the morning off school on 21st July 1956 to watch Canterbury play the touring Springboks (Canterbury won), and the masters postponed a complete round of school rugby fixtures so that all the players – and the masters of course – could travel back to Lancaster Park to watch the All Blacks repeat the trick.

This was a school where the boys were encouraged to participate in the District Stock Judging Competitions, and in June 1957 a boy called J.H. Greenwood did so well in the Fat Sheep Judging that he was selected to represent the Christchurch B team in the Council Stock Judging Competitions later that year (there was also a C team). It was a school where, on a visit to Borthwick's Freezing Works, the boys were encouraged to try their hand at slaughtering the sheep. One can only imagine what Ofsted would make of that today.

A notable member of the Board of Governors at the College was Capt. Charles Hazlitt Upham, who had attended the school himself in the 1920s and would occasionally give the chapel address on ANZAC Day. It is hard to conceive of a more inspirational role model for the boys – Upham was the last of only three men to win the Victoria Cross (VC) twice, both during the Second World War, and the only combat soldier to do so (the other two recipients of the VC and Bar were both army medics). Given only fifteen VCs have been awarded since WWII, Upham's achievement was extraordinary, and his legend was only enhanced by his heroism as a POW – refusing to allow an Italian doctor to amputate his injured arm, and escaping from the Germans on no less than four occasions. Those ANZAC Day addresses in the College Chapel must have been something.

Harper House was very strong at sports, winning the House Rugby and House Tennis cups in 1957, as well as most of the Athletics prizes. The competition between the houses was fierce: in the end-of-year report for 1957, School House describe themselves as 'an average house without anyone really distinguishing himself either in the class-room or on the playing-field' – this despite them winning the House Cricket Cup, the inaugural inter-house hockey competition, and the inter-house swimming relay in record time.

Boxing was popular, with 115 boys taking part in the 1957 championships. Bouts were comprised of two two-minute rounds. And these were amazingly vigorous:

J.G. Burdon showed the value of a right cross in the final of the lightweight against M.K. Stewart, and the fight was stopped in the first round. If Stewart could learn to attack more, his success would be multiplied. In one of the most closely contested bouts of the evening M.D. Sainsbury defeated B.G. Moore for the featherweight championship. Towards the end of the bout both boys had punched themselves to a standstill, and the decision could have gone either way.

...In the final of the heavyweight championship of the school, C.R. Bidwill ended the night with a bang, by knocking out A.S. Reekie. The fight might have been interesting if it had gone on a little longer but Bidwill landed a heavy left hook to the head which terminated the matter.

This ruthless competitive streak also found its way into the annual soccer match between masters and boys. The match report from 1958 includes some heroic cheating by the masters:

The match was to be in the charge of a prominent member of the staff, and there was some speculation whether he could interpret the rules of soccer as well as he could foreign languages. He was to be assisted by a panel of umpires, who would presumably act with the judgement of Solomon [Solomon was one of the masters].

At precisely thirty-one minutes past four hostilities began. The Masters' captain immediately showed his capabilities and directed the initial attack with Hector-like ferocity. From the outset it was apparent that this was no picnic party. The atmosphere in the forward line reached an almost Norman level of grimness [Norman was another master, known for being particularly stern].

The first half was uneventful except for two incidents. One of the umpires had, unknown to the referee, who however, was not in a position to see, produced a whistle, which he blew just as the School was about to score. This skull-duggery can have no peer. Late in the first half dense smoke covered the ground, reeking foully. It is thought that the Masters had bribed a gardener to make smoke at the appropriate moment.

The opening moments of the next half were marked by some heady arguments between opposing forwards. It was now that a keen-eyed spectator remarked on the seemingly large number of Masters. A quick count revealed twelve, a fact of which the referee seemed unaware.

The match ended goalless – probably for the best.

The College also catered for less physical tastes. There was the Film Society and a full-size cinema screen (although boys often complained about the frequent interruptions to change reels, "usually in the most exciting part"); the Camera Club; the Press Club; the Miniature Rifle Club; the Engineering Club; the Dramatic Society; the Young Farmers' Club (1957 highlights: a film on rabbit control and an illustrated lecture on lucerne growing); and the Junior Debating Society, which covered subjects as varied as tourist provisions in New Zealand, and Britain's H-bomb tests in the Pacific.

***

One contemporary of Kik's at Christ's College was Justice Andrew Tipping, who as 'A.P.C. Tipping' peppers the school boards and records as one of those extraordinary over-achievers: Head Prefect of Harper House, School Prefect, Captain of Hockey, Hon. Secretary of the Games Committee, the Dialectic Society, and the Kit Kat Club. Tipping went on to become a distinguished member of New Zealand's Supreme Court, and in an interview with *The Press* in January 2008 he said Kik was always popular and would have a go at everything – although often "with an enthusiasm unmatched by skill":

> *He had a certain charm and flair. He was a bit unconventional and this made him popular. If he spoke, people took notice. He was respected. He was a definite presence.*

Kik's enthusiasm on the rugby pitch earned him a regular place as a flanker in the Second XV, as well as the occasional appearance in the First XV – an impressive achievement in rugby-mad Canterbury. Roger House, another contemporary of Kik's at Christ's who went on to become a world-class surgeon in the US and UK, compared Kik to the infamous England flanker Lewis 'Mad Dog' Moody for the way he charged around the field without a thought for his – or anyone else's – safety. No doubt the legions of boys crammed in upon the wooden tiered benches running the full length of 'Upper', the main school rugby pitch, were thoroughly entertained by Kik's cavalier style.

Aside from sport, Kik's main extra-curricular interest was music. He captained the military band in his last two years at school, leading on the trumpet. The school report from June 1959 describes the spirit in the band as 'the best we have had for many years'. They wore a uniform of khaki drill shirts and longs, boots, gaiters and webb belts. There are photos of the band from 1959 and 1960, with Kik standing front and centre looking mightily impressive – like a young Indiana Jones.

Another photo shows Kik looking particularly dashing in bow tie and cummerbund, letting rip on his trumpet while playing with his group 'The Metronomes'. Kik was known affectionately by his bandmates as 'Woood', thanks to the heavily Gallic pronunciation by his French teacher at school (Kik and Richard would continue to call each other 'Woood' thereafter). 'The Metronomes' would travel all over rural Canterbury to play, squeezed into a Model A Ford coupé, singing loudly together, Kik leaning in at key moments for emphasis.

Bob recalls his bandmate Woood with great fondness:

We have enjoyed watching two top American classic big bands tour NZ in recent years, and as they play it all comes back. When the trumpet player stands to play his solo, what I really see is that gentlemanly, tall Christ's College fellow with his characteristic fair-haired fringe, trumpet raised there again, and the sheer joy he brought with his music and his company.

Kik also moonlighted as a guest trumpeter in the college Dance Band, which went by the name of the 'Black 'n' White Rockers'. In 1959 the band played at the dance hosted by St Margaret's College, the girls' equivalent of Christ's College, which Sally and Marianne attended. By this point Kik had become highly sought after by girls. In her tribute for the funeral, Sally recalled:

As Kik matured he became exceptionally good-looking. He even undertook some modelling assignments. Older girls started to seek us out to talk to us – about Kik! We were delighted to receive this attention, even if it was entirely on account of our gorgeous brother!

It was while attempting to impress some girls that Kik had his first brush with the law. In 1957 Kik and Richard had spent the school holidays working as potato-pickers, a muddy and back-breaking job but quite well paid. Instead of investing their hard-earned cash in more of their favourite Dinky toy cars, they decided to buy a real one: a 1928 Austin 7. It cost them 39 pounds and ten shillings. In those days in New Zealand you could get your driving licence at the age of fifteen so Richard was a legal driver – but naturally Kik would often get behind the wheel. It was his car too, after all.

The car had a canvas roof which had been painted stiff and therefore was no longer convertible. Thankfully, one day the family cat fell through the roof and destroyed it; thereafter the car was a convertible again, although permanently so.

And so it was that on a fine summer's day in 1957, during the school holidays, the two brothers were enjoying the company of four girls and took the opportunity to offer them a lift home in their prized possession. Kik, aged fourteen, took the wheel, with one girl sitting beside him, while the other three girls draped themselves with Richard around the back and side of the car with their feet perched on the back seat. Thus arranged, like two Metelli parading through Rome with a captured harem, the Woods brothers piloted their chariot down the high street in Christchurch.

Inevitably, this extraordinary procession attracted attention. A moment later a large black Humber Super Snipe police car drew alongside and motioned to the Austin to stop. Kik obliged. An exceedingly large and impressive police sergeant then got out and walked solemnly over to the vehicle. He told the occupants to get out. Once they had done so he pointed out that it was illegal to travel with people sitting on the back, and produced his notebook. He asked Kik for his licence, which of course was not available. There then followed a short conversation:

Sergeant: "How old are you?"

Kik: "Fourteen, sir."

"Fourteen?!" [This was written down.]

"What's your occupation?"

"Schoolboy."

"Schoolboy??!!" [Ditto.]

"Which school?"

"Christ's College."

"Christ's College*???!!!"*** [Scribble.]

"What's your address?"

"Sydenham Vicarage."

"SYDENHAM VICARAGE????!!!!"

He told the girls to make their own way home and sent the boys on their way, with Richard – who did have his licence – at the wheel. The boys went straight home and immediately told their father what had happened. Just as well, because that evening the Sergeant telephoned Sam and asked whether they had informed him. Sam confirmed that they had, and was left to deliver his sentence: they could not use the car for the rest of the holidays. Fortunately this was only a matter of days.

Despite this brush with the law, and a growing penchant for parties and girls, Kik was not a particular cause for concern for his parents. He got on well with both of them. Sam was calm and very considerate, and enjoyed discussing a wide range of subjects with all of his children; and while Sybil could certainly be demanding, particularly in terms of academic achievement, she was a devoted mother to them all. Christ's College no doubt deserves a lot of credit for Kik's promising development: their vision, even today, is to create 'virtuous men who make a positive contribution to society'. There were no signs of teenage strife – at least not yet.

***

In 1960 Kik was made a House Prefect, one of only five in Harper. By this point he had a strong academic record: he had won school prizes for French and Latin in 1959, and then won the Somes Junior Scholarship for his final year in 1960, despite Headmaster Hornsby noting he was still "not good at exams"; he was also one of only two boys to be invited to study certain papers from the University of Canterbury. Hornsby duly placed Kik in his Current Affairs class, reserved for the brightest students. The Nixon/Kennedy election of 1960 was a particularly hot topic, and mock debates were staged.

But it was Kik's general all-round contribution and positive character – perhaps the "presence" Justice Tipping recalls – which led Hornsby to recommend him for a unique scholarship to Dartmouth College, a prestigious Ivy League university in Hanover, New Hampshire. The Major John Wilfred Findlay Memorial Scholarship had been established by Helen Findlay in memory of her late husband, who had enjoyed professional links with New Zealand.

By offering this route out of New Zealand, Hornsby was perpetuating a trend at this time for the best of Kiwi brains to drain abroad as they approached their peak. In his *Penguin History of New Zealand*, Michael King notes this loss of NZ academic talent to international institutions, and cites the American scholar Margaret Mead: "[It] is New Zealand's role to send out its bright young men and women to help run the rest of the world. And they go, not hating the country of their birth but loving it. From this base they make their mark on the world." King also references another academic, John Mulgan, who attended Oxford University before WWII and expressed similar feelings when he encountered his Kiwi countrymen fighting Germans in the North African desert:

> *They had confidence in themselves…knowing themselves as good as the best the world could bring against them, like a football team in a more deadly game, coherent, practical, successful. Everything that was good from that small remote country had gone into them – sunshine and strength, good sense, patience, the versatility of practical men.*

In his nomination letter to the University of Canterbury, through which the Findlay Scholarship was administered, and then in a letter to the Dean of Freshmen at Dartmouth, Hornsby gives us a wonderfully honest account of the teenage Kik:

> *Woods is a very competent young man, with plenty of reserve character. He was pretty young when he came to us and went through a period when he did not know whether he liked New Zealand, or hankered for England, but he is now perfectly well adjusted and fits in very well with New Zealand life. He is a good strong boy, well-mannered and quiet to talk to; he is playing football* [rugby] *this year for the First and Second XV; he may, for all I know, get his Colours. He plays tennis in the Summer, and has been leader of the School band for two years; he is an excellent cornet player. I think he writes an extremely good essay.*
>
> *…He has not made up his mind what he wishes to be; it may well be business in some shape or form, though he has at times been interested in school-mastering. I think he is very likely to go into business.*
>
> *…He is extremely acceptable to his fellows, and I should imagine would go down well in America, but he has sufficient common sense not to be bowled over by the very different American approach to secondary schools and universities from that of New Zealand: he would in fact keep his head.*
>
> *…Emotionally he keeps his feet pretty well on the ground, is well adjusted as far as the opposite sex is concerned, has out of doors interests in the holidays, as have most New Zealand boys, enjoys games, has a genuine religious belief, and altogether a reasonable brain.*

***

We don't know what Kik thought about this opportunity. He could easily have decided to finish his schooling at Christ's and continued to the University of Canterbury at the end of the year like many of his peers, including the precocious A.P.C. Tipping. Richard – himself a prize-winner at Christ's – would follow a route back to the UK by winning a place at Brasenose College, Oxford.

Perhaps Kik saw Dartmouth as a chance to do something different to Richard. Or perhaps he saw the chance to live and study in America as just too good to turn down – it was 1960 after all, and Dartmouth was already gaining a reputation for being a good place to party.

Napier, Southport, Hatfield, Birchington-on-Sea, Christchurch – and now Hanover, New Hampshire. Life had certainly filled Kik to the brim with sunshine, strength, good sense, patience, versatility, practicality – and a penchant for having a good time. Now was his chance to go and make his mark on the world.

***

Out there things can happen
and frequently do
to people as brainy
and footsy as you.

And when things start to happen,
don't worry. Don't stew.
Just go right along.
You'll *start happening too.*

OH!
THE PLACES YOU'LL GO!

You'll be on your way up!
You'll be seeing great sights!
You'll join the high fliers
who soar to high heights.

You won't lag behind, because you'll have the speed.
You'll pass the whole gang and you'll soon take the lead.
Wherever you fly, you'll be best of the best.
Wherever you go, you will top all the rest…

— Dr. Seuss, *Oh, The Places You'll Go!*
(a Dartmouth alumnus)

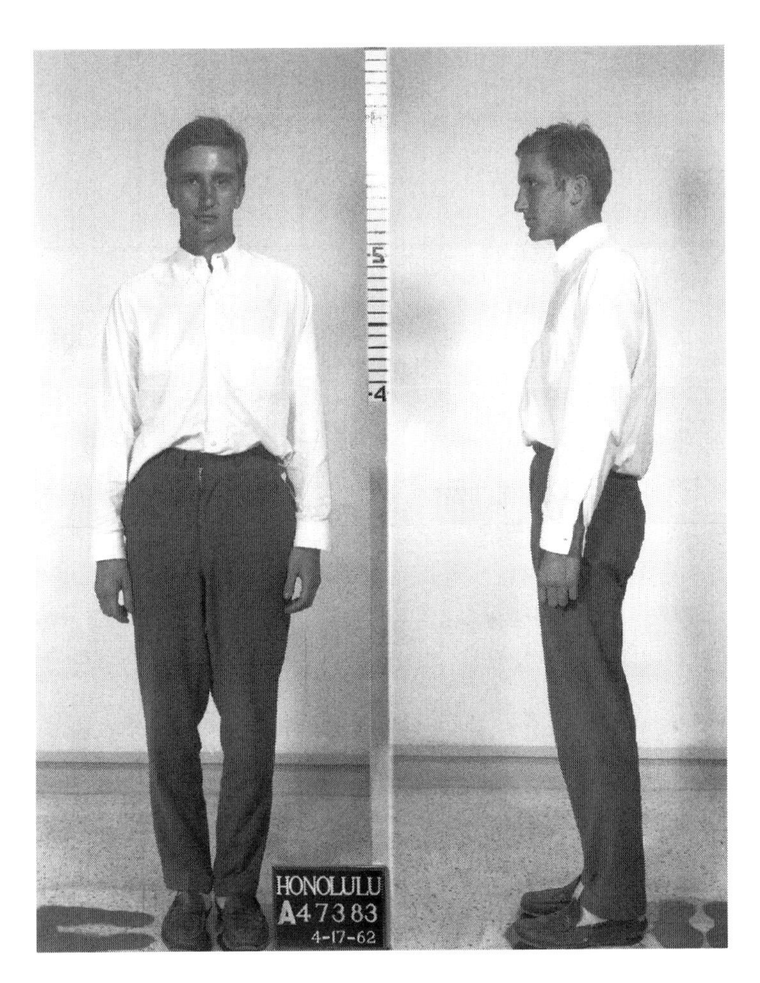

Prisoner K21875; Age: 19; Weight: 186lbs; Height: 6'1"

CHAPTER 3
Wah-Hoo-Wah!
(1960–1962)

...Except when you don't.
Because, sometimes, you won't.

I'm sorry to say so
but, sadly, it's true
that Bang-ups
and Hang-ups
can *happen to you.*

You can get all hung up
in a prickle-ly perch.
And your gang will fly on.
You'll be left in a Lurch.

— Dr. Seuss, *Oh, The Places You'll Go!*
(cont'd, HarperCollins, 1990)

Kik sits nervously on the end of a bench in the corner of the jail cell, elbows on his knees, hands clasped, head down, eyes fixed firmly on the floor, small beads of sweat stuck to his brow. He is sharing the cell with around twenty other prisoners, many of whom look like they're at the wrong end of a major moonshine binge, and they are penned in next to one another like the sheep at a Stock Judging Competition back in Canterbury.

There is one lavatory, in the centre of the room.

It's not too hot outside – around 28c, about average for this time of year in Honolulu – but Kik is heavy with emotion, his white shirt clinging to his back and his shoulders, bare feet moist in his brown leather loafers.

How did this happen? What on earth are Far and Ma going to say when they find out?

The thought of his parents' reactions – Sybil stern, Sam disappointed – makes his heart pound in his ears and his stomach churn. His mouth is dry and his hands are clammy. He feels the acidic burn of bile in the back of his throat. But he'd really rather not use the lavatory now – he's only used it in the dark of the night since he was placed in the cell three days ago.

That seems like an age ago now. The terrifying sight of the police officers at the airport. His pathetic attempt to avoid them. The arrest. The humiliation of being handcuffed and marched back out of the terminal in front of all those people. Being bundled into the waiting car and driven the short distance, along the beautiful harbour and past Honolulu City Hall, to the Honolulu Police Department. The conviction on a charge of 'Fraud – Misdemeanor'. The sentencing: 30 days' confinement. And the fine of 100 dollars, which of course he couldn't pay.

That was the whole point! I was trying to earn some money! How was I to know my US permit had expired? That hotel guy just wouldn't listen...he knew I'd been training for two weeks to sell those bloody saucepans...but if I can't work, how am I supposed to pay?!

Kik puts his face in his hands. His golden hair, now a little dank and dreary, still manages to catch the eye of one or two prisoners.

Suddenly a portly officer approaches the door of the cell, keys jangling. The energy in the room shifts. Everybody is alive, alert, expectant. "CHRISTOPHER WOODS!" shouts the officer. Kik sits bolt upright. The officer motions for him to come over. Kik's heart is pounding again, but this time in hope. "Your luck's in, kid," says the officer. "God's really got a sense of humour. The Bishop's wife is here for you. And she's taking you to church."

***

And so it was that Kik – Prisoner K21875; Age: 19; Weight: 186lbs; Height: 6'1" – was released from jail, 27 days early, on the good word of the Bishop of Honolulu's wife. It was Good Friday, 20th April 1962. And Kik was indeed taken straight to the Three Hour Service at St Andrew's Cathedral.

He was fortunate that Dartmouth had followed up on his premature departure from the University – after only five terms – with a letter to his parents. If they hadn't then Kik would almost certainly have spent a full 30 days in jail. The first Sam and Sybil heard, in terms of anything that was amiss, was the arrival of a letter dated 10th April and received in New Zealand on 16th April, from Robert K. Hage – Dartmouth's Director of Financial Aid, and quite a robust character by the sound of things:

Dear Mr and Mrs Woods,

I should report to you officially what you already know: that Christopher lost his scholarship because of a second term of exceptionally poor grades which led to his being put on probation. We gave him a non-refundable ticket to New Zealand and he left New York City on Friday, March 30.

It is not easy to tell parents that their son was a great disappointment, but I believe we owe that to you. Christopher is a boy of fine ability, but for some reason he never began to put it to good use here at Dartmouth. He didn't even try. Perhaps he's just going through a period of rebellion which many young people go through and we sincerely hope that he will redeem himself in whatever he does.

It is going to be even more difficult to tell you that Christopher left behind him an appalling number of debts…You'll be hearing more from me about this at a later time.

We all found Christopher a delightful person with talent and charm. His problems are serious but not insurmountable and I know will require much understanding and help from both of you.

I shall certainly be glad to hear from you if you would like to ask any questions or make any comments on Christopher's experiences and attitudes.

Sincerely,

R.K. Hage

Of course, Sam and Sybil did have a few questions – such as where on earth Kik was.

Some rather hasty enquiries revealed that on Friday 30th March Kik had indeed boarded Qantas Flight 501 at Idlewild Airport (renamed John F. Kennedy Airport the following year, after the President's assassination), bound for Sydney via San Francisco, Honolulu and Nadi International Airport in Fiji; in Nadi, on Sunday 1st April, he was supposed to transfer onto Flight 773 to Auckland; and once in Auckland he was to board Flight 125 to Christchurch. Somewhere along this route he had clearly gone missing.

After a number of phone calls with various contacts, including Director Hage and Harry Kennedy, the Bishop of Honolulu, they managed to track him down.

In a second letter, dated 20th April, Hage seems a little more contrite:

I can understand your anxiety as a result of having received my letter of April 10 without having heard directly from Christopher about his difficulties. When it was certain that he would leave, I gave Christopher some money with which to send you a cable to tell you he was returning home; and of course we expected him to reach New Zealand a few days after the cable and before my letter. Now that I know he did not follow through on either of these, I wish I had cabled you myself, though I am not sure this would have relieved you of any worry.

[This is followed by some practical details about Kik's departure from Dartmouth and their own attempts to find him via the US immigration department.]

When you do locate Christopher, please notify me by collect cable, as we too are anxious to know of his welfare. And if I can do anything further to be helpful to you, please let me know.

Sybil responded on 29th April, seven days after Kik's return on 22nd April. Ma – as she was known to her children and grandchildren – was a pretty serious character, occasionally a little foreboding to tell the truth, but she was also wonderfully protective of her brood. She would have had a few strong words for young Kik as he finally arrived home on Easter Day. Yet in her response to Mr Hage she came to the defence of her errant offspring:

Dear Mr Hage,

My husband and I were very glad to receive your second letter (of the 20th April) yesterday. Your first letter and our telephone conversation with you had been profoundly disturbing because they seemed to imply that Christopher had become a dissolute spendthrift, with no sense of responsibility to anyone. This was so different to his character prior to going to America that we were filled with apprehension and dismay. This, on top of our anxiety as to his safety, gave us four days of intense misery.

I think you should know that you entirely misjudged his reactions. When you told him that his scholarship was terminated he felt as though the world had fallen about his ears. His major worry was that he would leave the States with debts unpaid and so be a financial drain on us.

…On leaving New York his one idea was to get away quietly by himself, think things through and somehow try to clear his debts before returning to N.Z. He bought Mitchener's book 'Hawaii' in N.Y. and read it on the plane and decided to leave the plane in Honolulu and seek employment. This he did, not knowing it was illegal. The fifty dollars travelling expenses you had so kindly given him had dwindled to less than thirty before he left N.Y. because he had to send two heavy crates of books, linen, blankets and clothes by sea and pay his rail fare to N.Y. etc. You will see how wrong you were in thinking that he had got off at Honolulu in a nonchalant frame of mind 'to have a good time with your fifty dollars'.

He wrote us a long letter on April 1st (which he had to send surface mail owing to a lack of money) expressing his deep regrets and shock at the turn of events and telling us of his decision to stay in Honolulu and earn enough dollars to repay his debts and to give him something towards resuming his studies in this country. (Owing to the shipping strike we have only just received this letter.) He booked in at a cheap hotel and after a week selling Encyclopedias door to door for Collins Ltd. he answered an advertisement from a well-known steel firm and was taken on as a sales representative. The snag about this job was that it involved a fortnight's initial training without pay; but thereafter the pay was at the rate of 80 to 100 dollars per week. He completed his fortnight's training and all this time he was eating at a bare subsistence level – in fact for the last four days he was virtually starving.

On the day that he was to begin earning with the firm he was so hungry that he realised he couldn't carry on until he received his first pay check, so he went to the British consul for advice and assistance…On seeing his visa the secretary at the Consulate informed him that it was illegal for him to remain in the country and that he certainly couldn't earn there and advised him to return at once to N.Z. This he then tried to do but the people at the hotel wouldn't believe his story…and arrested him and he spent the next three days in Honolulu gaol. By this time we had the Bishop of Honolulu and Mrs. Kennedy searching for him and with the help of the Immigration people and the police he was eventually rescued and returned to us on Easter Day.

…Although he has been put back two years in his studies it has all been good experience, even the gaol, and he seems in no way the worse for all his adventures.

Yours very sincerely,

Sybil Woods

How had it come to this? What had turned the optimism of the summer of 1960 into the half-starved, incarcerated despair of Easter 1962? Why had the younger son turned into a prodigal one?

***

It had all started pretty well. This was of course a hugely exciting time to be heading to America. In 1945, Winston Churchill had declared that America "stands at the summit of the world" – and, if anything, by 1960 that summit had climbed even further into the stratosphere.

As Bill Bryson has pointed out in *The Life and Times of the Thunderbolt Kid* (his wonderful memoir of a childhood in small-town America, published by Broadway Books, 2006), the 1950s was a decade of remarkable prosperity for the US, which in 1959 appended the 49th and 50th states of Alaska and Hawaii (unfortunately for Kik). Competition between America and the Soviet Union resulted in unprecedented developments in space and nuclear technology. Between 1945 and 1960 the Gross National Product more than doubled, from $200 billion to over $500 billion. Rates of unemployment were low, and wages were high. The public had more money to spend than ever, and thanks to a proliferation in consumer goods, they also had more things to spend it on. By 1951, almost 90 per cent of American families had refrigerators, and nearly 75 per cent had washing machines, telephones, vacuum cleaners, and gas or electric stoves. By 1953, Americans owned around 80 per cent of the world's electrical goods. The 5 per cent of people on the planet who were Americans had more wealth than the other 95 per cent combined.

In some ways it is surprising that Kik was trying to sell saucepans at all, instead of some gargantuan nuclear kitchen appliance.

So by the summer of 1960, as Kik prepared to depart for Dartmouth, many Americans believed they were standing at the dawn of a golden age. This would have been exciting enough for a 17-year-old, leaving his friends at Christ's College before the final term of the year, on a prominent scholarship to a celebrated institution of the world's leading nation. But he was also going to fly for the first time – a thrilling prospect.

The 1950s had witnessed the start of aviation's own golden age. Aeroplane trips weren't just a means of going on holiday, they were a holiday in themselves. Passengers would dress up in their finest to fly. They lined up for group photos before boarding. On a two-deck, four-propeller-engined Boeing Stratocruiser Clipper – the type which flew the route Kik was taking from Honolulu to San Francisco – amenities included a lounge with leather walls, seven-course meals catered by *Maxim's* of Paris, and 'for the ladies, orchids'.

Air travel was of course prohibitively expensive – Kik was given $700 from the Findlay Memorial Scholarship to cover his trip, which equates to over $5,600 in today's money. It was also prohibitively unsafe: lower cabin ceilings and inferior seat belt designs meant that a bad patch of turbulence could leave you with a broken neck. Mid-air collisions were fairly unexceptional. Engines dropped out of planes so often that they weren't even recorded as accidents if the other engine could land them safely. On one tragic occasion in March 1960, a brand new Northwest Airlines Lockheed Electra *lost both of its wings* – they just fell off – killing all 63 on board.

***

In September 1960, it was in fact Northwest Airlines which carried Kik to Dartmouth College. He was seventeen, and although he had enjoyed plenty of privilege already in his life, it must have been quite something to arrive in the picture-perfect college town of Hanover just as the glorious New Hampshire forests were embraced by autumn.

This was the Ivy League at its finest. Dartmouth's stunning 269-acre campus resides on the banks of the Connecticut River, which divides New Hampshire and Vermont. The College's natural beauty had been noted by President Dwight D. Eisenhower, who visited in 1953 and announced, "This is what a college should look like."

Dartmouth was founded in 1769, the seventh of the eight Ivy League universities (and the furthest north) – the others being Harvard (1636), Yale (1701), Pennsylvania (1740), Princeton (1746), Columbia (1754), Brown (1764), and Cornell (1865). It was the last of the Ivy League universities to be founded under British colonial rule, established with a charter granted by King George III with funds donated by the 2nd Earl of Dartmouth and others.

Like Harvard, Yale and Princeton, Dartmouth's founder was a Calvinist, a minister from Connecticut named Rev Eleazar Wheelock. He himself had been educated at Yale. His primary vision was for a college where local Abenaki Indian men could be educated and trained for missionary work, although 'English Youth and any others' were also included in the charter.

As well as being Dartmouth's founder and first President, Wheelock also served as a Trustee, Professor of Divinity, and Minister of the College Church. And it took all of his entrepreneurial passion and skill to preserve the fledgling enterprise on the northern frontiers of the European settlement, particularly during the wars of the American Revolution. Dartmouth's motto, chosen by Wheelock, is *Vox clamantis in deserto* – 'A voice crying out in the wilderness'.

By the time Kik arrived in 1960, total enrolment at the College was around 3,000, with just under 800 in his year – the Class of '64. Even now Dartmouth only hosts a little over 6,000 undergraduate and graduate students, making it easily the smallest of all the Ivy League universities (Harvard and Columbia have well over 20,000 each).

Kik had been welcomed to Dartmouth in a letter from Davis Jackson, the Assistant Director of Admissions, sent in July. In it Mr Jackson outlined a few essentials:

> *We have every confidence that you will acquit yourself well academically and that you will find your undergraduate career at Dartmouth both challenging and rewarding.*
>
> *Under the terms of the Findlay Scholarship grant, Dartmouth will provide you with full tuition, dormitory room accommodations, and your meals while College is in session. In addition, there will be provided $400 in cash* [$3,200 today] *for miscellaneous personal expenses such as books, furnishings, clothing, laundry, entertainment etc. Your scholarship will be continued in subsequent years, so long as your record is entirely satisfactory, until you graduate with a Bachelor of Arts degree in June 1964.*

Kik was also required to fill in the usual plethora of information forms on his arrival, which contain a selection of fascinating titbits:

Best-liked subjects: *French, German, English*

Least-liked subjects: *Math, Science (Chemistry, Physics)*

Name of Faculty adviser: *Professor Sensenig, Major Ladd*

List the two most valuable part-time and summer jobs you've held: *Woolstore, Tannery*

In what ways was this of value? *Met other types of people from different ways of life*

Have you selected a Major? *Yes* If so, what? *French*

Is the problem of deciding what occupation or profession you ought to enter after college a source of worry to you? *Sometimes, but not seriously*

List in order of preference two or three vocations in which you are interested or which you have considered: *Foreign representative for company; Diplomatic service*

Reasons for interest: *Interest in people of all types, and also organization, experience of progressive organizations*

Have your parents or friends suggested any particular career to you? *No*

Kik was housed in 201A Little Hall, a smart, new redbrick undergraduate block located just behind the infamous Webster Avenue – aka 'Frat Row'. This would prove to be rather an unhelpful proximity in due course. Kik's roommate was a hardy-looking chap named Kevin McDonough, from North Syracuse in New York. At North Syracuse Central High, McDonough had won honours in Football, Track and Wrestling. His nickname was "Kev".

In his Classbook photo, Kev resembles the archetypal Ivy Leaguer: handsome, well-proportioned head and sturdy neck emerging from a pristine, pinned shirt and tie, and thick jacket; gaze steady and sure; dark, lavish eyebrows converging on a proud nose; and a firm short back and sides, all of which confidently declares "Let's roll". Kik, on the other hand, looks a little bit…disturbed. All of the ingredients of his considerable good looks are there: the cheekbones and jawline, the luscious lips, flaxen locks, and magnificent Woods snout; but his shirt collar is a bit skew-whiff, his hair a little dishevelled, and his deep, brown eyes carry a slightly haunted look. The look of a boy who has just realised he is sharing digs with Flash Gordon.

Still, there was plenty of reassuring guidance for the young foreigner in the College Handbook. A small, Dartmouth-green hardback running to over 150 pages, it contained everything Kik and Kev needed to know about life at this great institution. It opened with some vigorous words from the President, John Sloan Dickey:

> *Your own destiny and the destiny of something larger than you will rest largely in your own hands. From here on you will have increasing opportunities to be something finer by choosing on your own not to be a loafer, a lout or a cheater. In short, you will learn to be men worthy of Dartmouth by choosing not to be something less…You have been admitted to Dartmouth because we believe you have it in you to make the right choices. You now have the opportunity to show us – and yourself – that your performance is worthy of both your promise and your privilege.*

Hop Holmberg, student Chairman of the Freshman Orientation, backed this up by stating that "To attend Dartmouth is a privilege and we are proud to have you."

So far, so inspirational. But the Freshman Orientation was quick to bring boys back down to earth. There were twelve responsibilities outlined in the Handbook, including: "1. Freshmen must wear class hats and name tags at all times and in all public places 2. Freshmen must have name plates on their doors…4. Freshmen must attend all rallies and class meetings…7. Freshmen shall carry furniture and do odd jobs for the upperclassmen. This is a one-year investment for a three-year return 8. Freshmen shall build all college bonfires". And the excellent "11. Freshmen shall refrain from collective or individual rowdyism." Freshmen were left in absolutely no doubt as to the implications of failing to take these responsibilities seriously: "The Undergraduate Council considers these responsibilities very important. If you violate them, you will be interviewed by a board of upperclassmen. If they find that your violation was wilful and repeated, you will be taken before the Steering Committee. This Committee has authority to punish you."

One of the other responsibilities for Freshmen was to learn all the Dartmouth songs and cheers. The Official College Cheer was entitled *Wah-hoo-wah!*, and went like this:

Wah-hoo-wah!
Wah-hoo-wah!
Dart-muth!
Wah-hoo-wah!
Dart-MUTH! Dart-MUTH! Dart-MUTH!

The origins of the *Wah-hoo-wah!* are not clear. Different authors have claimed everything from the name of a patent medicine to several trees or shrubs, a tropical fish, a small town in Nebraska, or a fabled Indian warrior chief. You would imagine the college men preferred channelling the warrior chief at Ivy League sports events, rather than the tropical fish.

Dartmouth's Indian heritage was referenced in other official Dartmouth cheers, including one entitled the *Dartmouth Indian*:

I-i-i-i-n-n-n-n-d-i-a-n
I-i-i-i-n-n-n-n-d-i-a-n
I-N-D-I-A-N
Dart-MUTH
I-i-i-i-n-n-n-n-d-i-a-n
SCALP 'EM!!!

Presumably this one has been discontinued.

***

At the end of September, President Dickey addressed the Freshmen at the opening of the College's 192nd year. It was the dawn of a new academic decade, and the dawn of a defining decade for the country as a whole: before the Class of '64 would graduate, they would teeter on the brink of nuclear war in the Cuban Missile Crisis; experience the confusion and conspiracies of the JFK assassination; be dragged further into a fateful, futile war in Vietnam; and see the civil rights movement gain historic momentum, including the passage of the landmark Civil Rights Act. After the apple pie simplicity of the 1950s, life in the 1960s was about to get a lot more complex – and fast. Dickey didn't hold back:

> *The time permitted for solving a problem has always been one of the fundamental factors on any job. Whether the urgency of the brief sixty minutes permitted to you to shine on the all-too-familiar hour exam, or the fact that for nations war is a race to victory where the prize is survival, our mortal and finite world at every point is bounded by time factors.*
>
> *I believe that today's central challenge to man's moral and political development is that the time factor permitted to him in the past for a gradual evolutionary growth has been suddenly and drastically cut short by the scientific revolution and the cascade of physical power it has loosened onto a socially and politically primitive international community. Man's most ancient reassurance, that 'time cures all things', has become his most dangerous delusion.*
>
> *Leading by the light of reason in today's world is not child's play. Even we in this most fortunate America have some fast growing up to do.*
>
> *I do believe that leadership is man's only tried and trusted answer to great urgencies and that bold minds are his only hope for creative solutions. It is because I believe these things that I believe in you and in the greatness of the fact life now offers us for our appointed task – your education at Dartmouth.*
>
> *Your business here is learning and that is up to you.*
>
> *We will be with you all the way. Good luck!*

***

After all this preparation and galvanising rhetoric, it is baffling that young Kik's academic performance never really took flight. In truth, it staggered along the runway for a bit and then crashed into a bush. After his fourth term, with a grade of 1.7 (the maximum being 5.0), Kik was given an official Warning and it was agreed that he should achieve a score of

3.7 for the next two terms. When he only achieved another 1.7 in Term 5, including a zero for Life Sciences, he was put on Probation and his scholarship was suspended – and he left Dartmouth. (It is apt that Life Sciences effectively finished him off – our family has never had a talent for the sciences. Not one of Kik's five offspring took a single science at A-Level.)

Given his excellent academic record at Christ's College, the results were both disappointing and surprising. There were a number of potential contributing factors. As we have seen, his old headmaster at Christ's, Headmaster Hornsby, had informed Dartmouth in one of his recommendation letters that Kik was "a poor examinee" but did believe "he has sufficient common sense not to be bowled over by the very different American approach to secondary schools and universities from that of New Zealand; he would in fact keep his head."

However in a letter to the Christchurch Department of Education, dated 27th April 1962, with Kik now back in New Zealand and looking to continue his studies at the University of Canterbury, Hornsby drew attention to the contrasting educational approaches:

Woods has now returned to this country after a year and two terms at Dartmouth University, and he does not intend to return to America. At Dartmouth in his first year he did French, English, Government, Psychology, Geology, Art, and in the last two terms Music, French, English, History, Sociology and Life Sciences. This may well seem absurd to you, as it does to me, but this is the system of American Universities to do vast numbers of unrelated units.

There were other perspectives on Kik's performance. A year earlier in August 1961, the University of Canterbury had corresponded with President Dickey of Dartmouth to make arrangements for a visit, as they considered the next round of applicants for the Findlay Memorial Scholarship. In doing so they enquired after Kik: "We trust that Christopher Woods is proving a worthy holder."

President Dickey responded amiably, assuring Canterbury of a warm welcome for their visit, and took the opportunity to evaluate Kik's worthiness a little:

> *After receiving your letter I requested a preliminary report from the Director of the Offices of Financial Aid here at Dartmouth, Mr Robert K. Hage, about Christopher Woods' first year with us. Mr Hage describes his academic performance as 'spotty'...He ranked 347 in a class of 775 at the end of the year.*
>
> *Christopher also apparently had a somewhat 'spotty' experience with his finances, particularly in managing some of his personal 'extracurricular' expenditures but Mr Hage believes these difficulties were perhaps to be expected in the course of his adjustment to a very different kind of social life...*
>
> *In short, I gather that Christopher has had a reasonably satisfactory introduction to American life and I think there is a good prospect that from here on he will be able to show a somewhat more distinguished academic performance.*

***

The reference to Kik's financial eccentricities is interesting. This is certainly a recurring theme of his time at Dartmouth, and one which clearly got the formidable Mr Hage – Director of Financial Aid after all – very energised indeed. It's possible that the decision to remove Kik's scholarship, no doubt driven primarily by poor grades, was influenced by his reputation for 'dropping bad checks around town' as one report said.

In April 1962, after Kik had departed Dartmouth, Hage wrote to Professor Sensenig (Kik's Foreign Student Advisor) to explain why his scholarship had been withdrawn, and attached a memo entitled, 'The Financial Foibles of Christopher Woods'. It's the kind of memo you probably don't want sitting on your record in the archives, waiting to be discovered by your offspring 53 years later. In it Hage unleashes his frustrations at the lack of care and consideration shown by the young scholarship student, and opens with this:

I first became acquainted with Mr Woods' shortcomings in the handling of money when he reported to Mr McCurdy that three checks totalling $14.80 had 'bounced'...and that he had no resources to start with on his vacation. (Later he told me that he knew he did not have enough in the bank to cover the checks but 'I have to eat.') We asked him for a statement of his expenses and resources to date on the basis of which I gave him a lecture on finances.

In his subsequent correspondence with Sam and Sybil in May, Hage referred to "an appalling number of debts and checks drawn against insufficient funds", outlining a list of Kik's personal outstanding obligations to other students totalling $174.61 as well as "eight checks which Christopher wrote when he had nothing in the bank, the last one having been when he closed his bank account and was in Hawaii." Of course Kik eventually ended up in prison there, fleeing to the airport when confronted by his inability to pay his hotel bill.

Why was he struggling so badly? It wasn't for a lack of funds – Hage pointed out to Sam and Sybil that Kik's scholarship of $2,700 was the most generous in the history of the University. A clue would appear to be in President Dickey's use of the phrase "extracurricular expenditures" – and for this, there are three likely explanations: high society with Helen Findlay; girls; and his fraternity, Sigma Alpha Epsilon (SAE).

Firstly, Mrs Findlay – or "Aunt Helen" as Kik referred to her, which shows how fond she was of her young patronee. Aunt Helen lived in Manhattan, a wealthy widow residing on the refined Upper East Side. Her late husband had worked on Operation Deep Freeze, the joint US/NZ Antarctic programme based in Christchurch, and so she had retained a sentimental link to New Zealand.

She seemed delighted with the charms of her prototype model scholar. In January 1961, after Kik's first term, Hage sent a note to a few colleagues:

You gentlemen who are interested in Christopher Woods and/or the Major John Wilfred Findlay Memorial Scholarship should know of the life of a typical New Zealander at Dartmouth.

Apparently Mrs Findlay has taken an even greater personal interest in Woods than we would have expected. She has invited him to New York three times so far (once in early fall, once at Thanksgiving and once at Christmas). Apparently she treats him rather royally, but he has to take care of all out-of-pocket expenses such as transportation. When she invited him down for Christmas she told him he had to have a tuxedo and she actually paid for that. He stayed at her home for five days before she went to Florida and then she sent him to stay with a relative of hers in Philadelphia so that he could attend all of the debutante parties down there! He was moving in fast society – no doubt just what his minister father in New Zealand considers typical for all Americans.

I have had to increase his Findlay Scholarship by $100 to help him take care of some of the extra expenses he has incurred.

In the summer of 1961, Kik got a job on Nantucket Island, an exclusive holiday spot for the East Coast elite. Aunt Helen's residence there was No. 4 Lincoln Avenue (at the corner of Grant and Highland avenues), a large five-bedroom house set in half an acre of garden. It is now worth almost $10m. She subsequently moved to No. 10 Pleasant Street, in Nantucket's downtown Historic District; records show this was built in 1750, with five bedrooms and five bathrooms.

So Kik was living the high life, and earning $50 per week as a beach boy at Aunt Helen's private club. Ricky Nelson topped the charts in June 1961 with *Travelin' Man*, and it's easy to imagine the musical young Kiwi crooning along as he raked the sands on the pristine shoreline: "I'm a travelin' man / made a lot of stops all over the world / and in every port I opened the heart / of at least one lovely girl."

Back at Dartmouth, Kik was a regular visitor to the nearby female colleges, Skidmore and Smith. I say nearby – both are well over 100 miles away. But it was clearly worth the effort. In his fourth term alone, Kik spent five weekends at girls' colleges. By the end of term he had used up all of his summer savings, all of his Findlay Scholarship, owed $30 and had bounced three cheques – earning the wrath of Mr Hage, who in December 1961 vented his anger to Mr Richard Remsen, legal representative of the Scholarship in New York:

> *I got from him a detailed account of his expenses for the first term which included an entertainment figure of $130 (in addition to the $40 social dues at the fraternity). We normally figure that scholarship men should be able to get by on that amount or less for the entire year as far as entertainment is concerned.*
>
> *...I have just lent him $50 from a short-term emergency loan fund so that he can get down to Philadelphia for the Christmas holidays* [no doubt for more debutante balls]*...I am going to try to get him a job working at the Dartmouth Dining Association which will earn him $155 and which will keep him in town most of the weekends of this next term.*
>
> *...The thing that disturbs me most is that he can't see that what he has done is extravagant.*

In January 1962, Hage wrote to Kik to ensure that he sent a thank you letter to Mrs Findlay for a Christmas cheque she had given the young reveller, and to reimburse her for a laundry bill from Nantucket: "Needless to say, your dereliction in these matters just adds to our great disappointment in you."

***

As well as high society and sororities, at the beginning of his second year Kik was eligible to join a fraternity. Dartmouth is well known for its Greek system – perhaps explained by the lack of alternative social venues up there in the wilderness. The hugely popular 1978 film *Animal House*, set in 1962, was based partly on the fraternity experiences at Dartmouth of one of the scriptwriters, Chris Miller (Class of '63). Numerous other Hollywood productions – including *Old School, Revenge of the*

Nerds, Sorority Wars, Brotherhood, and the recent *Bad Neighbours* – have tried to capture the unique Greek culture of rushing, pledging, hazing, secrecy and general boisterous misbehaviour.

British universities are not exactly free of boisterous misbehaviour, and there are plenty of societies, clubs, and ingeniously destructive drinking games – but it's all rather tame in comparison with fraternities. Male Cambridge dining society activities consist almost exclusively of going for a curry every couple of weeks with a female dining society from another college. Attendees take their own wine or beer. And that's pretty much it. Bacchus would be bored stiff.

In contrast, Greek life in America is a little bit more intense. At the beginning of your sophomore (second) year, individuals 'rush' the fraternities and sororities, where each party appraises the other at various social events – and occasionally at formal interviews. Afterwards, existing members will convene privately to vote on whether to extend a formal invitation or 'bid' to the prospective applicant. Those applicants who receive a bid, and accept it, are considered to have 'pledged' the fraternity or sorority. Thus begins the pledge period, an extended phase of evaluation for the new pledges culminating in a second vote to certify whether the pledge is worthy of becoming a full member or not. Prospective full members are then invited to a formal and secret initiation ceremony in the private, sometimes secretly hidden, 'chapter room', with elaborate rituals often drawn from Masonic practice or the Greek mysteries. New members can then be furnished with secret mottos and identification signs such as handshakes and passwords. Possibly a few branded T-shirts too.

The 'hazing' of pledges and new members is the most infamous and contentious aspect of fraternities and sororities. Whereas the initiation of a new member of a Cambridge club might involve downing a pint or two of beer (potentially, if you're unlucky, a 'dirty' pint comprising various malts, liquors, crisps and bacon fries), the Americans are once again leagues ahead in terms of planning and effort. Partly this is just down to resources. The Dartmouth chapter of Sigma Alpha Epsilon (SAE) – the fraternity which Kik successfully pledged – has had its own custom-built mansion next to the college library since 1908 and holds more than $1m in a trust. Some fraternities have been known to spend $25,000 on beer and entertainment in a single term.

Indeed, fraternity expenditure is essentially about alcohol – vast, limitless, rhinoceros-flattening quantities of booze. It's not as if the entire chapter charters a private jet to Vegas for the weekend; most of the members are under the legal drinking age anyway. They simply convene at the chapter house and drink themselves into the floor.

According to the US National Institute on Alcohol Abuse and Alcoholism, the conventional definition of a 'binge' is five drinks in a two-hour period (which, let's be honest, sounds like a fairly average Wednesday evening in Chiswick). Modern frat boys at Dartmouth pride themselves on being able to drink six cups of beer in less than 30 seconds – this is called a 'Quick Six', and requires said frat boy to open the gullet and pour the beer straight down.

Of course, all of this feverish ingesting leads inevitably to a number of gestational responses, the main one being vomit – or 'boot' as it is known at Dartmouth. And, like the Romans before them, Dartmouth frat boys have embraced vomiting with gusto. In fact, it has become a ritual in itself. Puking and then continuing to drink is known as 'boot and rally'. SAE has a 'boot room', which is essentially a bathroom where brothers can go to stick their fingers down their throats – known as 'pulling the trigger' – and then resume festivities. A notorious game called 'Thunderdome' consists of two members doing multiple Quick Sixes until one of them vomits; the first person to vomit is the loser, at which point the winner celebrates by vomiting on the loser's head. Some brothers have even been forced to eat a 'Vomelette', which doesn't sound like something you would see on *Mary Berry Everyday*.

***

So the obvious conclusion from all of this masochistic mayhem is that this must have been what caused Kik's grades to drop off a cliff in his second year. It makes sense – it is presumably pretty difficult to concentrate on your exams when you have 'boot' dripping from your eyebrows.

And yet the memories which Kik related to his children years later – backed up separately by the accounts of his fellow brothers at SAE – suggested things were a little different in those days. That this reputation for serious debauchery is a relatively recent trend. In March 2016, the Dartmouth chapter of SAE was actually suspended and derecognised for a minimum of five years, the first time in their long history, due to 'violations of health and safety regulations'.

Back in 1961, Kik's experiences of hazing were a little more creative than this crude obsession with stomach fluids. They included swallowing a live goldfish; being blindfolded, placed in front of a toilet bowl, and told to scoop up and eat whatever was in there (it was a banana in a separate basin of water); having aeroplane glue lathered into the armpits and your arms then stuck to your sides; and lastly, most imaginatively, being instructed to sit on a large block of ice for a few minutes, wearing nothing but a jockstrap, and then seeing how far across the room you could carry a prune between your frozen buttocks.

Despite all of this, being part of a fraternity was actually considered to be a good thing for one's academic pursuits. Even now, many chapters require their members to maintain a certain academic standard – the culture, particularly at the Ivy League fraternities, is that you win, at everything, whether it be studies, sports, careers, or Thunderdome. In January 1962, when Kik was summoned to discuss his first term grades with Mr Hage, he claimed his fraternity were being "rough on him" because of his poor average. In Hage's letter to Sam and Sybil in May that year, after Kik's departure, he stated:

I actually thought joining a fraternity would be one of the answers to Kik's problems. Sigma Alpha Epsilon is one of the strongest fraternities on the campus (it has just been announced that they won the cup as the best all-round fraternity during the current year). They rank fourth in academic average of all the fraternities on the campus and take great pride in this standing.

So when we look at the "different kind of social life" to which President Dickey made reference – high society, sororities and SAE – we cannot be certain whether any or all of them explain Kik's poor grades. He was certainly living life to the full, but then a lot of his peers were too.

It is just possible, however, that the dashing young foreigner found it more difficult to combine Aphrodisia and Academia. The memories of Kik by his Greek contemporaries speak of a hugely popular and gregarious young man. One SAE peer, Tom Rand, recalls him thus:

Your Dad was one of the most engaging and interesting men ever to walk the planet…I take some considerable pride in the fact that I believe I exercised some considerable influence in his decision to rush and ultimately pledge SAE…

Chris participated gleefully in all of our rituals following that rush season…those included that silliness at the back door (our only permitted entrance) when we had to recite something I can't quite remember in the loudest decibels possible. The hazing he described to you was relatively innocent, though I had to go to Dick's House (the college infirmary) to get one of the nurses to remove the glue that one of the seniors had squeezed under my armpit.

…Funny the things you remember. One in particular for me is the vivid memory I've thought about often over the years of the time I asked Chris to read and critique a paper I had just finished. He was the picture of concentration, and when he finished reading he slapped the page and said, 'Tom, this is eloquent as shit!' I considered that a high compliment coming from your Dad.

Your Dad was a delight to be around as a young man, Francis, and I was really sorry that he didn't stick around and finish all four years with us. It was too short but I still value the memories of the good times and laughter we shared during those first two years at Dartmouth.

The young men who knew him for too short a time at Dartmouth are better for the experience. And you are most fortunate to have had him for a father.

Another friend from SAE recalls, "There was not a better party person than Chris. He was always first there and last out, and he liked to make things happen. Ladies liked him because he was infectiously enthusiastic." This may also explain Aunt Helen's particular fondness for Kik – good-looking, delightful company, and radiating an irresistible zest for life.

***

And yet, while Kik was clearly enjoying himself at Dartmouth, there are also clues to a deeper conflict at play – hints of an underlying self-doubt and search for purpose, struggles with his Christian faith, perhaps even a struggle with authority. These are themes which surface throughout the rest of his life, motifs in the minor key emerging to whisper an occasional warning, like Prokofiev's wolf prowling around the tree beneath the cheerful cat and the sprightly bird.

On Friday 2nd March 1962, towards the end of Term 5 and under pressure to save his scholarship – indeed, his very presence at Dartmouth – he was invited to see William S. MacNaughton, at the Office of Student Counselling. MacNaughton's notes are worth capturing in full:

Chris Woods came in today at my suggestion to discuss a number of things which have perhaps accounted for his difficulties, academic and otherwise, here at Dartmouth. At this point it appears he is headed for a C+ in History, a D in Life Science, and perhaps a B in French. This obviously falls short of the 3.7 which he had put as a goal for this term, but he remains confident of his ability to do better work, and continues to be optimistic, not only about the final outcome of this term, but the prospects for next term. Part of his difficulty in Life Science stems from the fact that he has not had any sciences since several years ago, as his recent specialization abroad in secondary school has been non-scientific in its orientation.

We discussed in some detail his neglect of his financial responsibilities and the obligations he owes to those who are responsible for his financial aid, including Mrs Findlay, Mr Remsen, and Mr Hage. At least at this point, things seem to be on an even keel financially, and he seems to be managing his affairs without getting into difficulties with his budget. He admits never having been a good manager of money, and I tried to impress upon him the need to pay close attention to such matters, and to the people who have been generous in helping him with his expenses.

Perhaps even more importantly, we discussed his attitude toward his work here at the College, and toward life in general. I will not go into detail in this memo about this, except to point out that Chris is undergoing a very important examination of values and questioning some of the basic precepts which were a part of his upbringing, including his father's obvious commitment to the Anglican faith. I am entirely sympathetic with the restless spirit of Chris' inquiry, and I think we can account for part of what appears to be irresponsibility by realizing that Chris has reached an at-least-temporary period of occasional ambivalence which prevents him from achieving to the degree of which he is clearly capable. In other words, this is not laziness, but rather a sort of restless questioning of the worth of the Dartmouth experience, or of any momentary aspect of it, and beyond that – the very definition of life's goals.

We probed into this area at some length, and all in all, I think we felt it was a good session. I expect Chris will be dropping in again from time to time, and I will certainly follow his progress with interest.

(Additional comments, for files of Office of Student Counselling only:

Chris's relationship with Mr Hage has been strained from the start of his Freshman year, and he now feels that Mr Hage is riding him in an attempt to get him to leave college at the end of this year. I expressed my doubts about this, and we discussed his good fortune at having Mrs Findlay's financial help. I do not think that Chris is ungrateful, but rather that he is indifferent at times to the meaning of this help.

He expressed a need to 'be with people' yet intimated that this was the first time in 20 months that he had had a chance to talk about things which were of serious importance to him. He seems very appreciative of the interest I showed in him, and he genuinely seems to be enjoying his life at Dartmouth, even though he readily admits not working as hard as he might. All of this is quite understandable in view of the occasional (every ten days or so) periods of indifference or depression which he experiences. He remarks about an occasional sense of futility, whereby he reaches a perspective in which college and almost everything else seems fairly inconsequential. He writes creatively, and has expressed an interest in going to England.

Much of his time on campus is spent in the company of others. He plans to return to New Zealand this summer, where he will discuss things with his parents, and he hopes a sense of direction will come out of this. He is passive to the extent that he seems to want things to happen to him, for instance, by this change of geography, or by an occasional meeting someone new, and so forth, but he is nonetheless a thoughtful boy who once stimulated, can do quite well on his own, I am sure. Despite his religious drifting, he claims to have good rapport with his parents, and especially with his mother whom he describes as being quite 'perceptive' and understanding. He has not been in touch with his parents except by letter for the past two years. This is an interesting boy, well worth spending extra time on, and I would hope that ultimately his experience here proves to be a worthwhile one.)

A few days later, on Wednesday 7th March, Kik wrote to Aunt Helen:

> *Now what is important in life, Aunt Helen? Is it two numbers on a sheet of paper at the end of a term, or is it an ability, acknowledged by those in contact with you, to organise, socialise, and generally assume responsibilities of certain kinds?*

***

The prodigal son had lost his way, and was seeking something more meaningful. He was still the life and soul of the party, but his own life and soul were crying out for something more.

Sadly, the arrival of his second term grades meant that he never had the opportunity to find the answers at Dartmouth, and on Tuesday 27th March he was informed by Mr Hage that he had been put on probation, his scholarship removed, and that they were providing him with a non-refundable ticket back to New Zealand.

Three days later, he was on the flight from New York.

Three weeks later, he was in jail.

Kik on his overland trip from Scotland to India and back, 1972

CHAPTER 4
Here, There and Everywhere (1962-1974)

In April 1962, back in New Zealand, Headmaster Hornsby dutifully succeeded in gaining Kik access to the University of Canterbury. Kik would have to wait a few months before starting in the autumn, and he clearly had a number of debts to pay off so Sam and Sybil encouraged him to find work.

To his great credit he secured a position at ICI, the British chemicals giant. He started in the Indenting Section, which had the responsibility of documenting all the company imports from around the world, primarily from factories in the UK. It was not the most thrilling occupation, but it allowed Kik to keep his head down in the midst of some Christchurch society speculation about the prodigal's return. "It was regarded as a bit hush-hush when he came unstuck, like a minor scandal. It wasn't talked about," recalls Judge Tipping. To his friends, however, including Roger House, he was a bit of a rogue celebrity: "Everyone thought it was pretty cool that he'd been kicked out and gone to jail."

Pretty soon Kik's zest for life started to fizz once again. Nick Bridge was a colleague of his at ICI (they were putting Nick through his undergraduate degree):

> *We had a lot of fun. He was an immense distraction to one trying to start his university career. Chris was doing no degree. On the contrary – he was fancy free of all such pretensions at that stage of his life.*
>
> *At ICI he was an irrepressible companion. He threw himself into repertory with a group at the firm who were talented thespians. He had a wide circle of friends. He was in a leading choir.*
>
> *It was singularly undemanding work, allowing plenty of scope for outside enjoyment, especially for one whose destiny was manifestly not in chemicals and plastics.*
>
> *Any memoir would probably not want to include some of the pranks that Chris instigated. Suffice to say he enlivened the lives of many of us who became his friends and enjoyed his excellent and exuberant company.*

One such prank involved a girlfriend, Angela Harvie. Kik had certainly been making the most of his newfound proximity to the opposite sex, taking a series of glamorous girls to various parties and balls in and around Christchurch, but he and Angela had become something of an item.

One day Kik decided to send Angela a very special gift, delivered by hand courtesy of the official ICI chauffeur, who was always kitted out in an impressively tailored uniform. The driver – complete with smart chauffeur's cap – arrived at the Harvie household on Bolton Street and rang the bell. Dulcie Harvie, Angela's mother, came to the door. "Parcel for Miss Harvie, Ma'am," said the driver, with perfect poise, holding out a beautiful ring box.

There was great excitement and surprise. Mother and daughter immediately sat down in the living room and, bursting with expectation, opened the ring box together. Whereupon they discovered a raspberry.

Kik's phone at his ICI desk rang shortly afterwards, and a volley of choice abuse was delivered. Amazingly he and Angela continued to be good friends – clearly his charm was a thing of great resilience even then. This may have been partly thanks to his fine features: fellow student Liz Cooney recalls Kik as being "extraordinarily, wonderfully handsome…we used to spot him occasionally around the Quadrangle [at Canterbury University] and say 'Wow!' to each other! We used to say he looked like a Greek god!" Another female contemporary, Mary Stamers-Smith, says, "He was so good-looking and we used to say that Adam Faith was a very poor second to Woods".

One girlfriend was Anna Szigethy, who had fled Hungary with her mother in 1956 to escape the Soviet invasion. Anna (now Anna Porter) went on to become a successful publisher and author based in Canada. She recalls Kik at this time:

> *I still have a few photos of your father from the early '60s when we were amazingly young. In one of them, we were going to a fancy ball, both of us looking rather stiff in our formal get-up. Chris is wearing a white jacket and, of course, a bow tie. When he came to pick me up at our house, he presented me with a lovely corsage of, I think, an orchid – and he knew exactly how ladies wore them on their wrists (I had no idea).*
>
> *He had a way of running his hand through his longish blond hair when he was worried about something, and of flinging his hair back when he was happy.*
>
> *In another photo we are both at the annual Canterbury University students' street-party, both of us wearing Canterbury scarves and, as far as I can tell, neither of us is particularly sober. He was a real party boy, loud, funny, a great dancer, not someone obviously yearning for a vocation as a minister. He did, of course, talk about that option. It was almost a family tradition, but he could not, then, see himself in the role.*

It would of course take a few more years for that calling to come to life. In the meantime Kik was very cheerfully living the life of Riley.

And yet, the wolf continued to prowl. After one particularly raucous evening with some of his old Christ's College buddies, Kik and Anna had a blazing row – whereupon Kik stormed outside and stole the pristine sports car belonging to Roger House's flatmate. When Kik returned, at 4am, the car was sopping wet: in his heated temper, he had driven it straight through a river on the outskirts of Christchurch.

Roger recalls Kik at this time as a bit of a "lost soul", drifting along, partying hard, generally content – but searching for something more.

***

In 1967, after four years at the University of Canterbury, Kik was still happily unencumbered by any kind of formal qualification. To have failed one degree could be considered careless; to fail two consecutively suggests monastic levels of abstinence from his studies. And yet, as Churchill had it, "Success consists of going from failure to failure without loss of enthusiasm" – and Kik was never short of that.

A change of scene was in order. Later in 1967 Kik decided to move to London – as we have seen, he had expressed an interest in working in England while at Dartmouth, and now, aged 24, it seemed like the right time to spread his wings and head abroad again. There were plenty of other family members to keep Kik company in the UK, particularly those belonging to uncle Robin, who by this point had been Dean of Windsor for five years.

Robin had thus continued the Woods family's contribution to the royal household. One of Robin's responsibilities as Dean in 1967 was to recommend where Prince Charles should go to university, and as Robin wrote in his autobiography (SCM Press), "It was not difficult to arrive at a recommendation of Trinity College [Cambridge], though I had to admit the personal bias of having been there myself" – just like Robin's father, uncle, and two elder brothers before him. There was also the fact that his sons Robert and Edward were then at Trinity themselves, and in an amusing Pathé archive film now on YouTube, there is Robert – a fine-looking third year student by then – assigned to show the young Prince around. It was another memorable Woods moment for Prince Charles, following his infant courtship at Hatfield with Robert's cousin Sally.

The Deanery became Kik's home from home as he looked to establish some sort of career. This meant he was treated very much as one of the family, and in later years he recalled the occasional informal tea or dinner party with the Queen and Prince Philip. Apparently Her Majesty has a feisty sense of humour and a delightful cackle.

Nevertheless, Kik being Kik, there were a few times when he fell short of behavioural expectations, particularly those of the formidable aunt Etta, Robin's wife, who treated Kik to a number of mighty bollockings whenever he turned up at the Deanery late at night, or drunk, or on one occasion completely covered in mud. As Robert recalls:

> *My mother was extremely fond of Kik, she loved him dearly, but these were always the sorts of things that would cause a fracas with somebody like my mother. There was a terrific relationship there, but he did piss her off.*

Kik soon formed a lasting brotherly bond with cousin Robert, and fell in with Robert's social group from Trinity College, including Richard Goode, Andrew Ritchie, Harry Boggis-Rolfe and Dugald Barr, all of whom would remain lifelong friends. Evening dinners often involved a challenge of some sort: Andrew recalls one evening enjoying the charms of the fixed price carvery at the Cumberland Hotel, where the game was to eat as much as was physically possible. Towards the end, Kik took a deep breath in preparation for a final assault, and caused all of the buttons on his waistcoat to burst at alarming speeds across the table.

The Cambridge crew would often go stalking in Scotland, or shooting in Pembrokeshire. On one occasion in Wales, late in the evening after a long, freezing, muddy and boozy day stomping along the Gwaun Valley, the boys made their way to the local pub in great anticipation of warmth and further refreshment – only to discover to their horror that it was closed. All attempts to alert the landlord to their presence failed. And so they decided to let off a shotgun volley in unison as a last resort. The deafening noise reverberated around the nearby hills. After a moment, a window above them opened and a lady's head emerged looking very angry indeed: "DON'T YOU REALISE THERE'S SOMEBODY DYING IN HERE?!" she roared.

Kik found work in the marketing side of publishing, first at Collier Macmillan and then with Associated Book Publishers. He travelled widely in Europe, with a spell behind the Iron Curtain. At one point, over several months, he tried to save some money in between work trips by having no flat in London and basing himself instead in his company Volvo.

Mary Stamers-Smith remembers meeting Kik in Sweden at this time, and witnessing the full force of his natural exuberance:

> *Sal Lawrence and I travelled to Moscow for the last May Day parade in Red Square in May 1969. We were travelling with the British Communist Party (unintentionally). Chris was selling books in Sweden and when the ship called into Stockholm on our return to London, Chris came on board the Russian ship and argued deep into the night with British Communist Party officials still basking in the glory from having witnessed the Red Square celebrations. We were terrified we would all be arrested.*

***

Kik was eager to travel further afield, and in the early 1970s became Africa Manager for Reuters Economic Services. Economic and financial services had been important functions in the global news agencies since their inception in the 19th century – fast and accurate information for trade and investment was in high demand as global markets expanded.

Reuters was no different: its founder in London in 1851 was a German entrepreneur by the name of Paul Julius Freiherr von Reuter, who combined a number of methodologies (including a fleet of 200 speedy carrier pigeons) to transmit stock market quotations.

Most of the clients for these services were in Europe and North America. But Kik, as a young thruster with a passable grasp of French, was given the nascent economies of post-independence Africa, from the Sahara to the Zambezi. Kik averaged about 50 flights per year, and on one business trip alone set foot in 21 countries, doing business in 15 of them.

His task could not have been more daunting. This was an immensely challenging period for the continent, as the optimistic winds of change which had blown away the colonial powers in the late 1950s and early 1960s began to subside, and were followed in turn by the bitter breeze of despotic brutality. In the first two decades of independence there were 40 successful coups and countless attempted coups.

Uganda and Zaire were two of the countries Kik visited regularly. In Uganda, the early years of independence were a time of considerable confidence: between 1960 and 1965 Uganda had booming exports of coffee, cotton and tea and achieved the highest per capita growth in East Africa. But by 1970 the Prime Minister Milton Obote had squandered this position of strength. Idi Amin, one of only two African officers in the army before independence, saw his opportunity and in January 1971 – by now full commander of the armed forces – he took power in a coup.

Amin can sometimes come across as an amusing eccentric, proclaiming himself 'the true heir to the throne of Scotland', and offering Edward Heath – a gifted musician – a post as bandmaster after his election defeat in 1974. But like many of Africa's enigmatic tyrants at this time, power quickly turned to paranoia and psychotic levels of violence. Kik would no doubt have been appalled to read about the bullet-strewn corpse of the Archbishop of Uganda, still in his robes, being dumped at the Kampala morgue shortly after making critical remarks from the pulpit. Amin's rule left Uganda ravaged, lawless and bankrupt, with a death toll put at 250,000.

In Zaire (now the Democratic Republic of Congo), the late '60s and early '70s were also a period of booming economic growth – and no doubt a major market for Reuters Economic Services. After his coup in 1965, General Mobutu had been given strong financial backing from the Americans to hold back the spread of Communism, which was flirting heavily with Egypt, Ethiopia, Angola, Tanzania and the ANC in South Africa – Che Guevara himself led a disastrous guerrilla campaign in eastern Zaire in 1965 after Mobutu took power (President Nasser of Egypt had warned him he could become "another Tarzan").

It didn't last. Mobutu plundered the national coffers for his own gain – in the 1980s he was estimated to be worth $5 billion – and when the price of copper plummeted in 1975 the Congolese economy collapsed with it. Mobutu later retreated to his $100m palace in the equatorial jungle near his small home village of Gbadolite, 700 miles north-east of Kinshasa, and was finally ousted in 1997. In a coup of course.

In this context of boom and bust and butchered bishops, Kik felt he was contributing something worthwhile to the fledgling states of Africa. As we have seen with Kik's forebears, there is something in the Woods DNA – an accumulation of Woods, Williams, Barclay, Buxton, Fry and Gurney – which inspires a keen sense of social justice. Even without an explicit Christian faith, the contribution of Reuters Economic Services to the likes of Uganda and Zaire was Kik's mission, and this sense of purpose allowed him to continue fulfilling a challenging role in a very challenging environment for almost three years.

Nevertheless, Kik had retained his ability to behave like Tarzan, charging through the urban jungles of emerging cities like Kinshasa, Lomé, Nairobi, Kampala and Yaoundé. On one trip to Kinshasa in 1972, Kik was staying at the Intercontinental Hotel and, having perhaps indulged in one Primus beer too many, decided to cool off by diving into the swimming pool. Unfortunately, the swimming pool was half empty and Kik plummeted straight into the pool floor. He was still complaining of a sore neck when he arrived back in the UK a few weeks later.

Kik would often enjoy the company of Richard Goode, who was then working for a British company, Bradbury Wilkinson (BW), selling banknotes to governments all over Africa – between BW and another British company called De La Rue they printed 85 per cent of the world's currency for countries that couldn't print their own. Generally, Goode's schedule was fairly flexible and he would try to coordinate his travel plans with Kik's more rigorous Reuters itinerary so that they could meet up, which they did a few times each year. However, if there was a coup then Goode would be on the next plane, ready to provide a service to the new regime – he managed to secure the banknote order from Idi Amin in 1971 but his agent, Anil Clarke, was then killed during Amin's purge of Asian Ugandans in 1972. Another BW agent, this time in Liberia, was on death row when Goode and Kik visited him.

Bradbury Wilkinson were very conscious of the need to preserve their premium brand, and would spend lavishly on Goode – first class tickets everywhere, the finest suits, and the best rooms in the best hotels. Reuters were not as generous so Kik was entertained on Goode's expenses. And they certainly made the most of it. "We were pretty irresponsible in terms of our employers," recalls Goode.

On one occasion in Kinshasa the two friends went to a notorious pub called the Kinois, where all the mercenaries would stay. They arrived at 11am and drank all the way through until midnight – "We were absolutely legless," says Goode. There they got chatting to a man who was the manager of a huge brewery – the biggest in Africa – on the outskirts of the city, and they were delighted when he offered to take them for a tour the following morning. It was incredibly hot, and Kik and Goode were both struggling from the effects of the previous day's revelry. As they staggered up and down the blistering iron staircases, bathed in the heavy pungent aromas of various hops and malts, they both began to feel rather queasy.

To recover, they went to the tasting room and had a few pints of the brewery's best export lager. With a sudden jolt, Goode remembered that they were – at that very moment – supposed to be having lunch at the British Embassy with the First Secretary. They immediately jumped into a taxi, sped erratically through the crowded streets of the Congolese capital – not helpful for their delicate constitutions – and as they arrived they realised the guests had already made their way in to have lunch. As the two friends lurched into the dining room, stinking of beer and sweat and apologising profusely, Kik tripped on a chair and collapsed face first onto the dining room table, sending all of its contents crashing to the floor.

They were not invited again.

***

In between his trips to the economic frontiers of Africa, Kik continued his travels in other parts of the world. Together with Robert and the others he would collect ancient vehicles (mainly Jaguars for Kik), fix them up in a garage in St John's Wood next to Lord's cricket ground, and then drive up to Scotland to go stalking, or over to uncle Robin's cottage in Pembrokeshire for the shooting season. There is a photo of Kik standing proudly outside the garage with two of his Jags, a Mk II and a Mk VII, with the latter looking pretty smashed up – this was the result of an impetuous reaction by Kik to a minor mechanical issue, which saw him drive it repeatedly into a wall to finish it off.

Kik loved cars (until his dying day, he never quite recovered from the blow of coming home from school to discover that

Sybil had given away his prized collection of Dinky Toys). Kik owned a total of five Jaguars during his time in London, but his favourite was always a hefty old Mk 7 in which he and the boys would drive all over the Continent.

One famous trip abroad in the summer of 1971, to Sicily and back, comprised four Jaguars: Kik's Mk VII, Robert's XK120, Richard Goode's E-Type, and James Mayhew's XK120. Driving such antiquated machines had its risks of course: on one occasion the steering wheel came clean off Mayhew's car and he barrelled off the road and into a field; he drove the rest of the journey with a wrench clamped to the steering column. When the touring party arrived in Rome they decided to leave the two XK120s with Kik's brother Richard – by then working at the NZ Embassy in Rome – as they were overheating too often.

They continued in the yellow E-Type and Kik's black Mk VII all the way down to Sicily so that they could watch the famous Targa Florio – the world's oldest sports car racing event. The Targa covered 277 miles around the mountains of Palermo, replete with treacherous hairpin curves at altitudes from sea level to 2,000 feet, around which the drivers would be competing for over sixteen hours. The event was an infamous test of concentration, endurance, and sanity.

The boys sat on the parched Sicilian hillside merrily consuming industrial quantities of local wine and hollering every time a Ferrari, Alfa Romeo or Porsche whizzed past. In those days racing cars would tear through the small mountain villages while spectators sat beside, or even on, the road.

One leading driver at the time called the race "totally insane", and the Targa Florio as a World Sportscar Championship race was finally shut down in 1973, after two fatal accidents: one where privateer Charles Blyth crashed his Lancia Fulvia HF into a trailer at the end of the Buonfornello Straight; and another where an Italian driver crashed his Alpine-Renault into a group of spectators, killing one. On the return journey, Kik and the others stopped for breakfast on Mount Etna, just as it was erupting.

When the Jags reached Paris, the cylinder head on Kik's Mk VII blew up. The boys decided to fly home, pick up another cylinder head (not an insignificant piece of machinery), and heave it back to Paris on the plane as hand luggage. Kik's expired cylinder head was removed and ceremonially dumped into the Seine from a bridge.

***

On 28th January 1972, a scrawny but prodigiously talented child was born in London by the name of James Christopher Woods. He was Kik's nephew. While based at the NZ Embassy in Rome, Richard had (entirely coincidentally, according to Richard) found himself sharing a lift in his nearby medieval apartment block with an attractive, aristocratic girl called Joanna Proby. Six weeks later they were engaged and after five months, on 3rd October 1970, they were married. James arrived fifteen months later.

Kik was travelling extensively in Africa at this time: from 2nd–5th February he was staying at the Mount Febe Hotel in Yaounde, Cameroon; from 5th–6th February the Hotel du Roi Denis in Libreville, Congo; and from 6th–9th February he was at the Intercontinental Hotel in Lusaka, Zambia. It was at his next stop, the Benin Hotel in Lomé, Togo, where he discovered that a telegram was waiting for him:

CHRISTOPHER WOODS CARE LE BENIN HOTEL
LOME TOGO

JAMES CHRISTOPHER BORN 28 JANUARY
UNIVERSITY COLLEGE HOSPITAL LONDON STOP
REQUESTS YOU BE GODFATHER STOP

RICH

It is interesting to pause and consider for a moment what Kik's reaction would have been. No doubt he was absolutely delighted to become an uncle for the first time, and to be given the privilege of acting as a godparent – he remained very close to James throughout his life.

But, as was first apparent at Dartmouth, when the student counsellor noted "a restless questioning of...the very definition of life's goals," Kik was still lacking that true definition. The news may therefore have given him pause to reflect, alone in his Togolese hotel, on the different paths he and his older brother had taken: Richard with an Oxford degree, a successful diplomatic career stationed in glamorous capital cities such as Rome (and later Washington, Tehran, Athens, Moscow and Paris), a beautiful and devoted wife, and now a bouncing baby boy; Kik, on the other hand, with his failed stint at Dartmouth, his criminal record, his failed stint at Canterbury, and now, nearly 30 years of age, hurtling through far less glamorous capital cities than his brother selling foreign exchange technologies to corrupt and brutish regimes.

Whatever his initial emotional response to the telegram, it did not deter him from heading home to participate in his godson's baptism. On his way back to London, Kik spent the night of 25th February with Richard in Rome and then he, Richard and their sister Sally, who had also been staying in Rome, drove Richard's yellow Alfa Romeo GT 1300 to London together. James' christening took place on 4th March at Elton Hall, the ancestral home of the Proby family. The ceremony was conducted by his grandfather Sam.

***

Aside from the strong bonds developed with Robert and the others, at the end of the 1960s Kik also befriended a tall, dark and cultured gentleman at a party in London. His name was Esme Howard. This was a particularly significant encounter for Kik, as we shall see in due course. Kik was introduced to Esme, along with Jimmy Trimble and Mike

Justice, by a hard-drinking colleague from Associated Book Publishers called Mark Harwood. Mike Justice recalls Kik thus:

> *I think it was for his gusty humour and the waves of energetic enthusiasm which emanated from Chris that I remember him most. There was also a Woodsian vocabulary in which the term 'heavying in' seemed to feature quite a lot. This was used variously about parties, drink and other social activities; probably the Woodsian equivalent of 'getting stuck in'. The word 'slay' or 'slew' also featured, almost always in association with groups of friends in search of lunch: as in 'We just went into the pub and slew the entire contents of the food cabinet'. I think that a number of pubs suffered in this way.*

In April 1970, Mark Harwood invited Kik, Jimmy, Mike and Esme to the Île d'Yeu, a tiny island community just off the Vendée coast of western France, ostensibly to help Mark demolish and rebuild a house. In practice, very little work was done. Instead, a great deal of wine was consumed along with extraordinary quantities of the local seafood. The shoals of the French Atlantic certainly got a slaying.

Esme was then enjoying a successful career at Bankers Trust, but his real interest was in the arts – particularly painting, music and film, all of which he practised personally with considerable panache. Following the Île d'Yeu escapade came a trip in the summer of 1972 to Italy, with Kik and others, to make a film written and directed by Esme.

The medieval castle town of Sermoneta, long associated with the noble Caetani family, and once owned by the Borgias, is situated south-east of Rome along the western flank of the Lepini mountains and at the northern end of what used to be the Pontine Marshes. The Marshes, a vast malarial swamp that was finally drained in the 1930s, are now an area of creeping urbanisation and industry, with some farmland and occasional wild beauty. Sermoneta overlooks the flatlands from a vantage point atop a towering promontory at the foot of the mountains, with a resplendent 13th century castle.

The Caetani family connection to the Howards was secured through the marriage in 1952 of Esme's uncle Hubert Howard to Lelia, the last Caetani heiress. Her father, Roffredo, was the last Duke of Sermoneta. Hubert's own Italian heritage came through his mother, Princess Isabella Giustiniani-Bandini (Hubert's father – Esme's grandfather – was also named Esme, born at Greystoke Castle, great-nephew of the Duke of Norfolk, British Ambassador to the United States 1924–1930, and later made 1st Baron Howard of Penrith). Upon Roffredo's death in 1961, Hubert and Lelia (who did not have children) took on the various Caetani properties in Rome and in the countryside,. These included Sermoneta Castle, and the sylvan, magical gardens of Ninfa nearby, created by Lelia's English grandmother in the 1920s and nurtured into a botanical paradise by Hubert and Lelia after their marriage.

The gardens are now world famous, set among the ruins of a medieval town whose name goes back to the Roman era, receiving thousands of visitors per year. Ninfa's turbulent history has been long associated with popes – the Zacharias of the 8th century, Pope Alexander III and the Caetani Pope Boniface VIII. The Holy Roman Emperor Frederick Barbarossa sacked and burned Ninfa in 1171 after his nemesis Alexander III took refuge and was crowned there, but it recovered under the Caetani, reaching its urban and military zenith in the 14th century – before being sacked once more, this time against the background of the papal wars. The ruins lay fallow for five centuries and were only reclaimed by the Caetani family at the beginning of the 20th century.

Up at the castle in 1972, Esme had assembled a crack troupe of family and friends to perform in what would become his second most important film (after *The Gang Show*, a family masterpiece, featuring Kik and Kathy and family in St Helens, circa 1986). *My Kingdom for a Saucer* is an episodic parody highlighting the intrinsic role, in some of the most important events in human history, of the humble Frisbee. Esme describes Kik's performances thus:

Kik, versatile as ever, played the tough guy in one scene, a convincingly syphilitic William Tell in another, before crossing seamlessly into the part of an unmistakably gay/gigolo waiter-type in a Cinzano ad in the courtyard.

There is also an iconic scene in which Kik, dressed only in a pair of washed-out jeans, blond locks stuck to his sandy brow, crawls through the desert crying out for water. Even in such a vulnerable state he is quite the specimen – he looks like something from a Dolce & Gabbana TV advertisement. He is saved by the sight of a Frisbee, which, like a mysterious plastic homing pigeon, leads him to the sea. He charges towards the surf, before diving in with the signature flourish of the head his children would copy mercilessly years later.

It was at Sermoneta that Kik first properly met Esme's youngest sibling, Katherine Isabella Howard (there are two more brothers in between: John and Anthony, who is known as 'Tonino'). Kik and Kathy had crossed paths briefly the previous year at Jerome Cottage in Marlow, home of Kathy's parents Edmund (known as 'Mondi') and Cécile. Kik had just been shooting with Esme at Dean Farm in Gloucestershire (home of Francis Howard, Mondi's elder brother) and was wearing a flat cap and plus-fours. The boys popped in for drinks on their way back to London.

As they breezed into the kitchen Esme asked Kik what he would have: "I'd like a gin and tonic, thank you Esme," Kik replied in a booming voice, before disappearing straight up to the drawing room and making himself at home. Kathy immediately summed him up: "Typical huntin'n'shootin' sort of guy, not my type. Besides, he never looked at me!"

Now aged 18 (almost ten years younger than Kik), wonderfully pretty, generously gifted at the piano and guitar, fluent in French, Italian, Spanish and English (just about), and fresh out of convent school in Rome – Kathy was quite the catch. However, Kik was already attached at this point, and Kathy was rather taken by one of Tonino's friends, who demonstrated his affections for Kathy by gifting her a Vespa. Hardly *La Dolce Vita*, alas, and that was as far as the courtship went.

In any case, Kathy thought Kik a little boorish. Dashingly handsome and winningly cavalier, yes – but his very British sense of humour and slightly barbarian, loutish habits did not impress the more delicate, cultured sensibilities of Esme's little sister. If she had learned one thing from her forebear, Katherine Howard – fifth wife of Henry VIII, beheaded at the Tower of London – it was that charismatic yobs should be avoided.

One evening Kik rumbled into the medieval banqueting hall of Sermoneta Castle, where the whole group had gathered just before dinner and, buoyed by several refreshments, crashed straight into a number of old wooden chairs carefully arranged in the middle, generating a deafening echo throughout the vaulted room. Kik thought this was hilarious; Kathy did not.

They did act together in one scene, where Kik plays the gigolo waiter to Kathy's Audrey Hepburn-esque punter in the courtyard. But otherwise they stayed closer to their different friends. On this occasion, the romantic citadels of Sermoneta and Ninfa did not have their way with Kik and Kathy. However, Cupid and his cherubs – patrolling the ancient battlements with arrows drawn – were patient. And they would get another chance.

***

After returning to London, Kik embarked on the most famous of his road trips: his overland tour from Scotland to the southern tip of India and back again (later in life, Dad never missed an opportunity to regale guests or parishioners – mostly, his offspring – about the fabled 'India Trip'). He conducted this trip without Robert and the Cambridge group, but with a few other friends, including his then-girlfriend Johanna Turcan and her pal Sarah Thomson. Johanna and

Sarah had both read History at Oxford, and both had done their special paper on India in the age of Warren Hastings, the first British Governor-General in the late 18th century.

Kik had met Johanna in September 1971 at her cousin's shooting lodge in Perthshire. She, like many girls before her, had been won over by his combination of good looks and charm: "such a zest for life, that wonderful laugh – he was just a huge enthusiast".

Nonetheless, as we have noted, he did have a more serious, contemplative side in private. Although normally with Robert and the gang Kik was hail-fellow-well-met, cars, pubs, 'slaying', and tales of derring-do in Africa, he could also be much more thoughtful. He and Robert would often discuss their family's church heritage, and the nature of faith and spiritual belief; Kik may have lost his religion, but he had a vague notion that there was something out there, some kind of cosmic truth, which demanded a high standard of human behaviour.

Before the India trip Kik had actually resigned from his Reuters position and applied to be a prison governor – this would be his chance to really put a dent in the universe for the right reasons. He thought prisons were in need of serious reform, as any respectable descendant of Elizabeth Fry should. In fact, Kik and Johanna scheduled the India trip so that he could return in time to be interviewed for the governor position. The clock had started ticking for Kik: like the prodigal son looking enviously at the pigs, something now was really stirring in his stomach.

Of course, there is nothing like a trip to India when you are trying to find yourself (and, indeed, nothing like a trip to India to find things stirring in one's stomach). Many youths have returned from Goa reeking of joss sticks and claiming oneness with the world. Kik was unlikely to be quite so trivial – he may have been excited by the idea of driving across ancient, far-flung lands in a terrific motorcar with attractive friends, but he never tried to be something he wasn't; whether consciously or not, he was still anchored to his family's traditional Christian values. In fact, the one blazing row that he and Johanna had on the trip was when he accused her of being frivolous for wanting to go and experience the Burning Ghats of Benares on the Ganges – he didn't approve of this at all. As Johanna recalls:

> *It's interesting – he was sort of reverential but also quite cautious about Islam, Hinduism and Buddhism; he kept it at arm's length. I think it might have been a kind of feeling of disloyalty towards Anglicanism. Equally, he really minded the spirit in which people approached it – I think he thought I was too curious and probably not reverential enough, and he wasn't prepared to be reverent because he thought the true God was something else. And he didn't like things to be too complicated.*

Johanna and Sarah had come up with the India trip idea on something of a whim, and like Kik had resigned from their jobs. Maps were collected and pored over; embassies were contacted; the RAC and the AA were visited; piles of guidebooks and history books were consumed; the route was debated at length; enormous quantities of food were procured; jerry cans were filled; and two tents were found – the trio would be camping for much of the journey. In Edinburgh, Johanna bought one of the first Range Rovers off the production line, in a glorious racing green, licence plate MJD 657L. And thus, on Sunday 8th October 1972, they took off.

First they drove down to Bournemouth and took the ferry to Cherbourg, and, along the coast in the picturesque fishing village of Barfleur, they had arranged to meet up with cousin Robert and his friend Ray Guest. Except that Robert and Ray didn't come by car, or by ferry. Or by any conventional means for that matter. Robert and Ray flew over the Channel in two Tiger Moths. They flew low over the masts of the sailing boats in the harbour, no doubt to the great annoyance of their French owners, and landed just outside the village. Johanna plumped to go up for a spin with Ray – and a spin she got. Ray, delighted to have such a glamorous passenger, decided to show off by flying upside down. Although no doubt thrilling and impressive, this rather unexpected manoeuvre led to Johanna's prized gold watch plummeting to earth with a crash. Fortunately Johanna herself did not.

After such an exciting start to the trip, the team made quick progress: they continued south through France and east over the Alps to Italy; then across the northern part of Italy via Milan to President Tito's Communist Yugoslavia, where they headed south-east via Belgrade to Bulgaria. In the capital Sofia, under the Communist rule of Todor Zhivkov, they encountered the terrifying reality of a Big Brother state as they were tailed by government officials (fortunately Kik chose not to present his arguments against Communism on this occasion). They were appalled by the sight of so many dreadfully long queues for bread, and as they progressed out of Bulgaria towards Turkey, the Range Rover was caught in a flash flood and got stuck in a ravine – Kik, calm and unflustered, was able to extricate the vehicle before it filled with water.

And so they continued, through Istanbul and over the Bosphorus to Asia, advancing 1,500 miles east through Turkey's remote and dangerous Kurdish region to Iran, camping along the way in what were known as 'BP Mocamps' – campsites with basic loos and a tap. When they reached Tehran, under the rule of the Shah, they arranged to have dinner with some of the British consular staff to discuss their onward journey into Afghanistan. Kik, Johanna and Sarah were all desperate to visit the world-famous Minaret of Jam on the banks of the Hari River, in Ghor Province, on the treacherous route through the centre of Afghanistan from Herat in the west to Kabul in the east. The Minaret was built in 1194 by Sultan Ghiyas ud-Din, at the site of the ancient city of Firuzkuh, and is covered in extraordinary Kufic inscriptions on turquoise tiles. It stands 215 feet high at the centre of a dramatic maze of valleys and gullies – just the right spot for a muezzin to stand and proclaim the call to prayer.

However, the consular staff advised that the route through central Afghanistan would be unwise given the high risk of robbery and murder. Instead the Range Rover proceeded south-east from Herat into Helmand Province, and its capital Kandahar. They were in fact stopped on one occasion, just outside Herat, by a rather menacing group of men. Once again, Kik remained cool and unflappable, and the judicious donation of a watch allowed them to continue safely. By and large they were met with wonderful hospitality and friendliness as they proceeded north-east to the capital, Kabul, and from there took the old Silk Route road west to visit the monumental Buddhas of Bamiyan, carved straight into the sandstone cliffs and standing 115 and 175 feet tall. Sadly, these were blown up by the Taliban in March 2001.

The two real points of danger on the trip were in fact caused by accidentally insulting Islam. The first occurred in the eastern Iranian city of Mashhad, when Kik was busy fixing the car and Johanna and Sarah decided to go and observe the processions on the Muslim day of mourning known as *Ashura*. They were careful to ensure that they were dressed appropriately, but things turned ugly when they came upon the ceremonial self-flagellation, where young men tie knives to chains and whip themselves into a frenzy. Women – especially foreign women – were not welcome at this particular point in proceedings, and Johanna and Sarah were attacked and pursued by an angry mob. They were lucky to escape with nothing more than a few bumps and bruises. Kik, needless to say, was not impressed with their attempts at spiritual tourism.

Kik had his own mishap in Afghanistan. He stopped the Range Rover in a village to buy some chickens, and, having done so, did what Kiwis do and wrung their little necks before tossing them breezily into the boot and driving off. After a few short moments, Kik noticed with some alarm that the rear view mirror was filled with furious villagers in hot pursuit, including a man on a horse brandishing an AK-47. Kik gunned the V8 engine into life and took off at full pelt in a cloud of dust. It was only then that he realised his mistake: by strangling the chickens instead of bleeding them he had committed an offence under Quranic law. The next time they bought chickens, Kik very publicly slit their throats and strapped them to the roof rack, where they bled freely all over the back window.

The party continued east, up and over the extraordinary, winding, ancient Khyber Pass to Peshawar in Pakistan, via the capital, Islamabad, and up into the contested region of Kashmir. Here they went shooting in the snow-filled mountains, but unfortunately nothing was added to the food stocks. This was particularly troubling to the girls, as Kik was prone to serious bouts of grumpiness and bad temper whenever he got hungry. He would tolerate the subcontinent's fondness for vegetable curries, "but periodically there was a kind of carnivorous yell" and they would head off to find him some meat.

From Kashmir, they proceeded 1,000 miles south through Punjab and Rajasthan in India in order to visit a friend of Harry Boggis-Rolfe in Gujarat. That friend was the Maharana of Danta, royal ruler of a princely state dating back to 1068, full name His Highness Maharana Sri Prithvirajsinhji Bhawanisinhji Sahib Bahadur. The Maharana took his guests duck shooting – there is an excellent photo of Kik in a canoe on some kind of lake, his reliable Indiana Jones-style fedora perched handsomely on his head, shotgun at the ready, Indian manservant at the other end of the canoe holding a paddle and looking a little nervous. Unfortunately for everyone, the meat stocks again went unreplenished.

Finally, after another 1,500-mile drive south from Gujarat, and after approximately 10,000 miles on the road overall, Kik, Johanna and Sarah at last came to their destination: Cape Comorin, on the southern tip of India. They didn't stay long – Kik had to get back to London in time for the prison interview. However, they did make time for a detour on the return journey, firstly to Sri Lanka, then Nepal. Here Kik contracted an appalling bout of dysentery, which for two weeks left him near-comatose in a rather sordid hotel in Kathmandu. Despite losing almost two stone, he insisted on continuing with some wonderful walks in the Himalayas. Due to his weakened state, he carried a small wooden chair with him for regular breaks until one morning it collapsed unceremoniously as he was taking in the stunning panorama outside their tent.

On the way home, the trio stopped in Florence outside an immaculate Gucci store. There is an amusing photo of Kik and Sarah standing in front of the shop window, dressed head to toe in kaleidoscopic Afghan shirts and waistcoats. Kik looks like a cross between Robert Redford and Dame Edna Everage. The filthy Range Rover was parked right outside, caked in mud and dust and a few leftovers of dried chicken blood. As they entered the premises, the hippy youths were treated to some wonderfully snooty looks by the Gucci staff – until Johanna put down her bank card next to the till and ordered a number of lavishly expensive items, including a pristine pair of Gucci loafers for Kik.

The grand tour ended a few days later. The Range Rover, by now named Ganesh after the Hindu elephant god, was still only six months old but had already notched up 28,000 miles in some of the world's most glamorous locations. She was a rare prize, and Johanna sold her for a profit.

***

It was now early 1973, and Kik was able to attend the interview for the prison service. He was tremendously excited – this was something he was genuinely passionate about. However, he was dismayed to hear shortly afterwards that he had been unsuccessful.

This was a blow. Kik was now 30, with no academic qualifications and no career to speak of. By contrast, Richard was making impressive progress with the NZ Diplomatic Service (he would become Ambassador to Iran a few years later); Robert was developing a successful career at P&O (he would eventually become CEO and Chairman); Richard Goode was making great strides at BW, and captaining the British Aerobatics team in his spare time; Harry and Dugald were building names for themselves at the Bar and in the City respectively; while Andrew (known as 'Reg') was starting to make some headway with his invention, the Brompton Bicycle.

Expectations of family and friends can be a mixed blessing. On the one hand they can persuade and inspire to achieve great things; on the other, they can sit heavily on one's shoulders like a fat chimpanzee, hairy and uncomfortable and yapping away incessantly in the ear as one staggers, like the Pilgrim, through the Slough of Despond. We know that while Kik was generally a larger-than-life character, he was also a man of hidden depths, restlessly questioning his life's goals and searching for his true calling – something which would allow him to become, as St Irenaeus wrote, 'fully alive'.

We don't know how Kik responded to the setback of the prison service interview. No doubt his parents had some words of advice – and no doubt Sybil made it clear that coming home to New Zealand would be a sensible option. Richard and Joanna, with godson James and a new baby boy on the way (Samuel, born on 7th May 1974, also lean and precocious), were by now based just north of Wellington; Sally lived in the capital itself, while Marianne had married and was living near Dunedin.

And so it was that the prodigal son at last got up and went to his father.

His Father was waiting.

ANNO DOMINI

Kik, and truck, in Wellington, 1973

CHAPTER 5
The Road to Otaki
(1974)

CHRISTIAN: Why, truly, I do not know what had become of me there…as I was musing in the midst of my dumps; but it was God's mercy that he came to me again, for else I had never come hither.

— John Bunyan, *The Pilgrim's Progress* (Wordsworth Editions)

Amazing grace! How sweet the sound
That saved a wretch like me!
I once was lost, but now am found;
Was blind, but now I see.

— John Newton

The road from Wellington to Otaki is 45 miles. It winds along the attractive Kapiti coastal route at the south-eastern end of New Zealand's North Island, taking in places such as Porirua, Paraparaumu, Waikanae, and Te Horo. Compared to the glorious landscapes normally associated with New Zealand, it is relatively unremarkable.

Yet it was on this unremarkable road, on an unremarkable weekday morning early in 1974, as Kik was driving alone to a work assignment in Palmerston North, that a very remarkable thing happened.

It happened very suddenly – Kik later said it was "between one lamp post and the next":

> *I didn't see a face. I certainly didn't see Christ. I hadn't even been thinking about God when I suddenly became aware of being taken over by him. I sensed some immense, overwhelming power outside the vehicle. This was a totally overwhelming personal experience for me.*
>
> *I can't say I saw a light or anything in particular. But I was on my own. If somebody had been with me, I wonder if they would have noticed anything, as happened with St Paul's companions. But I remember I just rose up in the driver's seat, grinning! Something completely life-changing had happened to me. Instantaneously I also knew my vocation. I knew then I would become a minister.*

He pulled over, got out, and fell to his knees.

***

Richard and Joanna happened to live a little further up the road in the small town of Otaki, in a charming pink house nestled among the Pohutakawa trees opposite the racecourse. As Kik made his way there to tell them about his experience, he noticed Joanna at a nearby service station, standing beside the road as the attendant filled her car with petrol. Kik screeched to a halt and jumped out, grinning from ear to ear:

"I am going to be ordained!" he announced, without any kind of introduction.

Joanna was flabbergasted. "Why don't you come and have a drink?" she replied, hoping that a slug of brandy might bring him to his senses.

"I will have a drink," said Kik, "but I am going to be ordained."

***

If this encounter with God was a flashbulb moment for Kik, it most certainly came as a blinding shock to his family and friends. Other than Christmas Day, and the occasional wedding and christening (and of course the Good Friday service in Honolulu in 1962), Kik had not attended church since leaving home fourteen years earlier. Indeed it may be true to say that in those fourteen years Kik had actually spent more time in jail than in church. Unlike his clergy predecessors, there was certainly nothing inevitable about what had happened.

As he enjoyed a very generous refreshment with Joanna, Kik called his sister Sally in Wellington to tell her the news. She was so amazed, she had to put the phone down to recover before calling him back. When Joanna later informed Richard of the day's events, he was absolutely staggered – and at first not totally inclined to believe it.

In the months since Kik had moved back to New Zealand, there had been little sign of the coming conversion. He had grown a beard, and developed a beguiling reputation as a male model and truck driver. When he applied for a respectable position in Wellington as a sales manager with AH & AW Reed, New Zealand's leading publisher, he turned up to the interview in his overalls, changed into a suit somewhere on the premises, took the interview, and changed back into the overalls again to leave in his truck. Not only did they give him the job, they also gave him the large Holden station wagon he was driving on the road to Otaki.

His life of girls, parties and trumpet-playing had continued with gusto. At a house party in 1973, he had been introduced to Richard Lavers, the First Secretary at the British High Commission. They hit it off immediately and became great friends (Kik assisted at Richard's marriage ceremony in Antwerp many years later; Richard is godfather to Madeline). The two suave young gents enjoyed numerous weekend fishing trips with various pretty girls to stunning locations such as Lake Taupo and the Wairarapa region. They drank lots of the local wine, in the days before it became a more sophisticated commodity: "It was total plonk, but it didn't seem to bother us too much," says Richard. On one excursion to Porangahau beach on the east coast, they were rather drunkenly caught out by the speed of a giant sea elephant and had to run for their lives.

Kik and Richard fell in with a pretty raucous group of Kik's old friends from Christ's College. These young men were from well-established Canterbury farming families and had resources to play with. They would fly up to Wellington from Christchurch in their single-propeller planes, party all night, and then lurch back into their cockpits at first light to find their way home.

One morning, John 'Honk' Bristed was piloting from the rear of the plane while his brother sat in front. Feeling a little queasy, Honk – with absolutely no warning – decided to flip the plane upside down in order to release what Antipodeans call a 'technicolour yawn'. His sibling was not strapped in, and had to grip onto his seat for dear life as Honk relieved himself. Feeling much better, Honk duly righted the plane. His brother, rather stirred by these events, then proceeded to vomit himself – right into the face of Honk behind.

On another occasion, Kik and the boys spent a stag weekend at The Portage Hotel in the Marlborough Sounds. It was a rather pretentious place, with a rather pretentious pianist. Kik and his friends, looking perfectly presentable in their dinner jackets, eventually took offence to this pianist. They got up from their table and surrounded the piano. One of the boys asked rhetorically, "Do you like this music?" Another replied, "No I don't! It's horrible!" Griff Bristed kicked the pianist off the stool and started to play a few numbers himself – while simultaneously pulling the piano apart with his bare hands, strings and hammers flying in all directions. "He had a habit of dismantling the pianos he played," reflects his brother Honk.

As he continued with his skilful performance, the boys pushed the dishevelled instrument through the dining room – scattering dinner guests in their wake – and out towards the edge of the veranda, high above the car park. The hotel staff were surprisingly genial as they tried to prevent Griff from throwing the piano over the balcony. "The Portage people knew many of us pretty well and were prepared for most things," says Honk.

They almost certainly weren't prepared for what came next. The boys went berserk, jumping into their pickups and driving at speed across the immaculate lawns of the hotel. One of the group fell out of a passenger door and was lying prostrate on the grass, at which point another member of the party took the opportunity to run him over. Fortunately for him it had rained earlier in the day, and he was merely flattened into the soft New Zealand turf.

Encouraged by the miraculous survival of their kinsman, the stag party continued their rampage by abducting an enormous, muddy, slightly malodorous pig. They gave the pig a few drinks, and then escorted it to a nearby cabin, where they carefully tucked it into bed next to Richie Dillon, who had retired early for the night. As the huge sow snuggled down, they turned up the heating in the room, and to their delight she proceeded to emit a series of wonderfully warm, content, piggish grunting noises from under the duvet. "I don't have to paint a picture," says Honk, "but it gave the boys a lot of cheer when Richie and the pig woke up together in the morning."

***

And yet, perhaps it was destined that the son Sam and Sybil named Christopher – meaning 'bearer of Christ' – would eventually renew his faith and follow the family trade. When he telephoned his parents to inform them of his experience, they took it in their stride. His sister Sally thought it a fitting coincidence that he was living on Orangi Kaupapa Road – Maori for 'From Heaven to Earth' – when the divine intervention took place.

Indeed, it is clear that while the conversion came as a bombshell to family and friends, it was also, with the benefit of hindsight, not inconsistent with his overall character. One Dartmouth contemporary states:

> *On your question about whether there was any hint that he would eventually take the course he took that led him to his ministry in the Church of England. On that point I have to submit an unqualified no. I can say without reservation that that was the last thing I'd have predicted about your Dad's future.*
>
> *But on reflection it's not too surprising to me, given the fact that he was such a kind, good-hearted young man who had an uncanny ability to relate to the young men – and women, when he took his treks to Skidmore and Smith, among others – and to brighten their lives. That's a gift, and I'm sure he used it to great effect in his years in the ministry.*

Mike Justice also reflects:

> *Looking back, it should not have been a surprise when Chris announced he was taking Holy Orders. The fact that his father and his uncles were both in the Church could well have indicated the path he would eventually take. However, there were expressions of amazement that such a reveller could undergo this Damascene conversion. Would he now be 'heavying in for God?' one mutual friend enquired in some disbelief.*
>
> *His rumbustious good nature, sociability, and energetic love of life cloaked a deeper conviction. Sound good sense and good judgement about people were always evident even in some of the crazier*

adventures: he was never a fool and his consideration and humanity were always plain to see.

A sceptic could look at Kik's life and conclude that he was just looking for something to do with himself, searching for direction, and once he hit 30 with no other career prospects he simply chose to follow the family trade having had some kind of epiphany in the car. Plenty of people have life-changing epiphanies after all, with no apparent input from God, and there is nothing wrong with that.

But this kind of emotional or intellectual epiphany doesn't explain the "immense, overwhelming" spiritual dimension of Kik's experience on the road to Otaki – quite out of character for him. He could have come to an enthusiastic and reasonable decision to continue the family trade whilst taking a walk along one of Wellington's beaches on a windy Sunday afternoon, perhaps after Sunday lunch with Sam and Sybil, or after attending church for a period in order to find his religion. That would have been more in keeping with the manner in which Sam and the other Woods clergy had approached the cloth. It certainly would have been more civilised – and more compelling to his family and friends – than a rather baffling and disconcerting tale of being filled with the Holy Spirit in the car on State Highway 1.

Perhaps the most powerful evidence for the truth of his experience is the fact that he responded to an extreme call with an extreme commitment, devoting his entire 30 years of ordained ministry to a remote and impoverished corner of the Liverpool Diocese, refusing offers of promotion and preferment despite the immense hardships. Whenever times were too tough or the task too challenging, in the face of temptation to call it quits, he was able to remember his call from God on the road to Otaki that day.

And unlike Saul's very public conversion on the road to Damascus, Kik's meeting with God was a very personal affair: a quiet road in a quiet part of a quiet country, no flashing lights, no booming oratory, no witnesses – just an overwhelming, soft, tender embrace of one man by his heavenly Father, calling him back to His side, and asking him to serve.

***

The day following his Road to Otaki experience, Kik went to see Richard Lavers at his house overlooking Wellington harbour. The two friends stood beside the fireplace, drinks in hand. It was a setting they had shared countless times before, discussing life, girls, politics, literature, religion, treating all subjects with an equal measure of curiosity and wit. This time, their conversation reached new depths. Kik explained what had happened, and finished by saying that his life had been taken over by this extraordinary encounter – that he could not now resist the spiritual call of God. He was certain he had to abandon his publishing career immediately and return to England to get ordained.

Richard was "very surprised, but not totally dumbfounded". He could see that something fundamental, something spiritual, had shifted in his friend. And he therefore encouraged Kik to pursue this calling to its conclusion, offering him a room in his house while he made preparations to leave:

> *I have no doubt whatsoever about the sincerity and the reality of his conversion. There was no exaggeration when he described it to me afterwards. His whole life thereafter attests to the overwhelming power of this experience, for it changed his direction and compelled him to devote himself to the ministry of God.*

PART TWO - WITH CHRIST

Kik and Kathy on their wedding day, 15th January 1977

CHAPTER 6
The Pilgrim Progresses (1974-1979)

For it is one thing to see the land of peace from a wooded ridge…and another to tread the road that leads to it.

— St Augustine

The *Cumberland* was a big old girl: 560 feet long, 500,000 cubic feet of refrigerated cargo, 11,000 tonnes. She was operated by Federal, a New Zealand shipping company owned by P&O which in 1948 had built the biggest refrigerated ships in the world in order to transport New Zealand's burgeoning post-war economic exports of lamb and dairy. There were no containers on board; the lamb was packed in dry and loose. By the time Chris (the name by which he now became widely known) boarded the *Cumberland* in Port Chalmers, Dunedin, a few months after his conversion in 1974, she was coming to the end of her life – she was sent to the knacker's yard in 1977.

Chris had wasted no time in making arrangements to return to the UK. After staying with Richard Lavers for two months in Wellington, he travelled down to Oamaru, just north of Dunedin, to stay with his sister Marianne for a few days before departing. Marianne is married to Baxter Smith, and has two offspring: Andrew and Jacqui. Baxter is in many ways the archetypal South Islander: tall and strong, a talented amateur rugby player, an excellent horseman and keen hunter, and a pretty good sailor and fly-fisherman. He has been known to instruct visiting nephews in how to strangle chickens and chop trees with a chainsaw.

Baxter is also very content with a pint of the local Emerson's brew. On the day of Chris's departure, he took his brother-in-law for a few farewell drinks in the old stone pub overlooking the dock, with picturesque Carey's Bay in the background. Forty-three years later, Baxter took me to sit at the same table at the same window in the same pub – apparently the view hasn't changed one iota. Whereas he and I had a coffee, back in 1974 Baxter and Chris consumed jar after jar of Dunedin's finest beer as they waited for the *Cumberland* to be loaded. They were in very high spirits as they finally drove Baxter's hefty Holden Kingswood right up to the wharf where she was docked. "I had to pour your father onto that boat," Baxter said with a glint in his eye.

As they shook hands and said their goodbyes, Baxter asked Chris if he was really sure about his decision to get ordained. Chris paused for a moment. "I've never been more sure of anything in my life," came the reply.

It was Robert Woods, now a rising star at P&O, who had arranged for his cousin to travel on the *Cumberland* from Port Chalmers. By the time Robert and his wife Georgiana (Georgie) met Chris on the docks at Sheerness in Kent five weeks later, the old vessel had sailed the great circle route of the southern Pacific, around Cape Horn – some 12,000 nautical miles. Chris was in good heart, "looking very smiley". He had made great friends with the crew and the Captain (who sadly would later return to his home city of Liverpool a raging alcoholic). No doubt Chris enjoyed a few refreshments with them all on the long journey, but he spent the rest of his time on board the *Cumberland* satiating a very different kind of thirst: he read the Bible cover to cover, absorbing everything – including every introduction, footnote and comment.

***

Formal training for ordination began in the autumn. In discussions with Robert's father Robin – by now Bishop of Worcester – it had been agreed that Queen's Theological College, Birmingham, would be the right place to do this. It didn't hurt that uncle Robin knew the Dean rather well, but Chris impressed the Selection Committee with his recently-acquired biblical knowledge (although he still didn't know anything about the Church – as he said later, "I didn't know what the letters PCC stood for when I *left* theological college"). And so continued a strong tradition of Woods clergy being schooled, both theologically and on the job, in Britain's industrial heartlands.

Queen's turned out to be an excellent choice for Chris, perhaps more diverse than Ridley Hall (where Chris's grandfather Edward had been Vice-Principal) or Wycliffe Hall, a little less intellectual certainly, more practical and down to earth. The basic living arrangements prompted some sincere contemplation: it was as Chris squeezed himself into his tiny bedroom under the stairs, with just a suitcase and his Bible in hand, that he reflected on how his circumstances had changed – from living in a three-bedroom detached house in Wellington, with a large company station wagon, to a miniscule boudoir in Birmingham.

Humility was a central tenet of the teaching at Queen's. One of the first requirements was for ordinands to make a full confession. Chris approached this with some caution. Having given what he thought was a full and frank confession to the Dean, he was stunned (and not a little alarmed) to be summoned for a second round the following day. This time he really plumbed the full width, length, height and depth of his experiences, and let everything go. He recalled leaving the room as if floating on air – "my feet didn't touch the gravel".

A contemporary at Queen's, Melvyn Nixon, has extremely fond memories of the experience:

Queen's College in the '70s was a real melting pot. Not only was there an amalgam of Anglicans, Methodists, the odd Baptist and United Reform minister in training, there was also huge diversity within each of those church representatives. Some Methodists were inclined towards a churchmanship that was higher than the Anglo-Catholics, some Anglicans so low as to be beneath the rug, and there was a Greek Orthodox tutor thrown into the mix for good measure.

This latter gentleman was of a rotund appearance, thinning hair, and was an habitual snuff sniffer. He taught liturgy amongst other things, a subject about which he was well informed. The frequent pinch of snuff was always followed by a quick wipe with the handkerchief, watery eyes and two streamers of brownish snot making their way to his top lip. He was known to have a firm belief in an afternoon siesta. This he insisted must be an authentic pursuit requiring one to undress fully before slipping between the sheets, and he himself was certainly seen on more than one occasion proudly displaying his ovoid shape from the picture window in his upstairs flat, dressed only in his underwear.

The diversity of the churchmanship held by students, and the humour and respect it evoked, were best seen in chapel worship. Methodists naturally had more ritual to become acquainted with. Interestingly some Methodists developed a greater interest in the art of incense-swinging than many Anglicans. One such Methodist, eager to swing the burner during the Eucharist, found himself lost in clouds of incense and took a serious tumble.

One of the two lecterns was reserved for the reading of the Gospel. Behind this lectern were two light switches, one illuminating the lectern, the other the symbol of God's presence high in the chancel.

As they stepped up to read, many looked anguished at the prospect of inadvertently turning off the wrong light at the end of the lesson. To do so would bring whispers and sniggers from those alarmed at God having been extinguished!

Chris Woods was humorous, in ways unorthodox yet all the better for it, a true pastoral heart and passion for the gospel of Christ. He took his place along with others, giving and receiving, questioning, never quite in or fully out of his comfort zone, with a story to tell, a sense of calling and mission, times of productive doubt and more of confident boldness, courted by some and held at arm's-length by others. He was rich in spirit, if not materially, but then that never bothered him.

Prior to completing his ordination training, Chris approached uncle Robin once again for advice on his next move. His challenge to his uncle was typically forthright: "Which is the toughest diocese in England?" Robin replied that it was probably Liverpool, so Chris duly applied for a curacy there. The church in question was All Saints', Childwall, a parish on the outskirts of the city.

His ordination ceremony took place at Liverpool Cathedral on 21st December 1976. It is rather extraordinary to think that on the same day 31 years later – 21st December 2007 – he was at the centre of a very different ceremony in the same sanctuary, having dedicated his entire ordained life to that diocese.

***

Three weeks after his ordination, Chris was due to be married.

Eighteen months earlier, in August 1975, Esme Howard had gathered another party of friends and family at Sermoneta. His sister Kathy was there, having spent the previous two years working for family friends Malcolm and Anne Munthe, at their family homes in London and at Lunghezza near Rome. Chris was there too. The castle cupids at last had their second shot.

Kathy recalls the situation:

Rumour had it that this rather roguish man had undergone a Damascus Road conversion whilst in New Zealand the previous year, and was now training for ordination in the Anglican Church. Since I too was a keen Christian, albeit of the Roman Catholic variety, we soon found ourselves talking about our faith, away from the rest of the party, and discovering more than expected common ground.

Kik seemed a very different person to the one I had encountered three years' previously. He was gentler and humbler for a start – a man 'tamed by the Spirit of God', one might say, but still with a wicked sense of humour and strong personality. I began noticing his good looks as well...As a result, he was suddenly very attractive to me! Thankfully he too began to show more than a passing interest in me.

A slow dance at the cosy Charlie Brown nightclub in Sermoneta (to the tune of Don McLean's Vincent*) sealed our romance...*

Chris would later explain to his offspring that the actual moment when Cupid fired the arrow was in the banqueting hall of the Castle – scene of his previous drunken collision with the antique furniture. This time, it was his heart which was struck. Now seated at the enormous medieval dining table, waiting to be fed, he looked up to see an angelic creature entering the great hall with a seraphic smile on her face and a vast dish of steaming spaghetti in her hands. In that moment, he was smitten.

The following day, he decided to see whether Esme would approve of a courtship. He got his approach completely wrong. As the two friends walked up the steep, narrow cobbled street to the Castle on a glorious, balmy evening, Chris announced with his usual breezy confidence, "Esme, I think I may have fallen in love with someone not a million miles from yourself." Regrettably, Esme assumed he was talking about Diane, his girlfriend.

In farcical scenes reminiscent of *The Comedy of Errors*, the two friends – one pleading, one fuming, both completely baffled – continued their increasingly heated discussions as they made their way over the drawbridge, underneath the looming portcullis and into the ancient courtyard, where Esme was tempted to challenge Kik to some kind of duel ("safe enough, as I knew an escape route from the back of the Castle"). Eventually they realised their error, and Esme relented with great relief.

Unfortunately, after ten days of happy romancing the two love birds were then separated. Chris had to return to Birmingham for his final year of theological training, while Kathy had already accepted an invitation to join a Dominican community near Florence as a lay member in September 1975, initially for a year. She had attended a French Dominican boarding school in Rome in her teens and had been struck by the wonderful affection and sense of fun displayed by the nuns. Their love of God had shone through in their dedication to the pupils, and Kathy's own faith was enhanced immeasurably by theirs. When she had heard that the nuns were opening a community to welcome those who wanted to commit their life for a period of any length, working and praying at regular intervals with them, without charge, she had signed up immediately.

So Chris and Kathy were forced to pursue their courtship by correspondence. It didn't take long for various thorny differences between their denominations to emerge – you couldn't imagine a more Protestant or a more Catholic lineage. Kathy's ancestor Philip Howard (20th Earl of Arundel) was even made a saint by Pope Paul VI in 1970, having been imprisoned in the Tower of London for his Catholic faith, and dying there (the rumour in 1595 was that he was poisoned). Trying to resolve these tensions at a distance was hard. Chris visited Kathy twice at the Community of Ganghereto, the first time in the autumn of 1975, the second during the spring of 1976. On both occasions he asked her to marry him, offering a beautiful Edwardian ring of sapphires and diamonds which had belonged to his paternal grandmother Clemence – certainly an improvement on the raspberry given to Angela Harvie.

Still unsure of which future vocation to pursue, Kathy responded with a "Wait" on each occasion, which the eager young ordinand took with good grace despite the obvious strain. Three offers of marriage (not including poor Angela, but acknowledging a failed proposal he had made to Johanna Turcan before heading back to New Zealand in 1973) and not a single one had produced the right response. One can only imagine how gloomy he felt on the second return journey from Italy to Birmingham. Kathy still had six months to go before she finished her year of service. To make matters worse, her mother Cécile reproached Chris over dinner at Jerome Cottage in front of the guests, asking, "When are you going to do something about my daughter?!"

After this second visit, Kathy was in turmoil. She just could not make up her mind which vows to take: she knew the Dominican Order was not for her, given its emphasis on academic rigour and teaching; she knew she loved Christopher Samuel Woods, but he was an avowed Protestant; and she had lately been attracted to a little known Catholic order established by a French playboy-turned-missionary (clearly she had a type) called Charles de Foucauld, who had spent decades in the Sahara with the Tuareg before being kidnapped and murdered. His order, the Little Brothers of Jesus, had inspired a female equivalent, the Little Sisters of Jesus, which had expanded its mission from the deserts of central Africa to the industrial wastelands of post-war France. The life of prayer and practical work in marginalised communities was very appealing.

In a marvellous echo of *The Sound of Music*, Kathy was given the blessing of the Prioress, Mère Marie – a close friend, spiritual advisor, and her former headmistress – to leave her commitment at Ganghereto and go home to consider her true vocation. Mère Marie reasoned wisely that it would be difficult for Kathy to come to a clear-headed decision while residing in a Dominican community in a Catholic country. Kathy returned to England in May 1976. Chris promptly boarded a train to London and took Kathy out to dinner.

Once again he proposed. Kathy's response must have knocked him for six – she replied that she still wasn't sure, and felt that she might in fact be called to join the order of Charles de Foucauld. The trainee clergyman would surely have been forgiven for responding with, "What the Foucauld?!"

But his actual response was to change both of their lives forever – for it was so gracious, accepting humbly that if Kathy felt God was calling her to a different mission field then she should pursue it, that Kathy was immediately convinced that she should commit to a life with him instead. She agreed to marry him there and then, and at last they were engaged.

The engagement didn't become official straight away: Kathy wanted to relish her new status as a bride-to-be without immediate razzmatazz. When Richard and Joanna invited them on a road trip from Paris to Tehran, they accepted happily. And so in July 1976 they all set off in a sturdy old Land Rover together with the two boys, James and Sam, from Valmondois – Cécile's family home north of Paris – to Geneva. They then proceeded to Venice, Split, and Dubrovnik, camping all the way.

New Zealand's Ambassador to Iran took the opportunity of extended time on the front seats with his brother to discuss the ordination process, and as he listened to the depth and sincerity of Chris's calling and commitment to his faith and ministry, "for the first time in my life, I felt as though I were a smaller man, a lesser person, than my own younger brother". It was a defining moment in his understanding of the remarkable turnaround in Chris's life, and the authentic spiritual revelation at the heart of it.

Richard also took the opportunity to quiz his brother energetically about his intentions towards Kathy. At this point, in Dubrovnik, with its beautiful medieval palaces and white, polished marble streets, the betrothed young lovers decided to make their engagement public, to the delight of their travel companions. They rang their respective parents from a telephone booth on a street corner, and the announcement was greeted with jubilation at the other end of the line.

***

The wedding took place on 15th January 1977 – Chris's 34th birthday – at All Saints' Anglican church in Marlow, just beside the Thames. Around 70 close family members were present, including a number of Kathy's French relations. Sam and Sybil flew over for the occasion, as did uncle Frank (then Archbishop of Melbourne) and his wife Jean. Earlier that morning, a special Mass had been conducted in a nearby Catholic church, with just the bridal couple present, along with parents Mondi, Cécile, Sam and Sybil, and the best man, brother Richard. All received Holy Communion.

Then began a rather challenging sequence of logistical hiccups. Cousin Robert had intended to drive Kathy and Mondi to the church in his vintage Rolls Royce Phantom 1, but it had snowed heavily the night before. Consequently, on the morning of the wedding, he rang from his home in Berkshire to say that the snow on the road was too thick for the Rolls to make it through. So Father Francis Little, a family friend and Benedictine monk from Downside Abbey, kindly offered to chauffeur the bride and her father in his rather small, muddy and decrepit Ford Escort.

Kathy hoisted her modest, white cotton wedding dress and bundled herself into the back of the car with Mondi. It was freezing inside, and the tiny back seat was a little damp, prompting the father of the bride to mutter, "It's still not too late to say no, my darling!".

His beloved daughter reassured him that it would take more than a soggy old car to prevent her from marrying her man. Crucially they made it to the church on time – poor Cécile, on the other hand, ran out of petrol and arrived just moments before the start of the service.

It was a wonderfully ecumenical affair. Sam conducted the marriage; Father Francis preached; and the local Catholic priest, Father Strain, prayed for them during the signing of the register. Kathy's brother Tonino played the organ beautifully, while Esme took the wedding photographs.

When the newly-weds emerged from the church they found a parking fine on the groom's car, an ancient Ford Zephyr. He promptly tore it up and drove them back to Jerome Cottage, where a banquet prepared by Cécile and innumerable French aunts was waiting. A picturesque sprinkling of snow still lay on the ground, and despite the freezing temperatures the happy couple made their way into the garden for a few photographs organised energetically by Esme.

After the festivities that afternoon, Mr and Mrs Woods got ready to leave for Portofino, on the Ligurian coast of Italy, via Luton airport. Tonino drove them in the aforementioned dilapidated Ford Zephyr. Unfortunately, as they made their way to the airport the car suddenly came to an ominous and rather abrupt halt. The Groom immediately rolled up his crisp white sleeves, leapt out of the car, opened the bonnet, and discovered a snapped fan belt. Unperturbed, he quickly found a substitute – a pair of Kathy's tights – and soon emerged from the bowels of the engine, covered in oil, a triumphant grin wrapped around his face.

The excitement didn't end there. The runway at Milan's Linate Airport was frozen so the flight was diverted at the last minute to Malpensa, 70km away on the other side of the city. By the time the happy couple reached their hotel in Milan, it was 4 o'clock in the morning.

When Kathy, in perfect Italian, politely asked the sleepy night receptionist if they could check in, she was informed in grave and sombre tones that their room had been flooded. In return, and with exceptional Italian customer service, they were offered a tiny room with a single bed. Exhausted and – possibly – keen to get upstairs, they took it.

Thus began their married life.

***

Following the honeymoon, Chris and Kathy moved to Childwall and he began his curacy at All Saints' in earnest. They were both keen to help support the significant pastoral needs of the parish – it is important to remember how close Kathy came to a vocation with a Catholic order focusing on pastoral work with remote communities in Africa, and industrial workers in France. She was just as much a missionary as her husband.

However, the culture in Liverpool was almost as alien to them as the Tuareg must have been to Foucauld (and Foucauld to the Tuareg for that matter) and the couple certainly put their foot in it occasionally. Kathy recalls an evening when they had rallied a number of parishioners to attend a carols celebration at the Philharmonic Hall in Liverpool:

> *Kik and I sat next to an elderly lady whom he had got to know a little. She was glum all the way through the lively performances and rousing carols. Eventually Kik turned to her and said 'Come on Yetta, it can't be that bad sitting next to me!' to which she replied, 'My husband died a year ago today'.*
>
> *That little exchange, and my husband's look of dismay, forced me to look away and stifle irrepressible giggles. So much for our pastoral skills!*

Aside from gaffes with the flock, the time spent in Childwall – in an echo of Sam and Sybil's time spent in Southport thirty years earlier – was notable for two additions to the family. On 29th November 1977 a baby girl, Isabella Gabrielle, was born. She was the centre of attention with her glorious fair hair, bright blue eyes and rosy cheeks – talents she has retained throughout her life. She soon began to communicate happily and loudly, again a talent she has retained, developing a precocious vocabulary by the age of one. Madeline Bridget followed on 12th August 1979. She had delightful dark hair and beautiful brown eyes, and grinned, giggled and gurgled with gusto (talents she has also retained). The two little girls were an indescribable joy to their parents.

During his curacy, Chris decided to write to Helen Findlay, the benefactor who had sponsored his scholarship to Dartmouth College. Perhaps it was an indication of his new-found maturity and determination to right the wrongs in his past – he had also completed his Canterbury degree by correspondence while training for ordination at Queen's. It is worth citing the letter in full as it captures a personal reflection on his change of circumstances:

55 Woolacombe Road,
Childwall,
Liverpool L16 9JG
13th March 1978

Dear Mrs Findlay,

It has been in my mind a long time now to try and contact you again, and the way was opened this morning when I received a very kind and thoughtful letter from Mrs Muriel Ashwell, a friend of my Aunt Priscilla Firth. She says that she meets you from time to time, and so I am immediately taking this opportunity of asking her to forward this letter.

So much has happened since we last met that I hardly know where to start! But may I first of all say that I look back on my time at Dartmouth as a time of many rewards, and great fulfilment in my life, and I would like to make plain to you my warmest gratitude for making it possible. I am sorry to have to tell you that the sort of utter irresponsibility which marked my time there persisted for many years after my departure.

I have travelled in some strange parts of the world since then, and, as it turns out, this has been a pilgrimage towards God, and also towards myself. I now see and understand most clearly that it's only when we allow into our lives the reality of the spiritual presence of God that our own true personality is given a chance to come out of its shell. Until we realise this, all we are doing is shadow-boxing; and I certainly did my share!

I am now the blissfully happy husband of Katherine, and equally happy father of Isabella. I was ordained into the Church of England fifteen months ago (and married three weeks later!) and my first ministry is a demanding and rewarding one here in Liverpool.

It would give me the greatest pleasure to hear from you, Mrs Findlay, and even greater pleasure to see you again!

With every good wish to you,

Very sincerely,

Christopher Woods

Sadly we don't have a copy of Mrs Findlay's response, but she did reference the letter in correspondence with a friend later that year:

10 Pleasant Street
Nantucket Island, Mass. 02554
Oct 30th

Dear Ort,

…I have something to tell you that I think will interest Dartmouth. You remember my scholarship lad, Christopher Woods, from New Zealand, who had to be sent down from Dartmouth? Well, he is now an ordained minister in the Anglican Church with a parish of his own in Liverpool, England. Quite a change isn't it. So perhaps everything was not wasted! He is married with a small daughter and very well liked in his parish and apparently doing a good job! I thought you would be interested.

…All best wishes,

Helen Findlay

Both letters capture some of the joy of prodigal redemption – that while the young Kik may have been close to wasting everything, merely shadow-boxing, he had discovered his true calling from God and was now fulfilling his real purpose in life.

***

Reverend Woods was certainly keen to ensure that he was punching his weight. Before the end of his curacy in 1979 he started to look around for potential incumbencies. By this time, he had experienced another divine epiphany – namely a revelation about the Holy Spirit encapsulated in the Charismatic Tradition. Richard J. Foster's *Streams of Living Water* (HarperOne, 2001), which looks at the six great traditions of the Christian faith, describes how the Charismatic Tradition "centres upon the power *to do*". Given Chris's energetic, practical approach to his ministry – and indeed his long genetic heritage of Charismatic mission, including the Spirit-fuelled Quakers of the Woodses, Barclays, Buxtons, Gurneys and Frys – it seems he had landed on the right Tradition. He described it as the spiritual equivalent of a boiler: his conversion on the road to Otaki had turned on the pilot light, but his experience of the Holy Spirit was now more like a major gas ignition, firing him up.

Kathy, on the other hand, was bemused by her husband's new-found zeal and asked her father, Mondi, whether he was alright. "Yes," he replied, "it sounds very much like what St Teresa of Ávila and St John of the Cross describe". Kathy felt better after that, reassured that Chris hadn't gone off the rails, and was in fact walking in the footsteps of some excellent Catholics.

Mondi was right – Foster states that the pivotal figure in the Charismatic Tradition is St Francis of Assisi. His story is of course not dissimilar to Chris's – wayward youth frolicking with his friends before a divine encounter and a life then committed to Christ. And like Chris, St Francis had a natural instinct for action, borne out of spiritual devotion and compassion: he is attributed the famous phrase, "Preach the gospel at all times and, if necessary, use words."

As Chris began to look for a parish, he was invited by Rev Graham Cray to attend an Anglican Renewal Ministries conference led by Rev David Watson at St Michael-le-Belfry in York. There he happened to sit next to a vicar, Eric Hague, who had spent most of his ordained life serving as a missionary in Chairman Mao's China. After talking for a short time, Eric invited Chris to preach at his church in St Helens, where he had served for three years before recently announcing his retirement.

The church in question was Holy Trinity, Parr Mount – roughly eleven miles east of Childwall, and also part of the Liverpool Diocese. Chris duly went to preach there. At the end of the service one of the parishioners came up to him and asked if he might consider becoming the next Vicar of Holy Trinity. The invitation struck Chris like a sledgehammer. He suddenly knew that this was where he was being called to minister.

Later that day he arrived home in Childwall and bellowed up the stairs to Kathy, "I think we're called to go to St Helens!" "St Helens?! Where is that?!" came the reply.

And so, in September 1979, only a month after Madeline's birth, Chris and Kathy and the girls moved into the vicarage on Traverse Street, a large old Victorian brick dwelling built in 1863. It was situated just eight feet from the east end of the church. This was going to be an immersive mission, right at the heart of the local community known as Fingerpost. The local government ward of Parr and Hardshaw had the highest breaking and entering statistics on Merseyside – and Merseyside had some of the highest statistics in Europe. This was what the Church of England calls, with admirable politeness, an 'Urban Priority Area'. There were 83 UPAs in the Liverpool Diocese and the parish of Holy Trinity was one of the worst.

And yet Chris and Kathy were about to realise that the challenge was not just outside but inside the church. In his retirement statement at the Annual Parochial Church Meeting that year, Rev Hague – who had spent decades working in atrocious conditions under the appalling brutality of the Communists – declared:

> *After 43 years in the ordained ministry, I have to say that, without doubt, this is the hardest place in which I have ever ministered.*

Rev Woods and Rev Hopkins in front of Holy Trinity Church, Parr Mount

CHAPTER 7
Energetic Optimism
(1979-1994)

Shortly after their arrival in Fingerpost, Chris was sitting in his study with what he thought was a local resident:

"You're from round here?" he asked the man.

"Nah."

"So where are you from?"

"Bull's Head."

Bull's Head is a neighbourhood named after a pub at its centre. It is less than half a mile from where they were sitting.

It took Chris and Kathy a long time to get used to this way of understanding place and community. St Helens is essentially made up of a whole series of urban villages like Bull's Head, each with an incredibly tight sense of identity. This harks back to its coal-mining origins – it is well-attested that coal miners have a very highly developed sense of community, based on their shared experience in the mines. They rely heavily on their co-workers for safety down in the pit, and it is therefore vital that they know and trust their co-workers very closely. Any outsider, or stranger, may not be dependable in the harsh conditions underground. You work together, you drink together, you live together. Over generations this contributes to a hyper-localised identity based around each pit, of which there were 90 in St Helens at the height of its industrial output.

The result was a parish for Chris and Kathy in which their own perspective of the world was at the polar opposite end of the spectrum from their new parishioners. Though born in London, Kathy was part French and Italian, and had grown up in Spain, Colombia and Italy; Chris had been born in New Zealand, educated in England and America, and had travelled all over Africa and Asia. He once asked a member of the church if he had a driving licence: "Nah. What would I want one for?" came the response. It took quite some adjustment for Chris and Kathy to understand the needs of people for whom a driving licence was excessive, and to whom The Bull's Head is not 'round here'.

This mindset in turn contributed to a very insular demographic. It is clear from the statistics that St Helens has a very low rate of immigration – data from the St Helens Crime and Disorder Summary of 1998 shows that there were 175,086 White people; 130 Black people; 26 Pakistanis; 112 Indians; 12 Bangladeshis; 130 Chinese; and 185 other ethnic minorities – including, rather astonishingly, a man from Yemen who was our local newsagent. That's 595 ethnic minorities in total (0.3 per cent). By the time of the 2001 census, the percentage was still only 1 per cent, one of the lowest in the country.

For a northern industrial town of 180,000 people, this seems to be a tiny proportion – certainly when compared to somewhere like Bradford, which in the 2001 census had 33 per cent of the population as ethnic minorities, or Blackburn, which had 31 per cent. Interestingly, both of these populations grew around the textile industry – they were mill towns – whereas another coal-mining population just down the road from St Helens, Wigan, has a very similar lack of diversity (also just 1 per cent). It does seem to suggest that coal-mining communities are particularly tight-knit.

St Helens was built both physically and metaphorically on coal, the town's motto being *Ex Terra Lucem* ('From the Earth, Light'). The collieries in St Helens were able to plug into the emerging transport networks of the Sankey Canal, which connected to the River Mersey at Widnes, as well as the Liverpool to Manchester railway. This enabled the production of coal to be increased to provide energy for the Cheshire salt-field, and provided the raw materials for Manchester and Liverpool's Victorian heyday.

In a satisfying twist of fate, Chris's great-great-grandfather, Edward Woods, had been Chief Engineer for the Liverpool to Manchester railway from 1836 to its completion in 1852. In 1834, Edward's first responsibility as assistant to John Dixon (whose predecessor as Chief Engineer was the 'Father of Railways' and inventor of the Rocket, George Stephenson) had been to take charge of the section from Liverpool to Newton-le-Willows, which is now part of St Helens. It is rather lovely to think that Chris travelled this very route – 145 years later – when bringing his young family from their curacy in Liverpool to their new parish.

***

By the time they arrived, St Helens was unfortunately beginning to lose some of its *Lucem*. Although the collieries were still employing as many as 5,000 men in the late 1970s, the trend for pit closures had begun to take hold and the last two, Bold and Sutton Manor Collieries, came to a juddering halt in 1992. The town was also host to other industries, including Pilkington's Glass, Ravenhead Glass, United Glass, Greenall's brewery and Beecham's pharmaceuticals.

Now only Pilkington's remains – and only just: glass production at their Cowley Hill site shut down in 2013, having operated there continuously since 1871. The iconic Greengate site does still house their float glass manufacturing plant – the technique for mass production of flat glass which they patented in 1952, turning them into a global powerhouse – but having had a workforce of well over 10,000 in the 1960s, only 1,350 remain.

The social impact of such a devastating industrial decline was stark, and Chris and Kathy discovered quickly that their parish was a despairing mix of mass unemployment and limited aspiration, with extreme pastoral needs. The town had twice the British rate of teenage pregnancies, and Britain the highest in Western Europe. On a more sinister note, the town also had the highest number of at-risk children of any metropolitan authority in Europe – the main reason being incest (Chris was once called out in the middle of the night to a nearby residence, and when he arrived the mother pointed to the bedroom door and said, "He's in there with the littl'un"). Many of the pastoral issues Chris and Kathy faced were the result of broken relationships and abuse of various kinds.

There were also very high levels of adult illiteracy. The historical reasons for this were linked to the need to have the maximum number of breadwinners in the household, coupled with the ease of finding manual work in the coal mines and other industries. The high rates of domestic abuse were apparently linked to this illiteracy. Women in the area were shown by one study to have a command of approximately 1,000 words (to put this in perspective, *The Guardian* in 1986 estimated that the average British person's vocabulary went from roughly 300 words at two years of age, to 5,000 words at five years of age, to some 12,000 words by the age of twelve, at which point growth tails off to around 15,000 in an adult). Men in the area were shown to have a vocabulary of around 400 words. So, during the course of a routine argument, Man quite literally runs out of things to say. Woman carries on talking. Finally, Man snaps.

The local secondary school, Parr Community High School, had the highest truancy rate of any school in England and

Wales: 22 per cent. There were 540 pupils at the school, meaning that on any given day over 100 of them were not there. Some parents were threatened by the idea of their children becoming formally educated; others actively dissuaded their offspring from attending school as a symbol of defiance towards the government – particularly Thatcher's government; many parents were simply not around to monitor whether their children went to school or not. Parr High was finally closed and razed to the ground (by the authorities) in 2002.

The health indicators in St Helens were so bad that *The Daily Mirror* once identified it as 'The Sickest Town in Britain'. It was women who suffered most, with female deaths from lung cancer at 62 per cent above the national average, and 20 women each year dying of cervical cancer – 75 per cent above the national average. There was widespread heavy smoking and use of junk foods, including by young children, resulting in some of the highest rates of obesity in the country. Chris knew one three-year-old who would routinely consume five Mars Bars in one sitting.

Drug abuse was also pervasive: needles were often left scattered on the steps leading down to the church cellar; glue sniffing was common amongst the Church Boys Brigade; and as children we would often have to stop playing games on the grassy verge behind the Vicarage whenever the cadaverous figure of Wayne shuffled out from the next house along the street. Each time, he would bring us newspaper clippings of his junior national championship boxing match at Wembley, explain how he threw it all away with heroin, and then shuffle back inside. With such high rates of substance abuse, together with unemployment edging up to 25 per cent, crime went through the roof (sometimes literally).

***

Holy Trinity Church was consecrated in 1857, and is a physical manifestation of the town's industrial heritage. It is made from slag-stone, which is waste from the smelting of raw ore, and may therefore have been sourced from either the local coal or glass production trade. It is black, and extremely hard, and the chunks come in all shapes and sizes. Together with the lighter mortar, the overall effect is a church which looks like a very sunburned giraffe. And like any precious species, it is therefore protected – Grade II listed to be precise.

The Vicarage, fortunately, was built of regular red bricks. But it was built so close to the church that you would have been hard pressed to swing a hamster, let alone a cat, on your way to the morning service. The garden, approximately nine square metres, was squeezed into the external space between the walls of the nave and the chancel. These walls, given their uneven slag surface, made games rather exciting and unpredictable – you could bounce a tennis ball off the church for hours on end and never have two trajectories the same. The Vicar's two sons would later put these fielding skills to good use in the school 1st XI.

The Vicarage, although much larger than most houses in the area, was originally the end house of a terrace. The neighbouring houses had been demolished in the late 1960s, leaving it standing rather perilously on its own – new buttresses were repeatedly affixed to the north and eastern walls to stop it falling over, and they boarded up and demolished the place as soon as the family moved out. The fissures in the dining room ceiling were particularly impressive, if a little startling for dinner guests.

Many other similar streets nearby, with cobblestones and small terraced houses, had also been demolished in the 1960s. Some of these dwellings were certainly inadequate, with an outside toilet at the end of the back yard, or even, in some cases, communal toilets at the rear of a group of houses. There were no bathrooms or kitchens. When it got really cold, the residents were sometimes forced to break up the bannisters or the floorboards for firewood. Some parishioners remembered burning cast-off shoes for warmth.

In place of the old terraces, a new dual carriageway – part of the A58 – had been built. It acts as part of a ring road around the town centre. It passes right around the front and side of the Vicarage: the view from the boys' bedroom was a busy main road on one side and black slag stone on the other. With a charming canopy of cracks in between.

The Vicarage was certainly not what Kathy's mother Cécile was expecting – when she was driven past it on her first visit, she gasped and said, "Oh, darling!!" The grimy yellow windowsills didn't help, nor did the dazzling pink flamingo wallpaper in the downstairs loo.

The views were certainly a far cry from the lush woodlands around Jerome Cottage. Even if Cécile hadn't been the daughter of a celebrated painter (Charles Geoffroy-Dechaume), she may have found the vista unsightly: to the east, the dual carriageway, Parr Baths and The Glass Barrel pub (known as 'The Blood Tub', for reasons which will become clear); to the south, the dual carriageway, Parr Flats – mostly derelict, despite being only 30 years old – and two National Grid gas towers standing nearly 300 feet high (thus allowing Richard to coin a new name for the Vicarage: 'Gasworks View' – when one of the gas towers was later demolished, Chris wrote to the company headquarters to complain that they had ruined the outlook from his study). To the west was a fairly bleak black church within sneezing distance, and myriad industrial chimneys on the horizon; and to the north, an old, unused church school and playground, backing onto Fingerpost high street.

The high street is very much the same now as it was then: on the north side, there is Thrifty's convenience store at the east end, purveyor of extraordinarily cheap canned goods and shampoo, most of it from former Soviet states with sell-by dates well into the 23rd century; Tanfastic, the local tanning salon; a pie shop, now Gregg's, but formerly Pimblett's, one of St Helen's most iconic family firms established in 1921, which finally closed in 2008; a betting shop; the butcher – although one of their two premises was formerly a video shop, which in 1985 memorably had some poor soul stand outside all day dressed as the world's portliest Darth Vadar, with appropriate heavy breathing, to celebrate the release of *Return of the Jedi* on VHS; the greengrocer; Smarty's hairdresser, scene of Kathy's infamous gaffe in 1988 when she brought Madeline in for a haircut and said, "My daughter would like a shag, please" (the family had just returned from New Zealand where a 'shag' was the local equivalent of a crop) – Viv, the proprietor, responded with a loud "PAAARDON?!"; the Cut Inn hairdresser, which was never trusted again after they shaved off the Vicar's sideburns; the Co-Op store; Foster's DIY shop; and a pharmacist.

On the south side, there is the Roundhouse Pub (now boarded up); the Queen's Head pub; the post office; Barclays Bank; some sort of tyre outlet; the Fingerpost newsagent run by the man from Yemen; Chipmunk Chippie, another great St Helens institution, to which the children would invariably be treated by their father whenever Mother was away; and another pharmacy, bearing the name of Ian James, a friendly, intelligent, bespectacled bearded beanpole with the world's largest supply of Old Spice, and a Lotus sports car parked outside.

***

Chris and Kathy soon realised that Parr Mount was going to be a long-term project. It was Kathy who suggested, one day early on, that they would need to stay for "a generation" in order for the church to implement the changes and improvements that the parish, and its parishioners, needed. Given her artistic sensibilities, and her aristocratic background, this was an extraordinary commitment to a place which presented a very different culture – and that commitment was to prove vital for a community in which many carried a heavy sense of rejection due to pervasive family and relationship breakdowns.

For Chris, an early pastoral case fired his conviction and compassion to serve these families. It included a number of the key social challenges facing the wider parish: an alcoholic single mother; her fourteen-year-old daughter living with her boyfriend; theft, with the boyfriend accused by the mother; a fight, resulting in the daughter attempting to strangle her mother; and, eventually, the daughter attempting suicide by taking two whole trays of anti-convulsant tablets (which belonged to her twelve-year-old sister).

Chris was called to the scene at midnight on a Sunday, the mother's oldest daughter arriving at the Vicarage with her three infant children and a small dog. He quickly got dressed (he had already retired to bed) and drove them all back to the house, where he found the mother unconscious – but breathing. He decided this was probably the Special Brew, not the strangling. Down the street at the boyfriend's house, he found the girl, also unconscious. He carried her outside and lay her on the floor of the van, whereupon her sister's three small children burst into tears, and continued crying all the way to hospital.

The girl survived, but this had been a defining moment for Chris – a heart-changing moment. As he sped to A&E, he recognised that his parishioners simply could not get into such appalling situations on their own – there had to be darker forces at work. "I found myself making a sort of decision that I was going to fight whatever spiritual battles were needed, on behalf of, and eventually, God willing, with local people. The sound of those children crying at half-past-one on a Monday morning made my mind up for me."

***

Unfortunately, the church community that existed when he arrived in 1979 was not at all pastoral, or welcoming. In fact, it was actively hostile.

Soon after they arrived, Chris asked one of the Church Wardens why the previous vicars, going back fifteen years or so, had each lasted such a short time, typically three years or so like Eric Hague. He replied, without a trace of a smile, "We saw them off."

The congregation was made up almost entirely of people who had lived in the Parr Mount neighbourhood until many of the old houses were demolished. They had then moved to other parts of the town – Eccleston, Denton's Green, Windle, Haydock – but continued to run the church from afar, almost like a private club for themselves. When Maurice Jackson joined the Parochial Church Council (PCC) in the late 1970s, he challenged the fact that council minutes were heavily edited and did not reflect the true nature of their discussions. He had participated in union meetings, where minutes had to be accurate, and he was shocked. "This is how we've always done it," he was told.

The PCC could do this in part because of the church's unusually resilient financial situation – the two local primary schools were both invested in the parish itself, instead of the diocese as would normally be the case, and both generated a small but stable income. The Vicar's salary was covered by the Liverpool Diocese, and there were no other staff costs. So apart from various bills and maintenance costs, the Church Wardens were in a strong position.

Of the 26 people on the PCC when Chris and Kathy arrived, eighteen did not live in the parish, including both of the Church Wardens. People who had moved into the new social housing in the parish, such as Parr Flats opposite, were actively excluded. There was almost nobody in the congregation under the age of 65.

One of the great strengths of the Church of England is its commitment to every neighbourhood in the country. Every parish church is expected, by means 'pastoral, evangelical, social and ecumenical', to reach the people who live within the parish boundaries. This was the reason, after all, that Holy Trinity Church had been built in the first place: to reach the new communities emerging in this part of St Helens as new coal mines were established. So for Chris to discover that the Parr Mount congregation was made up almost exclusively of people living outside the parish was quite a blow.

He and Kathy immediately set about trying to put this right. At one of the first meetings of the PCC after their arrival, Chris thought he would challenge the members over the use of the disused church primary school next door to the church, including the playground. Children as young as two would regularly 'play out' unsupervised, sometimes playing chicken across the dual carriageway after dark. In due course, Chris would take the funerals of three young children killed in the street like this.

He began the PCC discussion by quoting Luke 6:38 (NIV), where Jesus says, "with the measure you use, it will be measured to you". He pointed out that they had the iron gates to the playground chained and padlocked against the local children, and asked whether they thought God's gates would therefore be opened to them. "It is a *playground*, for Heaven's sake," he declared.

Bearing in mind that the great majority of those present had not lived in the neighbourhood for many years, they then entered into a lively discussion on perceptions of the local people. Most of the arguments against opening the gates, even at certain controlled times, centred on possible damage to the buildings. This was a genuine threat, which had occurred on numerous occasions. But Chris was determined that the church community should respond with a more open-handed and generous attitude.

At this point, one of the Church Wardens – the same one who told Chris that they had seen off the previous vicars, who also happened to be Lay Chair of the PCC – made a defence of keeping things as they were by pronouncing, "We're not a charitable organisation, Vicar!" Chris was flabbergasted. He replied, "Out of your own mouth you've said it, and I'm closing this meeting now!" He then got up and walked out.

He was gobsmacked. Not a charitable organisation! About the Church of Jesus Christ! Chris went back into the Vicarage and poured himself a large whisky. He sank into a chair in his study in despair, wondering how on earth he could change such hearts and minds. Soon afterwards, from the pulpit at a Sunday morning service, he compared the experiences of the clergy at Parr Mount to voyagers in the Bermuda Triangle, "where good men set off in faith and disappear without trace".

A short time later, Chris tried again. He invited two local couples, not church members, to see if they could begin a youth club together using the school building. The two Church Wardens happened to come into the school while one of the couples was working inside, preparing one of the rooms for the club. This couple lived in Parr Flats on the other side of the dual carriageway, facing the church. Chris reasoned that as residents of the parish they were perfectly entitled to help the Vicar in what he was trying to do.

The couple were greeted with contempt. "What do you think you're doing in here?" asked one of the Wardens in a threatening tone. No attempt to be civil – or indeed to check with the Vicar first. When Chris heard about it from the couple, he went straight round to the Warden's house, two miles away. He was out, so Chris left a note through the door saying that he would like to discuss certain things. He then proceeded to the local hospital on a pastoral visit. There, he was told that a man was sitting in his car outside the Vicarage, waiting for him. This made him nervous.

On his arrival home, the Vicar and the Warden had a two-hour heated discussion in his study. The Warden threatened to write to the Bishop. The Vicar, never exactly a shy and retiring type, said he could write to anybody he wanted, before bellowing: "I'm spending 24 hours a day trying to get people into this church, and you are spending 24 hours a day trying to keep them out. There isn't room for both of us, and I'm not leaving!" At that point, the Warden stormed out – never to return.

In this early period, Chris had been pastoring a local young man who had been in and out of prison. One evening, they were having a pint together in the Queen's Arms round the corner from the church, and Chris was telling the man about the wonderful difference that the love of Jesus can and does make in a person's life. The man said, "You mean to tell me that if I come across the road to your church I'll find the answer to all my problems?" The Vicar thought for a moment about the attitudes he was fighting in the church, and, sick to the stomach, had to reply, "No, you won't. Not yet."

But in his own mind, he was optimistic that, one day, they would become such a church community, where people would be welcoming, compassionate, gracious, able to help in any circumstances.

***

St Helens has a strong Roman Catholic heritage: in the Metropolitan Borough of St Helens there are 27 Catholic parishes, compared to 23 Church of England parishes. Some of this Catholicism comes from Irish immigration through Liverpool; some of it is old Lancashire Catholic.

As a response to this, Anglican churches such as Holy Trinity followed a resolutely Low Church tradition: no candles, services according to the 1662 *Book of Common Prayer*, morning and evening, with one family service per month. Eventually, one of the great benefits of Kathy's Catholic faith was that she and Chris were able to work together as a 'mixed' marriage to serve the blend of allegiances in the local community – but initially this only served to heighten the level of suspicion from the congregation towards the newcomers.

By August 1981, Chris was quite simply in despair. Supporters of his such as Maurice Jackson had been threatened verbally and physically by members of the old guard – there was even a suggestion that some of the burglaries which had taken place at the Vicarage had been targeted at Chris as intimidation. The lavatory in the back yard of the Jackson household had been smeared with dog faeces, and a number of their windows broken. Maurice was ill with stress.

On top of this, people whom Chris was pastoring and praying for were not responding – in fact, they seemed to be getting worse. One man kept on trying to kill himself despite Chris's prayers and support; another man's marriage broke up. He was trying everything he knew in personal evangelism, which admittedly was not much, and was getting no results: "I would get up early in the morning and pray for an hour or more, literally lying on the carpet in the living room, gripping the ankles of Jesus and begging Him to do something." The last straw was when a young policeman, who was about to head off for ordination training with his wife and three children, came to Chris and told him he was getting a divorce.

On his next day off, Chris cycled out of town to his favourite walking spot on the higher ground in Garswood, where he could get a distant view of the parish and its landmark gas towers. He surveyed the scene through tears, and cried out to God: "I can't cope with this! YOU have to do it. You'll HAVE to do it from now on." The brokenness of his parish had begun to break him.

There is an important principle here, to which Chris would return throughout his ministry. He wrote about it in an *Anglicans for Renewal* article in 1990:

> *John 12:24, with Jesus speaking, says, 'I tell you the truth, unless a grain of wheat falls to the ground and dies, it remains only a single seed. But if it dies, it produces many seeds'. Paul says in Galatians 2:20, 'I have been crucified with Christ and I no longer live, but Christ lives in me'.*
>
> *I believe that there is an essential quality of brokenness needed in Christian ministry, especially in leadership, which will, in turn, 'produce many seeds'. They also will need to fall to the ground and die, and as they do they will again produce many seeds, and so on.*

This brokenness was vital, because it was only now – as Chris flung his arms in the air and began to realise the limits of his own energy and strength in an environment like St Helens – that things started to change.

***

It was in this humbled frame of mind in September 1981 that Chris attended the Anglican Renewal Ministries conference at Swanwick (ironically, the scene of some of his grandfather Edward's proudest moments with emerging PCCs from around the country).

There he met Barry Kissell. Barry is also a New Zealander, short, red-haired, bearded, and still today rather feisty despite having broken his neck while surfing, and surviving cancer (Barry would always take great pleasure in lowering the young Woods children head first into the dustbin, as he let out a demented cackle). Needless to say Chris and Barry got on like a house on fire. Barry explained that he led an evangelism team based at St Andrew's, Chorleywood, just outside London, and suggested that he come to St Helens to lead a weekend with the church congregation. Chris was thrilled. Then Barry told him the date for the next available slot: November 1982, more than a year away. "What on earth am I going to do until THEN?!" he demanded, with his usual vigorous emphasis.

Barry returned to Chorleywood after meeting Chris and jokingly said to his team, "You won't believe it! I've just had a meeting with Prince Charles!" However, he then spent the next week praying and fasting, at the end of which he told two of his team, Bob and Mary Hopkins, that he felt they were called to go and minister with Chris Woods at Holy Trinity. They had never even met Chris. They were well travelled as a couple – Bob had been a successful marketing executive with Shell and they were posted in various exotic places around the world, including Brazil. Once an avowed atheist, he had followed Mary in becoming a Christian, retrained as an accountant, and then they had both joined Barry's evangelism team.

Bob immediately called Chris to arrange a weekend visit. He and Mary both recall how Chris took them for a walk around the parish – an approach favoured by Woods clergy it seems – and were amazed at how he could name the people and the problems behind each and every door. The problems were particularly stark in comparison to what they were used to in Chorleywood: Chris had spent one entire night walking the streets with a man to prevent him from committing suicide. He had then done the same thing again the following week. On another occasion the man had called the Vicarage at 3 am and told Chris he had taken an overdose, and by the time Chris arrived at the house he was unconscious – Chris had to drag him around the living room by his arms until the ambulance arrived.

The level of deprivation was enough to make Bob and Mary think twice – Mary couldn't wait to get back to Chorleywood – but they were moved by their experience. They were attracted by the energy and vision of this unusual vicar, and also by the immensely kind and generous hospitality of the Vicar's wife. They began to feel that Barry might be right.

In October 1982, Chris received a phone call from Barry urging him to drop everything and head down to St Andrew's that weekend, to hear a man from California by the name of John Wimber speak on church growth and associated matters. It didn't sound particularly exciting, but Barry was so insistent that Chris and Kathy decided that they would at least attend the Friday seminar before heading back up north for the Sunday services.

They were both completely bowled over by Wimber. A former keyboard player and manager for The Righteous Brothers, he was now the figurehead for the emerging charismatic movement called Vineyard Ministries International. Wimber was immensely likeable, natural, laid back, funny – and the experience of the Holy Spirit that day was striking, unlike anything Chris and Kathy had ever seen or felt before. People (educated people, people in suits and ties, people from

Chorleywood for goodness' sake) were singing aloud spontaneously at the top of their voices, screaming, crying, shaking, laughing, dancing, wailing, rejoicing, falling flat on their faces. Wimber was serene throughout – this was God at work, healing mind, body and spirit as each individual required. And slowly but surely, it dawned on Chris and Kathy that God was saying something fundamentally important to them about their own ministry in St Helens.

As they drove back up north the next day, Chris reflected that he was the only person in the entire Fingerpost neighbourhood to read *The Times* newspaper. He enjoyed 40 pages of close print, and balanced, reasoned arguments on complex issues. The Yemeni newsagent had a standing order for one copy which he kept under the counter and brought out for the Vicar when he walked in each morning, like some kind of secret dossier. Everybody else in the area read *The Sun*, *The Daily Mirror*, *The Daily Star* or *The Daily Sport* (it is probably true to say that the great theologian Karl Barth didn't quite have *The Daily Sport* in mind when he encouraged Christians to hold a Bible in one hand and a newspaper in the other).

But it struck Chris, following Wimber's example, that perhaps God was trying to show him that people in their parish would respond better to the Bible if they could actually *see* God do something. They needed a tabloid version rather than a broadsheet, sensory rather than cerebral. They bought the tabloids because they were full of pictures; their television sets were on day and night because they preferred to watch stories rather than read them. And so it dawned on Chris that if the parishioners could see God at work, they would respond. After all, that is principally what happens in the Gospels and the accounts of the Early Church in Acts – people were moved to respond to the acts of God they witnessed.

Finally, in November 1982, Barry brought his small team – including Bob and Mary and a few others – to Holy Trinity. For the first time, Chris and Kathy saw local people from the church responding to the presence of God in their midst and coming to faith. And in the summer of 1983, they were joined in the parish not only by Bob and Mary, with Bob as a non-stipendiary curate (covering his and Mary's costs by working as a part-time accountant in Warrington), but also by a young university graduate with brilliant musical gifts called Tim Humphrey. Three months later, Rev John and Michele Walker arrived, with John as the full-time stipendiary curate. All of a sudden, there was a new momentum in the leadership team – all outsiders, but all sharing the vision of building a local church run by local people, a church of the poor for the poor.

Gaining the diocesan approval for Bob and Mary's move required the two of them, plus Chris, to pay a visit to the Bishop of Liverpool, David Sheppard. For most of the meeting the Bishop was decidedly cool, suspicious of the motives behind why this curate and his wife from Chorleywood should want to move to Fingerpost – he was understandably cautious about the idea of a middle-class enclave being created in an Urban Priority Area. Fortunately, the atmosphere brightened when Sheppard was assured that Bob and Mary would be entirely self-funded. Bob also explained that they only planned to be at Holy Trinity for three years, and would then move on to repeat the church-planting experiment somewhere else (in the end, such was their calling to Fingerpost that they stayed for over fourteen years).

Despite having lived abroad for many years, Bob and Mary felt completely out of their comfort zone in Parr to begin with. On arrival at their tiny terraced house in Lascelles Street, they found that they were the centre of attention for the entire street – cockatoos in a cage full of canaries. A group of unaccompanied infants approached and declared themselves 'The Lascelles Street Gang'. They were fascinated by the Hopkins' dog, which was fluffy and feeble, unlike the local breeds. A friendly gentleman then offered to help them unload their van, filled with precious Chorleywood chintz: "I drive a van. Just let me get in the cab – I'll jam it in first gear; jam it in reverse; and then we can just shovel it out!"

***

Buoyed by the new arrivals, Chris decided at last to address the problem of the PCC – and deliberately bent the rules to do so. No doubt he was aware of the ancestral paradox: we have noted that Edward Woods had been at the heart of the creation of Parochial Church Councils as leader of the Life and Liberty Movement following WWI, and spent every year training PCCs at the Swanwick Conference. Chris was in fact resolved to constitute a PCC at Holy Trinity which was more in line with the vision of his grandfather – namely, a group of local representatives working with the Vicar to promote the spiritual, social and pastoral mission of the church in the parish.

A key stumbling block was that the PCC cabal at Holy Trinity kept voting each other back in for new three-year terms, perpetuating their own control. And so, before the Annual Parochial Church Meeting in 1985, Chris told the PCC that all members up for re-election would have to take a year out before they could stand for re-election. He had no right to do this: the Church of England statutes provide for nothing of the kind. But he bluffed – and they bought it. Thus, as a significant number of vacancies came up that year, he and Bob corralled all of the new members of the church to ignore anyone linked to the previous regime and vote in new, local representatives. As Maurice put it, "He rigged the ballot. He said, 'You vote for him, you vote for him' and so on." The old clique realised their time was up, and gradually they began to leave. Chris had challenged them head on, and won.

There was an excellent team spirit among the new leadership group. Chris combined his big vision for the church with a working environment of low stress, including outrageous humour, which proved highly motivational. John Walker had studied at the Royal Academy of Dramatic Art (RADA) and was an exceptionally gifted musician, possessed of a tenor which could have graced the Royal Opera House – but which was instead let loose spontaneously around Holy

Trinity. He was also a hilarious mimic, with one infamous sketch based on the idea of 'Graveyard Ministries International'. Chris encouraged his broader leadership team, including local members of the congregation, to lampoon each other at every opportunity. One day Maurice Jackson was in the church enjoying a particularly feisty exchange with another member of the leadership team when an older member of the congregation approached and asked if they had fallen out. "No, no, the Vicar taught us to be like this," he replied. And when one particularly cantankerous member of the old guard passed away, Chris announced the sad news at a leadership team meeting. After a pause, he said: "I only went to the funeral to make sure she was dead!"

On another occasion, Chris and the team attended an event at Liverpool Central Hall hosted by a Nigerian evangelist and self-styled bishop. They had taken with them a number of parishioners from Fingerpost, including a woman called Doris who was severely mentally disturbed and prone to hallucinations. Even on a good day, it was rather difficult to discern what was spiritual and what was psychological with Doris. She had once called the Vicarage to report that she had been possessed by 6,380,726 demons. At the end of the Nigerian evangelist's lively sermon, she went forward for prayer – and who should approach her but the Nigerian himself. Chris and Bob watched on with juvenile anticipation. They couldn't discern what Doris said to him, but his heavily accented response was audible throughout the auditorium: "Demons?!...You have DEMONS??!!" This quickly became a favourite catchphrase among the church leadership.

Another favourite catchphrase was to say that somebody had been 'Titus Three-Tenned'. St Paul's letter to Titus, Chapter 3 verse 10 says, 'Warn a divisive person once, and then warn them a second time. After that, have nothing to do with them.' And so, whenever Chris was forced to eject somebody from the church for being persistently disruptive (perhaps another errant PCC member, or one of Doris's demons), he would announce to the team that they had been 'Titus Three-Tenned'.

Chris's natural confidence and security also made him a very approachable and engaged leader. He was very happy to receive other people's input – normally over a sherry after a Sunday morning service (he called this 'Thirst After Righteousness'). While he would take the lead on outlining what he felt God's call and vision was for the church, he would follow this by asking, "What do you think?" In this way, clear mission and direction were established while retaining the engagement and buy-in of those implementing it.

***

The team did of course have their difficulties: there were a number of different personalities trying to work harmoniously in extreme conditions. While Chris was happy to fly by the seat of his pants – he would sometimes only decide who was preaching a few days before a Sunday service – others required more planning and structure, and focused on ensuring there were proper rules and systems in place. Where Kathy was a natural listener and pastor (she was known for providing the best cups of tea – "Brilliant cup of tea, that," according to Maurice), Chris was the visionary focused on the overall goal, galvanising the team towards it, and heading out into the parish to evangelise. The team finally clarified their differences after conducting a Belbin personality profiling exercise (Chris was deeply suspicious of this, claiming he knew how to manipulate it). Thereafter they were at least able to name the inevitable tensions between them within a common framework, and deal with them openly.

Chris also had a strained relationship with the Bishop, David Sheppard (perhaps an echo of his struggles with Mr Hage at Dartmouth). Sheppard had been a talented cricketer earlier on in life, captaining Cambridge, Sussex and England. He had gone up to read History at Trinity Hall in 1947, before training for ordination at Ridley Hall in 1955 – he was the first ordained minister to play for England, with his last Test coming against New Zealand in 1963. There was no obvious reason for the tensions between Bishop and Vicar: they shared a similar background, and were both passionate about the urban poor. On Sheppard's first visit to Fingerpost, it is true, somebody had asked him if his stole was for mopping up the Communion wine whenever he spilled it – but it is unlikely that this was the cause of their uneasy accord.

Perhaps it was the fact that Sheppard was being sent a constant stream of angry letters by one of the old guard at Holy Trinity, a woman infuriated by the changes made by Chris since he had arrived. A quality-controller at a nearby biscuit factory, she would sit in the Sunday morning service making a list of all the things he was doing wrong, and then submit them to the Bishop every week. It was the Bishop's standard practice to respond to the Vicar in writing, to alert him to these complaints. Chris would then store them in the bottom of a filing cabinet somewhere in the vestry.

Eventually, Chris and Bob were hauled in to see Bishop Sheppard and accused of breaking their ordination vows. The latest letter from the biscuit-botherer had complained that they had stopped wearing their priestly vestments – which Chris called his "penguin suit" – and instead were wearing dog collars with jackets. It was all part of their attempt to make church more accessible for local parishioners (stoles were clearly rather distracting). As they drove back to Fingerpost from the Bishop's office, like two naughty schoolboys having been to see the headmaster, Chris turned to Bob with a grin:

"Well, that went well!" he said jauntily.

"Did it?" Bob replied, a little warily.

"Yes," said Chris with a glint in his eye. "He didn't say we couldn't continue."

And so they continued wearing what they felt like wearing, and continued providing the Bishop with plenty of correspondence from 'Disgusted of Fingerpost'. Dropping Fred Trueman in the slips on the 1962 tour to Australia must have seemed a doddle by comparison (Trueman famously turned to Sheppard and remarked, "The only time your hands are together is on Sunday").

***

Meanwhile, there had been new arrivals at the Vicarage. Named Francis Henry, I was born at Whiston Hospital on 20th May 1981 (12 months after the legendary Steven Gerrard was born in the same location), and Thomas Edmund Christopher followed on 13th June 1983. Both brothers dreamed of playing for Liverpool FC and St Helens RLFC, and the grass behind the Vicarage was the scene of some sensational goals and mercurial skills, with the occasional interruption from dear Wayne and his newspaper clippings.

While Chris continued to lead the ministry at Holy Trinity, Kathy's role was increasingly one of moral support, pastoral hospitality for staff and parishioners, and raising a large family almost single-handedly. She was immensely popular in the local community, always friendly and polite – and known for being a little eccentric. On occasion, she could be seen walking the pet rabbit on a leash. It was widely known that she had salvaged one of her jumpers from the gutter on Corporation Street, just near the canal. During a clean-up operation at Holy Trinity, she was photographed being hoisted by her ankles head first into a manhole.

She had form for this kind of thing: in Childwall – while heavily pregnant with Isabella – she had decided it was too difficult to carry the shopping bags home on her moped (itself a dubious choice of transport when eight months pregnant and visiting the supermarket). Faced with this quandary, she simply hooked the shopping trolley onto the back of the moped and whizzed home.

The children were given respite from this unconventional behaviour by Merton Bank Primary School, a ten-minute walk away. Merton Bank hosted all of the Woods children and did a pretty effective job of getting us to read and write – it was too much to ask, it always has been, to get us to count. The sports fields were spacious and well maintained, save the occasional stolen car crashing into the goal posts. The school also had a terrific music teacher, Mrs Bocock, who played the piano at morning assembly with the verve and gusto of Les Dawson in his pomp.

The Vicarage was a very musical place, not surprising given Chris and Kathy's own musical gifts. Mum's preference for classical music competed with Dad's collection of appalling 1970s records, which were stored in our old Grundig console in the corner of the drawing room. The children were particularly enamoured by the mysterious, soft-focus record sleeve of the Barry Gee / Barbara Streisand duet, overflowing with teeth and hair. For many years I actually thought that Barry was Barbara and Barbara was Barry. Our grandmother Cécile had been a highly respected concert pianist in her day. Mum was constantly playing the guitar and piano and singing to us, albeit mostly in French, which none of us could understand ("*Un kilometre à pied, ça use, ça use!*"); and occasionally Dad would seize his old trumpet and scare the living daylights out of all of us. Very occasionally, if enough whisky was produced, he would take over the piano and perform a rollicking version of 'The Vicar's Stomp', hands and legs bouncing along in unison.

Isabella blazed a trail for her siblings, achieving Grade 8 in the flute, piano and voice. Madeline lowered the bar for her brothers by flitting nonchalantly between the guitar and the clarinet, while singing beautifully. I lowered the bar further by taking up the cello of all things. On one occasion, our parents were out for the evening and the infant Lydia (born on 4th March 1989) was giving our wonderful nanny Beryl Appleton a hard time, so I descended the stairs in my pyjamas and treated them both to an emotional performance of *The Grand Old Duke of York*. Lydia's howls only got worse, accompanied now by

Beryl, and so I calmly packed up and returned to bed. I then packed in the cello altogether and took up the drums, and the sound of monotonous paradiddles could be heard throughout the parish. Thomas would later serenade Lydia much more effectively on the guitar. And then Lydia did what little siblings do, and outdid us all – even gaining a First Class degree in Music at university.

The various musical outputs of his children gave Dad immense joy. He would regularly demand a recital of some sort, normally after dinner with a stiff drink. As his offspring grew older, and therefore more self-conscious, his enthusiasm for these private concerts would increasingly be met with howls of embarrassed anguish and sulky performances – none of which mattered to him one jot. He would sit there, whisky in hand, eyes closed, a look of deep contentment on his face.

***

A growing brood also allowed Dad to channel his enthusiasm for motorcars – now with a much reduced budget – into a series of eccentric family vehicles in which we would drive all over the Continent. Our first family car was a white minibus with images of The Incredible Hulk and other biblically-inappropriate characters painted on the side. It was in the back of this bus that I, aged four months and perched happily in my pram, was thrilled to see the rear doors suddenly fling open as we sped along the motorway. A crate of milk bottles clattered past and crashed onto the tarmac, finally alerting my parents to the unfolding drama behind them.

The Green Van (a green VW camper van) was a dear member of the family for many years, exploding through five different engines. On one occasion, as we were driving back from Valmondois with my father and Mondi in the front, and Mum, Cécile and the four children lying on the bed in the back, we all sang French children's songs loudly to the camper van in an effort to get it up a particularly steep hill. To our great relief, it worked.

Dad was absolutely unequivocal with staff and parishioners about preserving his family time. They knew that, unless there was a crisis, Saturdays were off limits. As well as taking trips to nearby parks and farm trails, our parents did like to head further afield whenever possible. During school holidays we would go camping in the Lake District, courtesy of Mum's uncle Hubert, who owned Lyulph's Tower beside Ullswater (it is now owned by Mum's cousin Philip Howard, Lord Howard of Penrith). We would set up camp in the field down by the lake, and generally spend our time walking, building bonfires, playing games, and skimming stones on the crystal-clear waters of the lake. Glorious, sepia-tinged stuff.

Normally our holidays involved some kind of monumental road trip, with Dad putting in Stakhanovite shifts behind the wheel (and under the bonnet) at all hours of the day and night. But for Christmas 1987, we had our first major plane trip together – to New Zealand. Thirty-six hours with four children under the age of ten. And no interactive screens. Miraculously, through a combination of Lego, books, boiled sweets and gin, Mum and Dad made it through. We had the most wonderful three months visiting Sam and Sybil, including Christmas together with them and Sally (who married Gordon Rutherford a few years later), Marianne, Baxter, cousins Andrew and Jacqui, as well as Richard, Joanna, James and Sam. Dad – perhaps nostalgic for his weekend fishing trips with Richard Lavers – ensured my Christmas present was a fishing rod, and, from a nearby pier, the two of us somehow lured a local grey mullet into our laps. We didn't fish once on our return to St Helens – for some reason, Sankey Brook (known as Stinky Brook) was not so appealing.

On our return route from New Zealand we stopped in California to visit John Wimber's Vineyard church in Anaheim. Dad had taken a team from the church to visit Anaheim previously, but wanted to give the entire family a chance to experience Wimber's laconic leadership and the magnificent Vineyard music. As children, this was our first real experience of church outside Fingerpost, and it was a real eye-opener – thousands of people packed into an enormous building, professional musicians and sound systems, and Vineyard T-shirts for all of us as mementos. It was perhaps our first glimpse of the kind of vision our father had for St Helens, and as such remained an inspiration for many years thereafter.

As well as the chance to visit Vineyard, Dad was also very excited to be back on US soil. Despite being kicked out of Dartmouth College, he had retained a deep and lasting affection for America. The American culture of positivity and optimism; of doing things at scale; of keeping things simple; of driving cars everywhere and eating vast quantities of meat (at Ruby's Diner the burgers were bigger than Thomas's head) – all of these things made America great in the eyes of our father.

He was absolutely thrilled when, on our arrival, we were collected at the airport by our Vineyard hosts in a vehicle so new and hi-tech that it had an automatic seat belt for the driver which advanced rather ominously towards the driver's neck as soon as the door was shut. When the door was not shut, and the engine was started, the vehicle would bellow in a loud robotic voice, "YOUR DOOR IS AJAR! YOUR DOOR IS AJAR!" This made my father very happy. He was slightly less happy when, a few minutes into our journey, I erupted like a Thunderdome contestant at Sigma Alpha Epsilon: Thomas, petit, beautiful and blond, now looked like he'd been swimming in a vat of minestrone; Madeline got a good hosing; Isabella saved herself by holding up Mum's coat. Robocar had no response to this.

Dad's excitement went up a notch when he realised that Anaheim also hosts Disneyland. Disney films were regular fixtures at the Vicarage – *Bedknobs and Broomsticks* was a particular favourite, and Dad was known to indulge in repeat viewings of the anarchic football match featuring two teams of cartoon jungle animals. Fortunately, on the day we chose to visit Disneyland, it rained. This meant the Woods family had the park pretty much to ourselves.

By late afternoon, as we made our way to Mr Toad's Wild Ride, a chill was starting to penetrate our free PVC raincoats. We were inspired by the sight of a ride with such quintessentially British literary origins – and Dad was particularly enthused about Mr Toad's motorcar. We all piled in and charged off into the eccentric world of *The Wind in the Willows*. Sure enough, Mr Toad's driving became more and more erratic until, with a great shudder, we crashed headlong into a train. At this point, the cars jerked into a dark corridor…silence consumed us…it was pitch black, and we began to discern faint hisses and demonic hooting nearby. A red hue formed in the near distance – and then all of a sudden we plunged headlong into a fiery abyss.

Sulphurous clouds belched on either side, wicked fiends emerged from the depths laughing and screeching (some of them pointing miniature tridents in our general direction), and overhead a deep, satanic cackle washed over us. The children – and our parents – took all of this on board with eyes on stalks. Dad was heard to mutter "Good grief" under his breath.

Eventually we surfaced from the darkness, blinking into the afternoon light. The Vicar was looking a little conflicted. It certainly wasn't the kind of entertainment he would normally provide for his family – even with his outlandish sense of humour, he was fairly conservative when it came to spiritual matters. He was also a little nervous about the idea of his four children regaling our Vineyard hosts with tales of demons at Disneyland. And yet, it was so lovely and warm down there in the midst of Mr Toad's eternal damnation…certainly when compared to Snow White's spinning saucers outside. And so, with his usual authority, he made a decision: for the rest of the day, whenever any of us started to feel a little bit chilly, Dad would announce that we were returning to Mr Toad's Wild Ride and we would all merrily reheat in Hell.

***

Back home, things had started to heat up too. In March 1984, Eric Delve – a well-known British evangelist – led a three-week mission to St Helens entitled *Down to Earth*, after which 73 people were referred as new parishioners to Holy Trinity. Earlier, in the summer of 1983, Chris had been made Chairman of *Mission England* for the St Helens area; *Mission England* was a series of major evangelistic events in the UK from May to July 1984, led by the legendary American evangelist Billy Graham.

In doing so, Chris was following in the footsteps of his grandfather Edward, who himself had led a 14-night mission to Bristol in 1925, supported by a team of 85. Factories were visited during the day, and 4,000 people attended the Mass Meetings each night which, with titles such as *Question Night for Trade Unionists and Others*, positioned Edward as the ecclesiastical Dimbleby of his day. He was thrilled with the connection being made between Church and community:

> *For once the Church was right down in the arena…More keenly than ever before do I feel that the great mass of people in this country are absolutely ready for vital Christianity, if only the churches would give it to them; if you put the thing in any sympathetic and attractive and intelligible way, they simply lap it up as if it is the very thing for which all along their souls have been athirst.*

One of the *Mission England* events was held at Anfield football ground in July 1984, with a capacity audience of 36,000 every night for six nights. Cliff Richard spoke and performed alongside a host of others. This was the year before *Live Aid*, but even bigger in scale. Fifty-two people were referred to Holy Trinity from Anfield, but it was particularly memorable for Chris for another reason.

Chris was there as part of the pastoral team (he had the excellent title of 'Supervisor Captain') and during the session when people were invited to come forward onto the pitch for prayer, his job was to patrol the back of the crowd to make sure everyone who had come forward was being attended to. On average, 10 per cent of the crowd would come forward each night, approximately three and a half thousand people – quite a number.

On the fifth night, as Chris was on patrol, he noticed two men at the back, one of whom was chain-smoking manically and looking very troubled. He approached them and asked the man if he was OK. "Fine," came the reply. "Let's sit down," said Chris. They sat on the coconut matting which had been laid down to protect Anfield's hallowed turf (Liverpool FC had just won the League title for the seventh time in ten years). It was a mild summer evening.

> Chris continued: "What's the matter? You don't look too well."

> The man finally looked at him. "I'm under orders from the hierarchy to kill my pastor."

> "Oh yeah?!" Chris thought. "We'd better go inside," he responded.

So he took the two young men into the media room behind the main stand at Anfield, where there were no windows (no doubt to help the journalists file their reports on time). He sent for two sizeable young parishioners from Holy Trinity, Craig Jevins and John Atherton, each of whom would have had a pretty good chance of stopping penalties at the Kop end. When they arrived, Craig asked Chris what was going on. Chris explained. Craig replied, "Oh shit!"

They closed the door and another volunteer was placed in the corridor outside. Later, in a seminar entitled 'Ministering in the Power of the Holy Spirit', Chris described what unfolded:

> *I was sitting on a chair, let's say here; the man was sitting over here, with his friend. I hadn't had any training. I just raised my arm, sitting on the chair, I just raised my arm and said, 'The name of Jesus is far above every other name' – and this man back-flipped right off his chair. I mean the whole chair flipped over*

backwards onto the floor; he somersaulted back onto the concrete, on his back.

John and Craig went and sat on him – we don't do that any more you'll be pleased to know – and the man was frothing at the mouth, and an evil voice was coming out of him, and this man was <u>completely</u> demonised.

[Craig has since explained that he and John, who was 18 stone, were both lifted off with unnatural and terrifying ease by the man, who himself was not large.]

But I felt complete calm, the peace of the Lord was just amazing and you just sense the authority of Jesus – 'authority' means 'the right or the power to enforce obedience'. And so I sensed I had the authority, the right and the power to enforce obedience on these demonic things, you see.

John and Craig were with him; I sat on a chair next to him, and I thought of Jesus and the Gadarene Demoniac, and I thought I'd ask this demon its name first of all, and it refused to give it to me. I made sure that the man himself knew I was talking to the demon and not to him; I'd ascertained his real name beforehand obviously. And so this went on for about half an hour and I said something like, 'Well you better tell me your name because we're going to stay here all night if necessary', and I meant it.

This demon finally came out with its name, which was the name of a Greek god. And then I addressed it by its name and commanded it to come out in the name of Jesus, and he sat up weeping and crying.

Meanwhile, his friend was absolutely <u>appalled</u> at all of this of course; he had no idea what was going on. Anyway, we stood this chap up. By this time Peter Horrobin [a good friend, who runs Ellel Ministries International] *had come in, and Bill Flag, who'd been a South American Missionary Society bishop, and we made sure that this person received Jesus and was filled with the Holy Spirit. He lived in Bolton, which was too far away from us, so we sent him on his way.*

Chris then called the man's vicar in Bolton to explain the situation – including the death threat. His response? "Oh! I had my doubts about him, you know!"

The man came back to visit Chris at Holy Trinity two months later. Bob was present, along with two other parishioners. It was at this point that the man explained he was a Satanist high priest, and had been so for ten years – he was only 24, but had been initiated into it by his grandmother at the age of fourteen. He had been on Pendle Hill (in east Lancashire, famous for the trials of twelve witches in 1612), where he had consumed human blood. He knew 800 demons by name; the hierarchy he had referred to, which had ordered him to kill his vicar, was a demonic one. He then started ripping up Bibles right there in the room.

Chris decided he couldn't minister to this man at such a distance, along with all of the new arrivals in the church. The vicar in Bolton would have to deal with him now that he was aware of the situation. As Chris drove the man back to Bolton that night in our green VW camper van, he turned to Chris from the passenger seat and said ominously, "Aren't you scared here, sitting next to a Satanist high priest?" In truth, Chris was certainly afraid – this was the first time they had been alone together, and Bolton was a good half-hour's drive away. But he said, again with great spiritual authority, "The one who is in me is stronger than the ones who are in you". At this, the man recoiled violently against the seatbelt, his body convulsing, and once again he began frothing at the mouth.

***

While Holy Trinity was having its heating system fixed, the entire church decamped to the church hall half a mile down the road in Peasley Cross. A couple from Haydock, Alan and Cath Kirkham, decided to join Holy Trinity at this point – they knew they would like it when they turned up at the main church on a Sunday morning to find a sign on the door saying simply, "We're not here any more."

The church hall was a simple room with a stage and a parquet floor. And it had the extraordinary effect of liberating the congregation from some of the entrenched views and behaviours they had held at the main church in Fingerpost. The leadership team made the most of this new-found sense of community by establishing small groups with specific responsibilities for welcoming, food and testimonies; they also instituted Thursday night evenings of music and prayer, which became immensely popular. On top of the significant increase in numbers generated by the *Mission England* events, Holy Trinity was flourishing: congregations of 200 or more were not unusual on a Sunday – almost ten times what they had been when Chris and Kathy had arrived.

One of the leadership team's key values was acceptance. Chris explained this later:

So many churches expect newcomers to behave like Christians as soon as they step across the door of the building. If they are smoking as they walk in, everyone throws their hands up in horror. But what do we expect? We must accept people as they are and then we will gradually seek to see change in various areas. Smoking comes about number 147 in our list of don'ts. One of our top ones is, 'Stop punching your wife.' That's a good one to start with after you've become a Christian!

The experience on a Sunday was completely different to anything anybody had seen before. Craig Jevins, a parishioner from Fingerpost who became a long-standing local leader, says:

I used to go to Holy Trinity before Chris was there, and even though I didn't know God then I used to think, 'There's got to be something better than this'. It was just a case of turn up, sit down, stand up, say a prayer, put some money on a plate and then go home. I'd miss the sermon because I'd always be asleep.

Maurice says the new Holy Trinity "felt spiritual, free. It had a spark. It was exciting." Chris's sermons were very much part of this – they were vibrant, funny, down to earth, and relaxed. He once showed the congregation his sermon notes and they were in fact a shopping list. His preaching was exhortational, not theoretical: instead of asking the congregation to understand complex theology, he explained the Bible simply and clearly – just as his grandfather Edward had to the British public over the wireless – and asked them to try the same things he was doing himself in pubs and homes around the parish. He applied the Bible to real life in Fingerpost, and created a sense of shared mission. It was both progressive and very pragmatic.

In an article published in New Zealand at this time, Chris described his approach:

> *People are not interested in formal religion but in a relationship with Christ. If the organised Church is a barrier between Christ and the man in the street then we should be asking ourselves, 'What is wrong with the organised church?' So many people tell me they believe in Christ, but they cannot believe in his Church. I think this is a terrible indictment.*
>
> *Many churches are like bottles. The pew-sitters are the sediment; the choir, the vestry, the church wardens et cetera are in the middle; and the minister is the cork jammed in the neck through whom everything must go in or out. So often the whole lot needs a great shake-up so the cork flies off and the new life begins.*

A central tenet of Chris and the leadership team's vision was to develop a localised leadership, where he as the cork would get out of the way. Chris was fond of saying to the congregation that he was the Vicar, but they were the ministers. It helped that parishioners in Parr were action-orientated: the question they would often ask was, "Does it work?" If they believed you, particularly if they had seen the ministry in action, they would just go ahead and do it. Chris loved this black and white simplicity – he was not dissimilar himself.

In this way, he released local people into all kinds of pastoral activity. The hospital visiting team was led by one parishioner and had twelve people involved, visiting St Helens

Hospital twice per week (one of the benefits of high unemployment rates was that people had plenty of time on their hands); Barry Dodd learned to read as a lay reader by reciting the Bible and the liturgy during Sunday services; Maurice Jackson was empowered to go and offer Holy Communion in the local old people's home, despite not being ordained – Chris simply blessed the bread and wine, blessed Maurice, and sent him merrily on his way.

Irene Whitaker developed an extraordinary gift of prophecy, became a local magistrate, and then got ordained; Craig Jevins and Anthony Burns were lay leaders and also ran for ordination; Betty Wales, against all odds, secured her national qualification in counselling, which she then used in the local surgery run by Dr Carl Consiglio, also a member of the church. And John Atherton – one of the burly men who sat on the Anfield Demoniac – got a job with Mercy Ships, travelled the world, and married a Maori lady before settling in New Zealand.

The empowering of the local parishioners came with its challenges of course. One week, Chris and Kathy brought along a very sophisticated couple to the Thursday evening session at the church hall. The couple were old friends who had come to stay, and were fascinated by the lifestyle chosen by the Woodses. At the end of the evening, the impeccably dressed wife decided to go forward to receive prayer – she had been troubled by an eye condition for some time. A local man named John, who had been unemployed since leaving school seven years earlier, stepped forward to pray with her and ask God for healing. John rightly remembered that when Jesus prayed for the blind man at Bethsaida, he spat in the man's eyes. And so, to Chris and Kathy's horror, they looked over to see John – with righteous certainty – spitting straight into the lady's eye as he prayed for her. She had an eye infection for the next three months.

The culture of lay leadership, and the consequences for excellence in the process, was very much in line with Chris's instinctive leadership preference for delegation and bringing together the team, the congregation and the community in one vision. Cath Kirkham recalls, "He was inspirational, he made people feel like they could do anything. If they failed, he'd encourage them to do it again. He never condemned failure – he would talk about his own failures in life instead." This was also very much in line with John Wimber's concept of being 'Free to Fail'. As G.K. Chesterton once wrote, "If a thing is worth doing, it is worth doing badly."

For people like Bob and Mary, coming from the very middle-class, professional context of Chorleywood, where there was huge pressure to get everything perfect, the freedom in Fingerpost was inspiring. They observed a key difference between the two contexts: whereas Chorleywood was full of successful people trying to be successful for God, Fingerpost was full of broken people perfectly happy to be broken before God, embraced just as they were – not as they should be.

***

Like his grandfather Edward and great-uncle Theodore, Chris was always very happy in the company of the local working men. He had worked in various manual jobs himself while growing up in New Zealand, which he felt gave him a natural affinity with many of his parishioners. He had stacked grain in enormous warehouses, carrying eight hundred 200lb sacks every day. "If you were starting with a hangover, which was often the case, you soon sweated it out!" he later recalled. Alan Kirkham – owner of a successful local engineering business – says that the fact that Chris had led a life rich in professional and personal experience before becoming a vicar was certainly a huge factor in his popularity: "People could relate to him, and he to them."

So in many ways, Chris – despite being an obvious outsider – felt quite comfortable ministering in a place like Parr Mount. He was very fond of the Glaswegian brothers Jimmy and Callum (names have been changed), who lived together in Parr along with Jimmy's wife and kids. Jimmy was the older brother, and slightly more responsible – Callum proved to be more problematic. The first time Chris met the brothers was after Callum's girlfriend had been admitted to a battered women's refuge in Warrington. Callum had come to the Vicarage to ask if Chris would deliver a letter to her, and then report back.

Chris knocked on the door of the house and a man he had never seen before, missing two front teeth, answered. Jimmy looked up and down the street as Chris asked if Callum was there.

"No," came the blunt reply.

"My name's Chris. I'm from the church at Fingerpost, and he asked me to deliver a letter for him."

"Oh right. CAALLUUUUUM…!" he shouted into the house. Callum promptly arrived at the door.

Jimmy and Chris became good friends, but they had some further dealings with Callum. On one occasion, Callum came out of prison and went straight round to the Vicarage to talk to Chris. He said he was trying to get work as a landscape gardener in Widnes and wanted to borrow the Subaru to get there (Kathy's father Mondi had passed on an ancient Subaru coupé, rusty but mechanically sound, and it had been gratefully received). It was a Wednesday, and Chris said Callum could keep it for 48 hours and then bring it back. The following morning, Jimmy came to the Vicarage:

"Did you give Callum that Subaru?"

"No, I lent it to him until tomorrow."

"Well, he was trying to sell it in The Ramford last night. I said to him, 'That's not your car. I know whose car that is – it's Chris Woods's.' And me and my other two brothers got him outside and gave him a thumpin'. Then I got this lump of concrete through my windscreen at 3 o'clock this morning!"

Chris had plenty of interesting experiences at The Ramford pub. One afternoon, after a christening, Chris was sitting at the bar with a number of local people, including Callum, enjoying a pint. Suddenly there was a loud screech of brakes and tyres outside in the street. Callum leapt up, looked out of the window, and then sprinted across the room, vaulted the bar like Red Rum, and disappeared out of the back of the pub. Four big men carrying baseball bats came in off the street and asked where he was – the Vicar was able to say, with some truth, that he didn't know, and off they went.

After another christening, again while standing at the bar of The Ramford, Chris reflected aloud to those gathered: "Of course, the reason we drink so much is to try and deaden the pain of living, isn't it?" At this, a girl sitting next to him looked at her boyfriend and said, "God! You must be in agony!"

The Glass Barrel pub, just on the other side of the dual carriageway, was nicknamed 'The Blood Tub'. Three people had been murdered there, one of whom was buried by Chris – he'd had his head smashed repeatedly on the flagstones just outside the front door. Chris was inside the pub one evening with a member of the church, sitting at the bar. It was crowded, and all of a sudden there was a commotion as a giant, red-faced man pushed his way through and stood in front of them. He then yelled at them at the top of his voice, sending the whole pub quiet:

"YOU'RE THE FELLA WHO REFUSED TO CHRISTEN ME KID!"

Chris was thunderstruck to be singled out publically like this, not least because he knew the man, Albert, and the christening had eventually taken place after a short delay. Chris managed to clear up the baptismal misunderstanding and the three men struck up a conversation which lasted long past closing time. Albert performed card tricks, despite his vast beer consumption, while the three of them discussed spiritual matters. At the end of the night, as they finally got up to leave,

Albert looked at Chris and said, "You know, I just *love* hearing you talk about God."

During their conversation, Albert had mentioned that he wanted to write – he was an intelligent man, but made a living by getting his girlfriend to drive him round to the back of large supermarkets: he would walk in through the rear doors and come out with microwaves and other electrical appliances, which he would then sell in the pubs. Chris decided to give him his electric typewriter to encourage him with his writing. Unfortunately, shortly afterwards, Albert was badly beaten by a group of men, one of whom was convicted for five years. Albert died a few months later.

Brutal, casual violence was a hallmark of the neighbourhood. One day a man called Dave (name changed), who had recently become a Christian, arrived at the front door of the Vicarage in a terrible temper. Kathy and the children were down in Marlow with her parents and so Chris was alone.

Dave had a reputation for ferocious outbursts of aggression. He had recently shredded his wife's dresses and smashed her shoes with a claw hammer. For reasons unknown, he was apoplectic about something Chris had done. He had two massive men with him. Chris showed great courage in stepping out of the front door and onto the driveway to engage with Dave as he paced up and down, shouting and swearing.

The scene was reminiscent of one his ancestor Henry Williams faced in an encounter with the enraged Chief Tohitapu and some of his men. Marianne Williams captured it in her diary:

> *After dinner a most troublesome chief, Tohitapu, put us all in confusion.* [He] *began to stamp and caper about like a madman…flourishing his mere (a greenstone club)…and brandishing his spear…Henry, upon joining them, told him his conduct was very bad and refused to shake hands with him…Tohitapu stripped for fighting…Henry beheld his capers with great coolness…*

Tohitapu then walked towards the store [and] *snatched up an iron pot…he made for the door. Henry dashed at him, snatched the pot out of his hands and set his own back against the door to stop his retreat, and called someone to take away the pot which Tohitapu made several attempts to snatch away, at the same time brandishing his mere and spear over Henry's head with furious gestures.*

Henry folded his arms with a look of calm and determined opposition only resisting his sudden grasp upon the contested pot and occasionally telling him to beware or exclaiming gently, 'Sir, that is enough.'

I think you will agree that only a man of physical courage as well as strength of mind would have dared to stand up to Tohitapu in this way. Probably the angry chief realised and respected this, and so although he continued to rage at and threaten him he did no actual harm. Had Henry shown the least weakness or sign of fear it could have gone very badly for him.

And so it was with the savage Dave. There was something about the situation which made the Vicar *very* scared – Dave was pacing up and down in front of the house in an uncontrollable rage. Chris's instinct told him there was going to be violence, and he didn't know if one of the three men was carrying the claw hammer. Nevertheless, he stood before the Vicarage and beheld Dave's capers with great coolness.

After a final volley of wild abuse in the Vicar's face, Dave suddenly stormed off through the gate and down the street. Chris's knees were literally shaking as he staggered back into the house and collapsed into a chair in his study – only to find that the two burly men had followed him inside. This was it.

As they stood there looming over him, filling the room with their imposing immensity, one of them said softly, "We just want you to know, Chris, that we didn't want to have anything to do with this. We didn't know it was going to be like this." They then turned on their heels and walked out, leaving the Vicar slumped in his chair, speechless and breathless.

***

The closest Chris came to actual physical aggression was when he himself caught a burglar. The Vicarage was burgled a lot – we stopped counting after the twentieth incident, which was after about ten years. The Vicarage had razor wire around the back yard and iron bars on some of the windows, but we remained a rather visible target.

On this occasion, a man had asked if he could speak with the Vicar after church one Sunday. While Chris was upstairs, changing out of his dog collar, the man took the opportunity to rummage through Kathy's handbag in the hall. Kathy had been in the kitchen preparing lunch – but she suspected something, and as the man and Chris began to talk, she checked her bag and discovered that her purse was missing. After shouting, "HE'S GOT MY PURSE!" at the top of her voice, the thief took off and the Vicar gave chase. He pursued the man on a circuitous route around the parish, before a cunning shortcut down a back street allowed him to close in on the villain as they approached a park.

Chris then demonstrated majestic sporting skill by hurling his umbrella like an Olympic javelin and knocking the man over a hedge, before leaping on top of him like Giant Haystacks. Various primal instincts were pulsating through his body at this point – mainly the urge to give the thief a good hiding. But just in time, Chris looked up to see a row of his parishioners' houses and realised that it might not be the best demonstration of Christian virtues if he were caught punching somebody in the face. At length, and with some reluctance, he regained his composure and called the police. As he sat on the villain, awaiting their arrival, he recovered the purse and the bank cards from the man's coat – but once it became clear that the cash was stored in less accessible parts of the man's person, he decided he would leave that to the cavalry.

Kathy also proved herself spirited in the face of felony. The family returned from a walk one Sunday afternoon (clearly the

Sabbath was a popular working day for local thieves) to find a police car parked outside the Vicarage. Apparently a man had been spotted lurking in our bathroom window on the first floor. Kathy took the lead, charging into the house and up the stairs to confront him. Aged seventeen, and rather protective of my tiny mother, I ran after her and grabbed a hockey stick on the way for good measure. At this, the policeman right behind me said sternly, "You won't be needing that 'ere, son".

When we got up to the bathroom, we discovered a homeless man with a scruffy white beard and a very red complexion, standing beside the window in a large overcoat. He was struggling to breathe. The two police officers seized him and handcuffed him, cautioned him next to the basin (rather too close to the toothbrushes for my liking), and we all made our way downstairs. All the while, the man was wheezing heavily.

The police took him away, and Kathy was asked to conduct an inventory of her possessions by a detective who remained behind. Sure enough, she discovered that three of her rings were missing. The detective immediately contacted the police car, which diverted to the hospital.

The following morning, the detective called. "Mr Woods, I'm pleased to say we have recovered two of the rings…and we are waiting for the third!" After a week, they were delivered in a clear, plastic bag marked with a yellow 'HAZARDOUS' sticker on the front – not only had the rings been on a journey worthy of Tolkien, but it turned out that their host, the vagrant Gollum, also had HIV. Kathy was assured that they had been decontaminated but nevertheless spent four days disinfecting them, firstly by boiling them in Savlon, then pickling them in alcohol, then scrubbing them with an old toothbrush, before finally soaking them in a jewellery cleansing solution.

Years later, I used one of the rings to make a proposal of marriage to Emma. She was thrilled.

***

Chris's ministry in Parr Mount began to gain the attention of church leaders further afield. Eventually, Chris and Kathy agreed to host a series of ordinands on placements from their theological colleges. This link began when Chris – in an echo of his first encounter with Barry Kissell – sat down at a breakfast next to Rev John Collins, during the Fellowship of Parish Evangelism annual conference in 1986. John had been the Vicar of Holy Trinity Brompton (HTB) until the previous year. And they were both delighted to discover that not only did they share a vision for charismatic renewal of the church, particularly in urban areas, but that they were in fact distantly related.

John explained that he, along with the new Vicar of HTB, Sandy Millar, had a passion for church planting. Chris was thrilled – this was a key area of ministry for Bob and Mary. He later introduced them to John and Sandy, and out of that random encounter came the first National Church Planting Conference in 1987, hosted by HTB, co-planned by Bob and Mary, and chaired by Chris.

This led to a series of HTB ordinands coming to serve at a very different Holy Trinity church. Some stayed for a month or so – including Tom Gillum, Steve Melluish, Justin Welby, Simon Downham and James Nickols. The culture shock when they arrived in Fingerpost was just as stark for them as it had been for Chris and Kathy. But that was partly the point. They came in order to allow themselves to step out of the rather comfortable London bubble and see what ministry looked like in an Urban Priority Area up north.

As a family, we were always thrilled to receive these bright young things. No doubt part of the challenge for the ordinands themselves was surviving a month at close quarters with the Woods tribe. It was a brave man who could survive ten rounds of Racing Demon in the dining room, emerge unscathed from the bottom of a stack of children during violent bouts of 'Pile On', descend the stone steps into the freezing, claustrophobic cellar for hours of table tennis beside the coal pile, or negotiate with the Vicar's daughters for access to the bathroom. One of the ordinands went on to become the Archbishop of Canterbury, so it was clearly worthwhile.

These outsiders (including Bob and Mary Hopkins at first) were forever amazed by the freedom from rules in Chris's ministry. This included his absolute insistence that Wimbledon, or Test cricket, should take top priority over work – sometimes for days at a time. He knew he was giving 200 per cent at all hours of the day and night for the rest of the year, and during these sporting extravaganzas he would always be on call to deal with a crisis as required. But otherwise he would be indulging his passion for sport, thank-you-very-much. It reflected his focus on vision and mission and the plans the team had agreed, his confidence in the team and the lay leaders to fulfil them – and, fundamentally, his complete satisfaction with unpolished, imperfect church. For the outsiders, this was a revelation.

Simon Downham recalls one example of this fascinating mix of family life and mission: having spent all afternoon watching Wimbledon with the family, howling at the television together, he and Chris were then called urgently to a house in the parish where an alcoholic man was attempting to commit suicide. They stayed there all evening, talking and praying with the man and pastoring him through the situation. They then returned to the Vicarage and had a whisky together. Just another day on the front line in Fingerpost.

One winter, another very pleasant ordinand named Andy Wooding-Jones came to stay for ten days, on a short placement from Oak Hill Theological College. Chris took him on a Marriage Preparation visit. The local couple in question were both aged 21, and had lived together since they were 16. They had four children. Chris took Andy round to their home on foot. As they approached a decrepit council house, Chris pushed open the front gate and they were faced with a gauntlet of rusting bikes and wrecked baby buggies in the front yard, which they navigated with care.

Inside the house there was no carpet on the floor, no wallpaper, no paint on the walls, and one L-shaped sofa with various ominous stains on it. All four children were present, though two of them were of school age. There were two television sets, an enormous one which was not working, and a smaller one on top of it, which remained on throughout the 45-minute visit. One of the children bounced back and forth on the sofa in a kind of catatonic state. The two parents chain-smoked throughout, and the four adults discussed Christian marriage and their life together under God's blessing.

When they judged that the time was right to leave, Chris and Andy traversed the stroller graveyard to the gate, and out onto the street. At this point, Andy paused for a moment and then said, "I wish my Director of Pastoral Studies at Oak Hill could have seen *that*!"

***

So this was what it was like trying to 'do church' in Parr Mount. In many ways the parish suited Chris's rumbustious, down-to-earth nature, and satiated his Charismatic missionary zeal in a way no suburban or rural parish ever could. After all, he was from a long line of missionaries in his mother's line – and all of his more high profile and celebrated Woods and Fry forebears had prioritised the importance of serving the industrial poor. Chris would often remind other clergy at seminars that to be an apostle means to be sent by the Lord to serve in a place far from home. Not one of the clergy in St Helens were from St Helens.

The successes of the 1980s – with the church transforming from a small, insular, hostile congregation to one which was growing, full of life and pursuing all sorts of ministries in the community – did attract attention from the Church of England hierarchy: Chris received five offers of preferment in the first nine years alone. In 1988, he was offered the role of Area Dean of Bootle, in the heart of Liverpool. It was an obvious opportunity to further his career, and follow in the Woods tradition of taking on senior clergy positions. For more than sixty years – from Theodore becoming Bishop of Peterborough in 1917, via Edward as Bishop of Lichfield and uncle Frank as Archbishop of Melbourne, up until uncle Robin's retirement as Bishop of Worcester in 1981 – there had always been at least one Woods bishop serving in the Church of England. Chris was the heir to that dynasty.

He declined. He and Kathy felt that the job was not yet completed in Parr Mount. In 1990, he laid out a new five-year vision for Holy Trinity. Having already established a flourishing local congregation, a children's team, a worship team, a hospital visiting team, and a prison visiting team (which included a Bible study once a fortnight in the notorious Risley Prison), he planned to create a community counselling team which could be trained to meet many of the myriad social needs in the parish such as debt, marriage breakdown, care for the elderly, and those with addictions of various kinds, including drugs, alcohol and gambling.

The vision also included the construction of an extension onto the north side of the church, for community use; the acquisition of a local residence to provide shelter for single mothers; and the conversion of the Glass Barrel pub (the infamous 'Blood Tub') into a hostel for the temporarily homeless. The vision was based on the three 'Cities of Refuge' in the Book of Deuteronomy – these were places of sanctuary for those who had committed manslaughter and were in need of protection from the avenging family. This was represented in the three key sites in the parish, where the mission of the church to the poor and vulnerable could be targeted.

The church extension was a great success, creating a kitchen and café area for the internal and external parish community. The café was open every day and provided a hub for local workers and church members to meet, where they could enjoy baked beans on toast and a cup of tea. A local care charity was able to provide its Down's syndrome patients to serve as staff.

The extension project, having raised £200,000, was then overseen by a church construction team led by a building manager who had been out of work for thirteen years. To have raised such a large amount of money for a church in Fingerpost was extraordinary, and although the vast majority of it came from outside sources, the congregation did chip in. This from a group of parishioners who had once been offered the opportunity by Chris to take money *out* of the collection if they were in need (a gesture which became so well known that *The Daily Telegraph* telephoned to see if it were true).

Indeed, by 1994, the Diocese was so cash-strapped that it asked every parish to come up with ideas to save money. The alternative was drastic reductions in clergy numbers. On this occasion, it was the *Church Times* which took an interest in the Vicar of Holy Trinity: in an article on 8th July entitled 'Sending the Vicar out to earn his daily bread', the focus was on Chris's unorthodox offer to reduce the financial burden on the Diocese by getting a part-time job. As a taxi driver.

> *Well, I was a businessman before I was ordained, and it has always seemed to me that the Church of England should be more flexible about this. I used to own a personal minibus, and I thought then that I could be running a taxi service to the airport…I could charge £50 for a one-way trip…You can see how the money would roll in; and I could begin to provide work for other men, build up a fleet…I know I could do this, but it's not even contemplated in the options put out by the Diocese.*

In the same article, the Diocesan Secretary said he would "reflect" on the idea.

Chris's growing network of church leaders had also resulted in a number of mission trips abroad, including to India, Uganda, Ukraine and Finland. Chris and Barry Kissell travelled together to Calcutta and had a hoot. One evening, they were collected at rather short notice by the Bishop of Calcutta's team to take them to an event at which Chris would be speaking (they took it in turns). Barry was caught slightly unawares, and hastily decided to throw on a white robe (which the Bishop had presented to him earlier) over the towel he had been sporting in the house due to the intense heat. Later that night in the Cathedral, after Chris had finished his sermon, Barry was invited to the front to lead the prayer ministry. After a few minutes, he noticed that Chris was looking at him and pointing to his nether regions, shaking with laughter – whereupon Barry looked down to realise that his towel had fallen off, and the white robe was almost entirely transparent.

After forging a strong friendship during his placement in Parr Mount, Justin Welby and Chris then took a team from Holy Trinity to Uganda to visit the Anglican community in Kampala. The party travelled on SABENA Airlines, which Justin memorably christened Such A Bloody Experience Never Again. With Chris's usual energy and determination, the team attempted to do the entire Alpha Course from start to finish in two weeks (it normally takes ten), with sessions every day as soon as they landed. Alan Kirkham did an entire weekend on 'Inner Healing'. "Absolute chaos," he recalls.

***

Chris's vision, energy and unpretentious leadership saw a number of seeds bear fruit in the 1990s and beyond. His deep inner security, in part based on his encounter with God on the road to Otaki, meant that his focus was continually on what he felt God wanted to do, not his own personal agenda. He was always looking to see how God would develop a mission and then seek to release others within it, devoid of personal ambition or success. He was an opener of doors.

Chris's idea for a Youth With A Mission (YWAM) base at Parr Mount had been developed with John and Michele Walker during their time on the leadership team. The vision was for an urban training base – in contrast to the usual YWAM rural manor houses – where YWAM students could be forged in the furnace of front line mission. As was his way, Chris injected huge energy and optimism into the project at first, and then handed over the leadership to Bob and Mary Hopkins – he knew he could not lead the parish and the new YWAM school at the same time.

Yet although he had opened the door for Bob and Mary, the initial effort in doing so was significant: he led negotiations with YWAM nationally and regionally, and with the Diocese, to bring it to birth; he gained all the ownership and permissions for the property (a derelict secondary school in the parish); he developed the mission as a genuine partnership between YWAM and the church; and he delivered the parish side of the ministries (Discipleship Training School, School of Church Leadership, and the Community Counselling School) – all these training processes were developed with students in parish placements under his leadership.

The YWAM partnership lasted a full ten years from 1987 to 1996 and has had a significant impact all around the world. Bob and Mary still meet people in mission and ministry who trace their journey back to YWAM's Parr Mount Base. Accounting for around 30 schools that were delivered at the Base, approximately 500 participants came through the parish of Holy Trinity, from all over the UK and the world. At the time of going to print, two are currently canons and one a lay reader of Liverpool Cathedral.

And as we have seen, the fruit was not only in those that came through the YWAM Base from elsewhere, but also those from the local area who were inspired by the global identity of YWAM to pursue their own missions away from the neighbourhood – people like John Atherton, who got a job as overseer of the deck crew on a Mercy Ships vessel, and settled in New Zealand. Jean Hucker also served on a Mercy Ships vessel and then planted a church in Chile; she is now working with indigenous Australians in Darwin. None of this would have been possible without Chris's entrepreneurial vision and vigour, and his willingness to release Bob and Mary into the YWAM enterprise.

Bob and Mary were also benefiting from Chris's visionary leadership on church planting. The initial conference held at HTB in 1987, which Chris instigated with John Collins and Sandy Millar and then chaired, led to annual and later bi-annual National Church Planting conferences which lasted until 2004. These conferences played a significant part in fuelling a national momentum around church planting which led to the 'Mission Shaped Church Report' in 2004, and to Archbishop Rowan Williams establishing the Fresh Expressions team in 2005. As with the YWAM vision, Chris handed over the main role in managing these conferences and their later developments to Bob and Mary, but as Bob says, "They would never have happened without his faith, vision, support and networking."

In 1989, another pioneering initiative was birthed. Through links with the Chief Secretary of the Church Army, Captain Philip Johanson (now OBE), Chris piloted an eight-week mission context school in Parr Mount involving placements for all final year EITs (Evangelists In Training). Their programme included living together in the converted YWAM Parr Mount Base, and sharing various spiritual and practical ministry assignments in the parish and deanery, which were brokered by Chris. This was a radical departure from their usual training context in a leafy, enclosed college in Blackheath, south-east London. The success of this new approach led, in part, to the Church Army developing a whole new campus in Sheffield – and all EITs are now trained in urban mission contexts.

His door-opening continued in 1991 when, together with Rev Chris Byworth, the Rector of St Helens Parish Church, Chris established SHINE: St Helens Inter-church Neighbourhood Evangelisation (you can see why they used the acronym). This was an ecumenical body bringing together churches from all denominations within the town to share information and work together on missions and community-based projects, as well as creating a major prayer network. Ecumenism ran in the blood – uncle Frank was a self-confessed "Ecumaniac", while grandfather Edward was a key founding member of the British Council of Churches. The SHINE model has since spawned other ecumenical partnerships around the country that now go under the name of FEASTs (Fresh Expressions Area Strategy Teams).

Last but not least, Chris was very much plugged into the emerging New Wine church network, established by his friend Barry Kissell along with Rev David Pytches from St Andrew's, Chorleywood. Barry felt it was important to have someone on the leadership team representing a different church perspective – and Fingerpost was certainly different to Chorleywood. In 1989, New Wine hosted the first of its annual church conferences at the Royal Bath & West Showground in Somerset, with 2,500 people camping in the surrounding fields. It was a far cry from the Holy Trinity church weekends away, which Chris had started on a whim when he bought eight enormous tents in the sales for five pounds each, and transported as many local parishioners as he could to a campsite out of town.

As a family, we were not able to attend 'New Wine '89' due to the arrival in March of Lydia Mary Charlotte Woods (aka 'New Whine'). But from 1990, the summer New Wine conference in Shepton Mallet became an annual fixture in the family calendar, and we always left feeling inspired – our father referred to it as his annual faith "booster". It helped that Barry had asked him to play the role of Pastoral Host, looking after the different church 'villages' around the site, for which he was given a quad bike. He was incredibly pleased about this.

Later on, Chris also worked with Barry and the New Wine leadership to help establish a sister conference in the north of England – called, unsurprisingly, New Wine North – to cater for the growing numbers travelling south each year to Somerset. Today, around 25,000 people attend the New Wine summer conferences each year.

***

So by 1994, fifteen years after Chris began his ministry at Holy Trinity, there was much to savour. The impact of Chris's leadership could be seen both in Fingerpost and further afield. But if he thought in 1990 that brokenness was an essential quality in a church leader, he was about to experience just how painfully true that could be.

Penlan Cottage, Pembrokeshire, Wales

CHAPTER 8
"Failure and Death"
(1994-2003)

"We were under great pressure, far beyond our ability to endure, so that we despaired of life itself. Indeed, we felt we had received the sentence of death. But this happened that we might not rely on ourselves but on God..."

— 2 Corinthians 1:8-9 (NIV)

"When Christ calls a man, he bids him come and die."

— Dietrich Bonhoeffer, *The Cost of Discipleship* (SCM Press)

At the end of January 2003, Chris and Kathy started their sabbatical at Penlan, uncle Robin's small, simple cottage on the Pembrokeshire coast. On the first morning, Chris sat down alone at a small desk in a room overlooking the sea and poured out his heart to God. He was exhausted, mentally, physically, emotionally, spiritually – with no energy, and no optimism. They had died. This is what he wrote:

The difference now is that I know intellectually that God has chosen me, but because of the death of optimism over the past eight years I feel powerless to continue in his calling. I feel abandoned by God. I'm like a fish thrown by a wave far up the beach flapping uselessly and in fact getting weaker rather than stronger. God's call and presence are too challenging and, I have to say it, threatening.

This is where I fail. I am afraid because of God's call, and in my lack of strength I am unable to respond. I am dismayed because I cannot cope with what he has called me to be and to do – I am an incapable servant. I cannot respond to the commands 'Do not fear' and 'Do not be dismayed'. How can I when I simply am afraid and I am dismayed!

The Lord says 'I will strengthen you, I will help you, I will uphold you' but it's all in the future – what about now? When I'm feeling so weak and depressed. It's all very well saying 'will' but what about now? Today? What form will the strengthening and upholding take? Always assuming I can hold out until they start to be experienced by me! A big assumption given the way I'm feeling at the moment: powerless, weak, unmotivated.

These are difficult words to read. In some ways they do not reflect the man we have come to know – assertive, galvanising, full of enthusiasm whatever the circumstances. But in many ways they reflect him perfectly: they are brutally honest, they challenge God directly, and they bear the hallmarks of a man still desperately seeking to respond to God's call on his life.

***

Chris wrote these words as he reflected on a Bible passage which had come to define his time as a vicar. Twenty years earlier, in 1983, he had taken another quiet journey – this time to the Lake District – to have some time alone with God. One might have expected a chirpy mood on this occasion: Barry Kissell had just made his second visit to Holy Trinity with the team from Chorleywood, and many people in the parish had come to faith. But no – as he drove up the M6 in the VW camper van to a secluded campsite at the heart of the Great Langdale valley, he cried out to God in anger:

> *Look, we've been here for four years and nothing has happened. Barry comes for ten days and look at the result! Why don't You get BARRY to come and be the Vicar?!*

Early the next day, he awoke in the camper van, made himself a cup of tea, and read the *Anglican Lectionary* (a set of daily Bible readings comprising Old Testament, New Testament, and a Psalm). He practised this routine, without fail, every single day of his ordained life. The Old Testament reading that particular day was Isaiah 41:8-20 (NIV):

[8] But you, oh Israel, my servant, Jacob, whom I have chosen, you descendants of Abraham my friend,
[9] I took you from the ends of the earth, from its farthest corners I called you. I said, 'You are my servant'; I have chosen you and have not rejected you.
[10] So do not fear, for I am with you; do not be dismayed, for I am your God. I will strengthen you and help you; I will uphold you with my righteous right hand.
[11] "All who rage against you will surely be ashamed and disgraced; those who oppose you will be as nothing and perish.
[12] Though you search for your enemies, you will not find them. Those who wage war against you will be as nothing at all.
[13] For I am the LORD your God who takes hold of your right hand and says to you, Do not fear; I will help you.
[14] Do not be afraid, O worm Jacob, little Israel, do not fear, for I myself will help you," declares the LORD, your Redeemer, the Holy One of Israel.
[15] "See, I will make you into a threshing sledge, new and sharp, with many teeth. You will thresh the mountains and crush them, and reduce the hills to chaff.
[16] You will winnow them, the wind will pick them up, and a gale will blow them away. But you will rejoice in the LORD and glory in the Holy One of Israel.
[17] "The poor and needy search for water, but there is none; their tongues are parched with

thirst. But I the LORD will answer them; I, the God of Israel, will not forsake them.
[18] I will make rivers flow on barren heights, and springs within the valleys. I will turn the desert into pools of water, and the parched ground into springs.
[19] I will put in the desert the cedar and the acacia, the myrtle and the olive. I will set junipers in the wasteland, the fir and the cypress together,
[20] so that people may see and know, may consider and understand, that the hand of the LORD has done this, that the Holy One of Israel has created it.

As Chris sat there sipping his morning brew, still grumpy about God's apparently preferential treatment towards Barry, these words spoke directly to him. "I took you from the ends of the earth" certainly got his attention, and he found reassurance and inspiration in the sequence of commanding, affirming declarations. The context of Isaiah 41 – words of reassurance to a people in exile – also rang true. This was God in all his faithful strength and power, a God to whom he could submit once again. He captured his reflections on this experience of the spiritual wilderness in a letter to family at the end of that year:

I had to confess to the Lord that I just couldn't succeed here; not even by prayer, and certainly not by straight force of personality…I conceded defeat in the struggle, and finally gave the whole thing over to God.

Of course, this is what I should have done from the outset, but clearly some of us can only learn the Lord's lessons through the most painful breaking process. The more stubborn we are (a useful quality in God's hands, and one not lacking in the Woods family), the more painful the breaking process.

Isaiah 41:8-20 became a key reference point for Chris's ministry over the next two decades, particularly during the desert times. And on the morning of his 60th birthday twenty years later, 15th January 2003, in the midst of his exhaustion and despair, he awoke, made a cup of tea, and opened the *Anglican Lectionary* – to find that the Old Testament reading was none other than Isaiah 41:8-20. The same reading, twenty years apart, delivered on both occasions precisely when he had conceded defeat.

His response to the text a few weeks later in Wales demonstrates just how broken he was this time round: "powerless, weak, unmotivated". Even though Chris was conscious of his own limitations in 1983, embracing the need for a church leader's brokenness to allow God's spirit to move, in hindsight he was still possessed of much more of his natural, youthful vigour and verve. He could still make things happen – and he did. What we see twenty years later is a whole new level of vulnerability – the "most painful breaking process" writ large. A 60-year-old apostle who has run a long race, with many hurdles, and is shattered, spent, hollow.

***

In the preceding eight years, Chris and Kathy had felt they were experiencing a period of serious spiritual depression – in some ways, spiritual exile. Chris summarised how it felt in a talk at New Wine in the summer of 2003:

> *Depression: you don't feel you can get out of bed in the morning, but you've got to because you have a funeral at half past nine.*
>
> *No faith: that God will do anything today, or even this week, or month or this year.*
>
> *No strength: Revelation 3:8 'I know that you have little strength'.*
>
> *Bitterness: in my case that goes down into feeling like I've failed the test. Now that may be a personal thing for me – somehow I feel that God has constantly had me in some kind of exam room – that's partly my upbringing possibly. But I think in Britain we do function like that. We feel we haven't pleased somebody.*
>
> *No reward: I've failed the test so God's not going to give me anything despite all my efforts.*

More bitterness.

My life's wasted: I was 36 when I came to St Helens and I'm 60 now. What a waste of a life!

Refusal to be comforted.

Further depression: back in the cycle again.

Chris had been tempted on numerous occasions to give it all up and go back into business. It just wasn't worth the effort. In business terms, he just couldn't see the return on his investment. As it says in Isaiah 49, he felt his life of Christian service had been 'in vain and for nothing' (NIV). Ultimately, he had remained loyal to his calling – to that divine encounter on the road to Otaki. But only just.

On other occasions, he and Kathy were tempted to move on to another clergy role outside St Helens. Each time, they would encounter a Bible verse which convinced them it was right to stay. Chris did continue to get offers of preferment over the years, and in the midst of his despair in the late 1990s he did pursue one or two by interviewing for them. But while his head said it was reasonable, his heart and soul told him he should stay. It was illogical on paper, given how long they had been there already. To family and friends it was baffling – even masochistic. Why on earth would they stay in a place like Fingerpost for such a long time? Why not move onwards and upwards like his forebears? Surely he could have more impact as a bishop instead of staying in some godforsaken corner of Merseyside? And yet, in that same family newsletter back in 1983, he had made something clear:

From the first in St Helens we felt that we should commit our whole lives to the job in hand, and not be looking around the corner for an opportunity to escape to greener pastures. One thing is certain, that greener pastures do not exist, unless God wants you in them!

Grandfar Edward could not have put it better.

***

What was it which had sapped him so heavily?

Much of the exhaustion was due to the unremitting pastoral demands in Fingerpost. Each household in the parish – whether members of the church, or a referral to the Vicar in a time of need – brought with it a particularly complex set of personal and spiritual challenges. In dealing with these for more than twenty years, often with no signs of improvement, they took a heavy toll. This was mission very much in the mould of the Early Church. Logical, educated, middle-class responses just didn't work.

One couple in the parish had been married for 35 years, yet for the last eighteen years they had not uttered a word to each other following an argument – they still lived together, but simply refused to give in. Chris spent many sessions with them, mediating and praying, but nothing worked and they continued to live in mutual antipathy until one of them passed away. Tim Humphrey spent three years in the parish as a youth worker, and led a Bible study group for teenagers. Just before he left to train for ordination, three of the fifteen-year-old girls came to him and told him they were pregnant (not by him, it should be clear). Tim, having spent years teaching them the Scriptures, threw up his hands in horror and departed for theological college (he went on to become Vicar of St Barnabas Church, Kensington, and Christ Church, Tunbridge Wells).

We can appreciate a few specific examples of these pastoral needs first-hand thanks to a number of interviews Chris and Kathy conducted. We will look at two couples (all names have been changed). These case studies are the true voice of Fingerpost, and they demonstrate first-hand the kinds of challenges and dysfunction that Chris and Kathy faced each day. These relationships were immensely rewarding in many ways, particularly when the benefits of Christian faith became clear. But over an extended period of time, across the parish, they were gruelling to process emotionally and spiritually.

Example 1 – Jemma

When I was about fifteen I had trouble with my brothers. I had three of them on my back all the time. If I didn't do what they wanted me to do, make them cups of tea or things like that, I got hit badly. When I told my mum, she used to say to me, 'You cause all the trouble in the house!' Two neighbours knew what went on in our house and they told my mum. But she still wouldn't believe me. I had hand-marks on my legs, and blood.

I was looking after my youngest brother Ned once, he was only about three. I wanted to see a friend who had a birthday on one night. I had to take Ned everywhere with me because my brothers wouldn't mind him. This night they wouldn't let me take his pram. When I was coming back Ned let go of my hand and ran in front of a car. He had a broken collarbone. When we got back from the hospital my brothers shouted at me again. My mum started hitting me.

Later I met Johnny. We got married. My brothers told me I was in a bad relationship.

A friend asked me if I would like to go and hear this fellow called Eric Delve at the warehouse down town. I said yes. At the end of this talk, this fellow asked if anybody wanted to ask Jesus into his or her lives. My friend said, 'Do you want to?' I said 'No.' I was ummin' and errin'. I felt a tap on my shoulder. It wasn't my friend. It was the Lord telling me to go forward! So I went to the front. At the end people prayed for us again. I was asked what I wanted prayer for. I said I had loads of bruises from my brothers and husband. I wanted prayer for our marriage. So we prayed.

When I got home, I had no key. So I knocked on the door. My husband wasn't very pleased because I woke him up. He started bawling. I said, 'I'm not having this, in Jesus's name!' I started talking to the Lord on my own, saying I was sorry for waking Johnny up. I was crying because I was frightened in case he hit me. I fell asleep in the chair. Johnny woke me up in the morning. I started walking upstairs. It felt as though I was walking on air! He said, 'Have you been drinking?' I said 'No, it's the Holy Spirit!' He said 'What are you on about?' I said, 'I have become a Christian!' He said, 'What, you mean you have joined all them lot? The Bible-bashers?'

Example 2 – Johnny (husband of Jemma)

I left school when I was 15. I started work at a little engineering place at the back of St Peter's Church. I worked there for about a year then got sacked. I can't remember why. I was on the dole for another year.

Every Saturday night I used to go to Parr Labour Club and Jemma was in with her Mum and Dad. I went over and asked her for a dance. She turned around and said, 'I can't dance!' It's been a joke ever since. She can't dance! We got married in December 1977.

From the start we had trouble in our marriage. I had played around with a Ouija board and I was into the occult in my teens, and that spilled over into our marriage. It caused problems. I was abusive towards Jemma, and when the kids came along I was abusive with them at times. In 1981 we were on the verge of being divorced. We had split up and I was living with me mum. But we got back together again.

Things carried on. We tried different methods of talking but nothing seemed to work. In 1984 Jemma became a Christian and that was OK by me so long as she kept it to herself. Chris would come knocking at our front door and I would go out the back! But by 1986 God had already begun to work in my life and Jemma asked me to come to a drama she was doing with her home group at the church. The only thing I can remember from that service was that they did one song, 'Rejoice, rejoice, Christ is in you' and I was singing every single word in that song. And I had never sung that song in my life before!

I saw a lady that I knew and she asked me how I felt. I told her I felt as though I was on fire. She said, 'That's the Holy Spirit!' I thought, 'Somebody get me out of here, quick! I want nothing to do with this!' I walked about a bit with Jemma and then came back and said, 'I can't keep on the way I've been going so something's got to change. I'll ask Jesus into my life and see what happens from there.' So I did. That was fifteen years ago.

God has done a lot in our marriage. We still had hard times. We fought and argued, got abusive with each other. We have been prayed for and received counselling and been able to talk to people. That's the blessing of being here with the church really. If you get down or depressed, you've got people to talk to. Chris has always been a good friend to us. We have always been able to talk to him and share problems, no matter what they have been. God has been good to us."

Example 3 – Betty

I'm the oldest of four children. The only positive memory I have of being a child is in a local shop where we used to live, and the shopkeeper telling my mum that he thought I was a very bright, intelligent child because I had totalled up the groceries upside down from the other side of the counter before he had. That's the only positive thing I can think of as a child. From five, six years of age I was sexually and physically abused by more than one man.

At the age of eight we were put in a children's home because my mum and dad had split up. We'd nowhere to live. After living in various relatives' houses for short spells, the last resort was a children's home in Lancaster. My mum went into what was then called the workhouse to give birth to my youngest brother. After about six months we were transferred to a children's home in Warrington.

I was being treated for very early periods at the age of eight, which they said was being brought on by the abuse, and treated with some sort of tablets to try and stop it. From Warrington we went to another children's home in Prescott.

I passed the Eleven Plus from the children's home to go to grammar school, but the children's welfare officer decided it was not right to go to a grammar school from there, so they got my mum a council house and we moved in on the Saturday. I started school on the Monday. The first twelve months were difficult because I had to adjust. The responsibilities in the house fell a lot on my shoulders, looking after the children, cooking meals, cleaning the house.

I had to take my baby brother with me to school at the end of the first year, which made things difficult. In my second year, I had to take him to nursery on the way to school and collect him on the way back. My mum started to depend on me, giving me her wages at the weekend to manage.

At the age of twelve to thirteen I had no normal childhood, no normal teenage years, didn't have records, didn't go dancing, didn't go to the pictures with friends. I had to stay in and mind the children and wait. I was sexually abused by my mum's fellow. I left school at the age of sixteen because of a nervous breakdown. I couldn't continue with the amount of work at home as well as schoolwork.

I was married at eighteen, had my eldest daughter when I was nineteen. I married because I wanted to get away from home, so I made it that I got pregnant. We had three or four different lodgings before we finally got a house, by which time I had another baby. My husband had various affairs during the time we were married. He was going out with one lady and her mother committed suicide when she found out. I had been to see her, and asked her if she knew the relationship her daughter was in. I got beaten up and told it was my fault that she had committed suicide.

In time I had a short, brief affair with a man, and I fell pregnant with my third child. That relationship didn't last. While being pregnant with the third child I met Bill, and he just accepted the fact that I had two children and was pregnant with somebody else's child, but it didn't matter. [Betty was to have four more children, with Bill.]

Times were very, very hard then. Bill worked very seldom. When he wasn't working he was in the pub. We lived in a three-bedroom council house with an outside toilet down at the bottom of the garden. Barbara was a problem teenager. She went out with a young man in the Navy. She didn't know him six weeks, she came out and said she was getting married. She was only seventeen. She got married just before her eighteenth birthday, went to live in Scotland. That marriage lasted eleven months. Her husband had a nervous breakdown with her demands for things – material things.

She came home for a short while but went back to Scotland and met up with another man, had her eldest daughter and lived in a one-bedroom flat with her partner and the baby. When she got pregnant with the twins they got married. She had the twins, but one died at three months of a cot death. The blame was put on me because I wasn't there to support her, I wasn't there to help her, she told me it was my fault the baby had died and for a long time I carried that. I did blame myself.

Then Burt started drug abuse, glue-sniffing, burglary, theft, house-breaking and was put into a remand home until he was eighteen. So we had little contact with him for over four years. He came out of care when he was eighteen and was given a flat and told to get on with his life, which he did the only way he knew how, by getting into trouble.

Our fourth child Brian left home for no apparent reason. He came home on the last day of school and said he was leaving to go and live with his gran. And he left. Relationships with him have been very, very poor. We don't see him; we don't see his children.

Brenda went to Scotland to stay with Barbara and found a job. But then Barbara found a job and Brenda stayed at home to look after the children and an affair developed between her and Barbara's husband. He left Barbara and went to live with Brenda, then decided he'd had enough of Brenda, and we came and brought her home. Again I was told it was my fault; if I'd been a good mother, it wouldn't have happened.

Barbara took to drinking and developed pancreatitis, which was at that time very, very severe – life-threatening. We made the journey to Scotland and was told she probably wouldn't survive the night. Three days later she had another operation and was told the same thing: 'Don't hold any hope of her coming out of this.'

The only thing that kept us going through that time was the fact that Bill and I had both become Christians about four or five months previously, and the friendship and care that we received from members of the church were the only thing that kept us going, because as we sat there at the side of Barbara's bed as she was dying, I didn't feel able to pray, all I wanted was to tell her I loved her…Bill phoned our church and a prayer chain was set up. People were praying for Barbara and we knew that the prayers were being answered because she came through the operation and out of intensive care so quickly. I sat down one day and thought about it – I was 39, seven children, none of them in any kind of secure relationships with partners, none of them having achieved anything, and I'd seen and been told that it was all my fault, my fault, I wasn't a good enough mother.

When Barbara's oldest was born, I wanted her christened at Holy Trinity, and I approached Chris. He had performed the wedding ceremony for Barbara the year before and I thought that's it, it'll all happen and be done with. But Chris said no. He refused to baptise the child because my reason for wanting a christening at Holy Trinity was that my mother had been baptised there, I had too, and I wanted Barbara's child baptised there. I wanted it, not what was best for her. And Chris's refusal really sort of raised the question in my mind: 'Well, if it's my fault we have all gone the way we have, I must be the one to go and make things right.'

So I started to go to church and got invited to an 'Abundant Life' course which Chris was just starting in a friend's house. That course was the breakthrough for me really, because I had never ever even thought about a God, was there a God. Apart from seeing Christmas cards and seeing the baby in the crib I had no understanding at all.

The Abundant Life course is a very straightforward, very simple course – and I very haughtily said to myself, 'It's too simple, this! Even a child can do this. What does he expect me to do, a 39-year-old woman answering a silly question like 'Who is God?' But in the first round, I had to say something about the Holy Spirit, and I didn't know what it was talking about. So I thought 'Chris is trying to trick me, but he'll not get me! I'll show him!' But as it happened the Holy Spirit got His way. I was the one that was humbled. I spent the rest of the night crying. Chris explained the reality, why it was that I was crying, because an awareness had been given to me of just how gentle the Holy Spirit was. The Spirit wasn't going to push his-self, wasn't going to force his-self upon me to accept. My tears were not anger tears, but they were a release in tears of frustration.

Over the next several years when the family problems seemed to grow greater and greater, I knew that the only thing that carried me through was the prayers and support. The number of times I have knocked on the Vicarage door. People rallied round. It was difficult for me, as somebody who still does manipulate things, used to finding the means of getting things and doing things, to have to be reliant on God. And it was really difficult, the teaching on forgiveness. I stood, and cried and cried all the way through the music time because I knew that there was something I had to do.

People had prayed for me to speak in tongues. I had prayed myself to speak in tongues and never been able to. And I knew there was something I had to do. I had to forgive the people that had abused me as a child, and

I found that extremely difficult. So, during this session on 'Unforgiveness' the Lord really spoke to me that the gifts were there for me to use and to take, but I had to accept them, and in accepting them I had to forgive. And as I stood there in the music session, crying my eyes out, knowing I had to forgive, and as I came to a point where I couldn't cry any more, people were happy and singing and joyful around me. So I just spoke out words of forgiveness towards the people that had abused me as a child. And suddenly something just snapped, and I started to speak in Tongues. And that was a first real experience of God, touching me as a person for myself, not for anybody else's benefit, but for me. I went home on cloud nine that night.

I know with certainty that I am a child of God in the head. Sometimes I don't feel it in my heart. But I do know that the promises of God are never broke and that one day I will see His promises fulfilled. That's the one thing I have to hold on to, that He will restore them years, and I'll have my childhood again."

<u>Example 4 – Bill (husband of Betty)</u>

I nearly died when I was three months old by what you call convulsions. I already lost two brothers through convulsions at three months old as well. It was difficult to make friends when I was growing up. The friends I had didn't last long. I never had much contact with my mum and dad cause they were always at work or too busy. I mostly looked after myself.

My uncle had a stick business, selling firewood door to door. We used to bundle it up and on Saturdays we used to go round with the horse and cart. When I got a bit older I used to look after the horse. Before I went to school I would take it to graze on a big field at the back, and then pick it up when I came home. I used to take one side of the street, my uncle the other side. We used to leave the horse parked up, and when we wanted some sticks when we had a customer, we would whistle the horse and the horse would come to us, like. It was very well trained. It was very gentle. Then it got something wrong with its leg. This big horsebox came for it. I led it in the horsebox, then they shot it there and then in the horsebox. It upset me at the time. It still does.

We also kept pigs. Sometimes we had to stay up, when they had a litter, all through the night, to watch they didn't lie under and get smothered.

When I left school, when I was about fifteen, I started work straight away. I lasted there about three weeks. Then I went to the brickyard making bricks. My mum worked there and it was more money, about £3.50 a week. I was there about six months. Then I got in the pub game. I started working part-time, doing a job during the day, then working in a pub at night. And that's where I met Betty.

We had our ups and downs, then we became Christians. It was about six months later, we were going through a rough patch, I would sleep on the settee, she was in the bed. I was going to the pub a lot. Barry Kissell came to the parish. Betty invited some people to our house. Bob Hopkins introduced himself and asked me would I like to stay for the talk. I was just on my way out to the pub. I said no, thank you very much. I went out. Then the week after, the same people were there again. Bob asked me if I wanted to stay. Anyway I stayed for a short while, then I went out. I got to like it, it seemed Bob had something which was missing in my life, because I had been alone all my life, not getting close to anybody, not even Betty, it becomes a habit. Bob had something that was missing, you know what I mean, which was Jesus of course. He had love and things like that.

I carried on with Abundant Life every week. Then I started coming regular to Thursday nights at the church hall. Then I started coming to church on a Sunday. Then they started inviting people to Eric Delve. He was preaching on stage. I went forward again. I don't know why I went forward. I just felt the urge.

The first thing that happened, I stopped swearing. I didn't realise I'd done it 'cause fellows in the pub, we'd get together, I'd have a smoke. We used to swear when we were at the pub together. Then I just stopped. Then when I was learning about John Wimber, things like that, small things happened. God started using me. I prayed for people and they got well! Some just had bad stomach aches at first, just instant felt well like. The most severe thing I prayed for, a woman was in a wheelchair. She'd been in a car accident and damaged all her hip. So I prayed for her and she got up and started walking around! I was amazed! 'I've got it!' God soon calmed me down!

My marriage got better. Betty and I started to heal our differences. We got very close. We still are, and get closer even now. The most important thing is that I have met Jesus. Since then I have a better relationship with my wife and made lots of friends, which I never had before."

***

These are just four examples of the chronic relational predicaments which Chris and Kathy were required to deal with on a daily basis. The entire parish was filled with all kinds of abuse and vulnerability – Chris knew them all, house by house. And a major part of Chris and Kathy's depression was the realisation that they were failing to see lasting, sustainable change in such a needy population. Members of the congregation fell out with each other; some of them fell out with Chris. Over time, the wonderful period of growth in the 1980s was almost entirely reversed. Chris wrote later, "We have been both the fastest growing and then the fastest declining church in St Helens!"

There were a number of contributing factors to Holy Trinity's difficulties in the late 1990s. It was partly a case of simple geography – a lot of the new additions to the church in the 1980s (73 from Eric Delve's *Down to Earth* and 56 from Billy Graham's *Mission England*) were actually from outside the parish. Over time, as these people moved on, it was impossible to replace those kinds of numbers from the local area alone. Not least because a number of local residents were still resentful of the changes the Vicar had made to 'their' church since he had arrived – one elderly gentleman said, "I'll never step in that church again until that bastard moves out."

But it wasn't just a numbers game – the underlying challenge was qualitative, not quantitative. Establishing mature Bible behaviours in the congregation was a key issue. Bringing local people like Jemma, Johnny, Betty and Bill into the church was one thing, but educating and sustaining them in basic Christian principles and practices was a monumental task. While the upside of such an emotive population was that they could be so receptive to spiritual engagement in the first place – perhaps more so than in other, more affluent parishes – the downside was that many then struggled to develop the solid grounding in scriptural understanding and disciplines which would have anchored their faith, and behaviours, amid their ongoing crises. Even in the midst of his own crisis, Chris's faith was underpinned by a knowledge of scripture which nurtured him throughout. For all his efforts, most of the congregation failed to achieve that – and were therefore more dependent on him.

One or two others who left perhaps did so because they were confronted quite directly on certain issues. Chris had created a church culture which was immensely loving, supportive and inspirational – in the Charismatic Tradition – but he was not a sentimental man and would challenge people if he thought it was right, particularly if he thought they would benefit. Chris and Kathy's ministry was marked by an unflinching commitment and compassion in Fingerpost, but they felt that part of their role was to hold people to account and ensure they took action to change their circumstances for the better. Tough love was often the order of the day.

One example of this was a 30-something homeless man called Michael who arrived at the Vicarage early one Saturday morning. The Vicarage hosted a daily procession of homeless people, and all received a sandwich and a cup of tea. A few – like John Smith, now famous in St Helens as 'Johnny Wellies' – became good friends. Michael was well known to Chris and Kathy, both at their doorstep, as well as those occasions when Chris provided a personalised taxi service when Michael needed it. When Chris opened the door that morning, Michael made the mistake of immediately and casually submitting his order: "I'll have two peanut butter sandwiches and a cup of tea with milk and two sugars, ta". He then sat on the step and waited expectantly. Chris was outraged: "What do you think this is – the bloody Hilton Hotel?! You're perfectly able-bodied – why don't YOU go and get ME a cup of tea?! I am choosing

NOT to give you anything today! Goodbye!" And with that he slammed the door.

Another example of Chris's ability to tell it like it is came when one individual decided to address what they thought were the key problems in the church – while giving a sermon. Quite quickly, things started to get a little awkward. After exchanging brief words with Alan Kirkham on the front row, who agreed it was inappropriate, Chris stood up, cut the gentleman off mid-sentence, thanked him, took him through a doorway, and then proceeded to reprimand him loudly. Alan did his best to continue with the service, but it was clear that the entire congregation was listening to the Vicar bellowing in the Vestry.

One congregation member had proved to be a persistent challenge, refusing to get a job, conducting a number of adulterous relationships, and was suspected of stealing from the church on more than one occasion. Chris continued to pastor him despite these issues, but at last ran out of patience. He told the man in no uncertain terms that until he secured a job – corroborated by a third party – he would not be allowed into the church, and furthermore, Chris would not even acknowledge him in the street. This caused quite a stir, but the leadership group and the congregation were supportive of this strong stance.

A culture of accountability is a good thing of course – Jesus was perfectly happy to confront disciples and Pharisees alike – and without it, Christian communities can fall into a spiral of passive, feeble niceness. But it was a difficult balance to get right, particularly when trying to model these disciplines in a parish like Parr Mount where a spirit of rejection was commonplace. And it is clear that while some of the congregation left because they had been 'Titus Three-Tenned' by Chris, others left because of confrontations with the lay leadership or with other parishioners, which could perhaps have been avoided.

A key factor in the decline of Holy Trinity was the challenge of maintaining a strong leadership group. As we have seen, the full time leadership team which was established in the mid-1980s after the arrival of the Bob and Mary Hopkins, John and Michele Walker, and Tim Humphrey, was an excellent group with complementary attributes, which enabled the church to flourish both inside and out. Once these staff members moved on – the Hopkinses to YWAM, although they stayed in the parish; the Walkers to lead their own church in Bradford; Tim to ordination training and his own ministry – it was extremely difficult to find replacements. Where Holy Trinity was a pioneer in charismatic inner-urban local ministry in the early to mid-1980s, by the early to mid-1990s there were lots of alternatives around the country. It was therefore harder to attract high calibre people who were willing to move to Fingerpost, as well as to find people with the right character and skills who could thrive in that environment.

There was also a sense that Chris had been a victim of his own success when it came to the indigenous leadership of the church. Almost as soon as local members of the church were built up and became key leaders, they would head off to pastures new: the wonderful worship pastor, Paul Barker, moved to Warrington to take up a new job; a number of others left to join Mercy Ships or YWAM; Maurice Jackson and his wife Janet, loyal friends and key leadership figures in the church, were unable to find suitable accommodation in the parish for their growing family and ended up swapping houses with a couple from Billinge, four miles away.

What all local leaders acknowledged was quite how difficult it was to minister in Parr. We have seen already what happened to Maurice when he joined the PCC – the personal threats and faeces smeared on the house – and even though the most difficult members of that PCC eventually moved on, those hardened behaviours were endemic throughout the parish. Craig Jevins and Alan Kirkham have both suggested that there is something uniquely tough about the people and environment of Fingerpost – even compared to neighbouring parishes. "You only need to move a few hundred yards down the road, and it feels completely different," says Alan – people are more encouraging, more supportive of each other as a community within the community.

One local man pastored by Alan turned out to be a witch, and he was convinced the church building was positioned on an intersection of three ley lines – fault lines in the earth's geometry which are thought by some to harness a kind of spiritual power. From Chris and Kathy's perspective, not the good kind. Like the parish, the church building itself seemed to be a uniquely tough place to minister – as we have seen, much of the church growth and spiritual liberation had taken place when the church had actually moved to the hall at Peasley Cross while the main building was having the heating replaced. The number of people attending home groups in nearby Parr Flats grew exponentially at this time, but very few ever attended church when Holy Trinity reopened.

In the mid-2000s, after Chris had left, there were advanced plans to demolish the building and replace it with a multi-functional community centre, including a small chapel; designs were sanctioned and approved; funds were applied for and secured – but the whole project was then scuppered by a local councillor who felt that the Grade II listed building was too much of a local landmark to lose. It stands there still, the heating broken once again, the few remaining members of the congregation holding their services in a small room at the back, ecclesiastical support coming from either the new vicar – who is covering a number of parishes – or a local volunteer from the Salvation Army.

The councillor's appreciation of the church was not always evident from the local community. There were periods when it felt as though Chris and Kathy were living in a war zone – part spiritual, part physical. The Vicarage garage was burnt down by a ten-year-old from Merton Bank Primary School (a contemporary of Thomas's). Having miraculously raised the funds to build the church extension, the builders would return each morning to discover that three quarters of the bricks had disappeared overnight. Once the extension had been completed, the roof tiles were broken on a daily basis, all of the down-pipes were pulled off, the gutters were smashed, and the attractive Plexiglas in the front doors was removed, forcing the church to board them up permanently. At one point Chris had to close the evening service because thunder-flashes were being thrown into the church; a branch of a tree then came through the window; on various occasions people were spat on as they walked out of the building; someone even got shot at by an air rifle.

***

On top of these challenges, over the years Chris had also faced some genuinely serious – and stressful – tensions with the church authorities, which again, over time, wore down his energy and optimism. On top of frequent letters from the Bishop, and his assertion that Chris and Bob had broken their ordination vows by not dressing properly, Chris was forced to endure not one but two Consistory Courts. These are essentially the Anglican equivalent of *Judge Rinder*, presided over by a Chancellor who must be over 30 years of age and have at least seven years of experience as a barrister.

Churches can go for hundreds of years without experiencing a Consistory Court. Holy Trinity hosted two in less than a decade. Chris, with his usual decisiveness and total lack of tolerance for red tape, had fallen foul of the authorities in the mid-1980s when he decided to get rid of the choir stalls and pews in the church. He didn't really like the choir, most of whom were insufferable and talked loudly throughout the service. In any case, chairs were far comfier than pews, and much more practical for when the church space was required for other events.

So when the heating system broke down and the church moved temporarily to Peasley Cross, he took the opportunity to make some major interior changes. Incandescent letters were written to the Bishop by the choir and other members of the church.

That prompted Consistory Court No. 1, held in the church itself – which was by this time a building site. During the court sessions, the level of abuse meted out by the church members was quite sensational. Even the Chancellor in his wig was not protected from the wrath of the old-timers, who had galvanised many in the local community to show up (despite not being members of the church) with the rhetoric that the outsiders were ruining 'their' church. At one point, a former Church Warden took the opportunity of it being a public meeting to accuse Bob Hopkins of embezzling church funds. The idea that Bob had given up a highly paid international job with Shell to volunteer as a curate at Holy Trinity so that he could pilfer the church coffers was screamingly mad. But to the established clique who had controlled the church as their private fiefdom for many years, the likes of Bob – with his fancy accounting skills – represented a serious threat.

At the end of proceedings, with countless arguments being heard for and against the removal of the pews, the Chancellor made his judgement. He began with a deep sigh. "Well, if I had my old powers, I would make those complainants walk around this building on their knees seven times. Because this has been a total and utter waste of time." And so, the ruling came in favour of the Vicar, and he celebrated by burning the pews in a large pyre on the field behind the YWAM school.

In the early 1990s, as the construction preparations for the church extension were being carried out, Chris decided that the stained glass in the western window of the church should be replaced – it wasn't particularly attractive or sacred anyway, and had been threatening to fall into the street for years. Cue more incensed letters to the Bishop by the few remaining stalwarts of the previous regime. Cue Consistory Court No. 2. Chris eventually came through this one with the ruling on his side once again. But the level of stress involved in being subject to these Consistory Courts – the preparations, the public scrutiny, the risk that injustices might carry the day – was immense.

***

Later on, Chris became something of a go-to figure when a talk was required on perseverance in times of crisis, conducting annual seminars at New Wine. There are plenty of biblical examples on perseverance, such as James 1:2-4 (NIV):

> *Consider it pure joy my brothers whenever you face trials of many kinds, because you know that the testing of your faith develops perseverance. Perseverance must finish its work so that you may be mature and complete, not lacking anything.*

Chris was perfectly happy to state how difficult those words are to hear, how threatening, from a position of exhaustion and burnout. "I mean, is he on the same planet?!" was his response in one seminar.

Two things stood out as he reflected on his own experience of perseverance in Fingerpost. The first was God's strange answer to prayer. In the book of Habbakuk, God seems to respond to his cries for help by sending the Babylonians to destroy everything. At Holy Trinity, while Chris was praying throughout the 1990s and early 2000s for a new stirring of faith in his church, the result was that large numbers of people left the church, including key congregation members, and those who remained often fell out with each other. The same thing had happened in the early 1980s when people he had prayed for died or got divorced ("You don't want me to pray for you tonight!" he said to the people gathered at New Wine).

The second reflection was Chris's attempt to square this kind of response with God's character – surely God can't, won't, wouldn't allow his church to decline like this? What about the promises in Isaiah 41? Rich Nathan, an American Vineyard pastor (and friend of Chris), has said: "The ultimate crises of faith are those experienced by mature Christians".

So in his wonderfully honest and heartfelt response to Isaiah 41, written in Pembrokeshire in 2003, we can see the crisis of faith writ large after so many years of perseverance and – apparently – so little progress. Chris was not the only clergyman in his family to articulate vulnerability: the wounded pride and searing authenticity are uncannily similar to those shown by his grandfather Edward in his diary in 1924.

After he failed to get re-elected to Convocation, and therefore the Church Assembly (which he had been leading for five years – his liberal views on changes to the 1662 *Prayer Book*, to make it easier for the laity to read, had not been well received), Edward wrote:

> *The news bowled me over: a really bitter disappointment. In my feeble attempts at self-analysis (which I am bad at, and don't often do), I see quite clearly that although I do mind very much the blow this gives to Prayer Book revision…I really mind more the blow to my own self-love and self-esteem…I must look this in the face. I think 'ambition' and 'success' have been getting at any rate some footing in my mind and outlook…it's time it was cut out, even though an operation is needed.*

In the late 1990s, Chris and Kathy decided they just had to get out. Their disillusionment about God's plans for them and the church meant that they were questioning their trust in God as never before – not to the point of denying their faith, but certainly to the point of struggling to make it through each day of soulful strain, devoid of hope. They felt completely trapped, living in a house surrounded by razor wire and prone to attack, and churning through a life of often cheerless ministry in a parish which was showing few signs of renewal.

There were signs that God had not forsaken them completely. One example was a 21-year-old woman who came up to Chris at the end of a weekend conference he was leading and asked him to pray for her. She had not had hearing in one ear since the age of two due to a degenerative disease. Chris countered that he was exhausted from leading the whole event, and was honest enough to say he didn't have much confidence or faith at that moment. But the woman insisted that God had told her specifically to request him to pray with her. Chris replied that out of obedience to God he would do so. He prayed a simple prayer for healing, and after a few moments the woman shouted an elated, "I can hear!" This gave great encouragement to the whole team.

Nevertheless, the overall feeling for Chris and Kathy was one of gathering despair at their lack of progress. Alan Kirkham had a number of conversations with Chris at this time about whether he should stay or go. During one particularly disheartened discussion, he asked Alan, "Is the church not moving on because of me? Is it time I went?" For all of the reasons we have seen, Alan said it was unfair to suggest that Chris was holding the church back – and that only he could decide whether he left or stayed. When one YWAM friend later asked Chris and Kathy whether they were hoping one of their children would follow them into the ministry, the woman was taken aback at Chris's response: "Oh no, I don't think so. It is just not worth it." Kathy added, "The price is a heavy one. I wouldn't wish it on anybody."

Chris decided to look into a number of clergy positions, including at St Michael-le-Belfry, where Chris's journey to Holy Trinity had started back in 1979 when he had met his predecessor Eric Hague. Another opportunity, this time in London, took him to the third interview stage. And yet both he and Kathy retained a nagging sense that they couldn't leave St Helens at such a dire time, that this would be escaping, that they should stay to see things through until they were called somewhere else.

Irene Whitaker was one of the local leaders in the church and came to the Vicarage without any knowledge of the interviews going on – as she was talking to Chris and Kathy she received a biblical book, chapter and verse in her mind, the details of which she didn't know herself. It was Jeremiah 42:10. Irene found a Bible and read it out loud: "If you stay in this place I will build you up and not tear you down, I will plant you and not uproot you, for I am aggrieved over the disaster I have inflicted upon you" (NIV). Chris immediately rang up and cancelled the final interview.

***

If the spiritual and emotional outpouring that Chris experienced on his sabbatical in 2003 was the culmination of many years of underlying strain and a gathering gloom at Holy Trinity, it was not obvious to his children. He and Kathy were adept at protecting their offspring from the depths of their depression.

In part, that was because by 1994 the first four children were away at boarding school. Rossall School had been chosen as an alternative to Parr High, with its 22 per cent truancy rate. Kathy's uncle Hubert had left money in a family trust to support the education of the wider Howard clan, having never had children of his own with his wife Lelia. This, along with some music scholarships, allowed all five children to board between 1989 and 2007.

Rossall is located on the Lancashire coast a few miles north of Blackpool, near Fleetwood, about an hour's drive from St Helens. It is appallingly cold and blustery all year round. The icy winds rushing in from the Irish Sea were occasionally strong enough to propel smaller, lighter children right across the main square, like tumbleweed. Dad would delight in coming to stand in the inclement weather to watch his sons play rugby. He could be rather vocal – cries of "NAIL HIM!" and "Go on! GO ON!!" were audible as far away as Fleetwood. On one of the rare occasions that Mum came along too, Thomas was knocked unconscious and carried from the field limp and lifeless after tackling a boy eight times his size. She never came to another match after that.

Rossall was not known for being overly academic (entrants to Oxbridge were minimal). Like most of the pupils and teachers, it was more of an all-rounder school, with a lot of outdoor pursuits – not dissimilar to Christ's College. It therefore suited the Woods offspring perfectly. Mum and Dad were particularly happy that there was such an excellent music school, named after old boy and celebrated conductor Sir Thomas Beecham (a member of the St Helens industrial family). This only increased Dad's desire to hear his children perform during the holidays, ignoring all appeals to leave us alone, eyes closed by the fire, whisky in one hand, the other resting contentedly on his stomach, as we warbled uncomfortably through medleys of *West Side Story* and – appropriately – *Les Misérables.*

Mum even joined one of the school choir tours, to France and Italy, where, in Venice, she made a name for herself by eviscerating a gondolier who had tried to scam one of the school staff. His face was a picture, horrified and immediately repentant, as Mum was called over and began to ask some initial questions in perfect Italian. The sight of her erupting in a torrent of outrage as she discovered the extent of his attempted manipulation, and seeing him cower before her, shoulders hunched and arms waving frantically, was a moment of immense pride – and prestige – for her brood.

Neither Mum nor Dad were particularly interested in their children's academic performance, possibly for entirely different reasons. Mum had been schooled in a fairly casual manner while growing up in Madrid, Colombia, Florence, Genoa and Rome; while Dad had been schooled vigorously, with a particular emphasis on academic achievement driven by his mother Sybil (herself top of the class). This produced the same result: none of the children were pushed to get particular grades, and all were free to choose their own path.

This partly explains why none of the five offspring went through a serious rebellious period – there was not a lot really to rebel against, and at the same time all were acutely conscious of the humble sacrifices Mum and Dad were making in their own lives to pursue a mission focused on helping those in need. This is not to suggest we were angelic – far from it. But misbehaviour at school was managed pretty sensibly: Dad was always able to say, rather frustratingly, that he had done far worse.

Dad continued to be thoroughly inventive when it came to family cars. The green VW camper van was replaced by a red Peugeot 505 estate, which certainly looked sophisticated, but had an alarming tendency to shed vital parts of the engine in transit. We then upgraded to a red Ford Transit van, with vaguely familial seating in the back, which allowed us to travel all over the Continent without the confines of a normal car – if you walked from the front seats to the back seats enough times you could get a perfectly good level of exercise while we bombed down the autoroute. Lydia, aged about six, once stood on the front passenger seat with her head through the sunroof like a chubby periscope, taking in the stunning views of the Amalfi Coast as her cheeks oscillated in the wind.

There was a rather unfortunate interlude in the mid-1990s as Dad decided he would be best served in his parish travels by using a motorbike. Cue the sudden arrival of a rather beaten up BMW with a punchy 650cc engine, for all of £80. Even in the mid-1990s, this was dubiously cheap. Cue wife and children standing in the disused playground next to the church (by now a car park) observing his jittery circuits with mounting anxiety. Whereas Dad was a master of four wheels – wonderfully smooth, tutor of the exciting double de-clutch gear shift, happy rolling up his sleeves under the bonnet – on two wheels he looked a little uncomfortable. Fortunately for all of us, he couldn't afford to transport it to Liverpool for his test and so gave it to a grateful parishioner.

However, it was the next family vehicle which really went down in history. Dad got the idea at a funeral. Specifically, a funeral motorcade. He was travelling with the grieving family in one of the limousines behind the hearse on the way to the crematorium, when he was suddenly struck by the idea that the limousine would make a fantastic family car. He knew most of the funeral directors in St Helens, and a short time later he became the proud owner of a dark purple, stretched Ford Sierra Sapphire.

Reviews were mixed – certainly the girls were appalled at the thought of arriving at Rossall in an undertaker's car. Mum was concerned that her parking at Morrison's might prove even more traumatic than usual. My brother and I were of course delighted to be transported around in such a magnificent machine. The parishioners were also thrilled, particularly Callum (ominously), and the car became a thing of great pride to the community.

A high profile vehicle comes with risks of course, and it wasn't long before 'The Limo' – as we named it, inventively – attracted the attention of some local youths. Having broken through the sitting room window to steal the TV and video player, the boys then gouged The Limo with a screwdriver. Most of the damage was in the form of long gashes all the way down the length of the car, but one scamp indulged his creative side and carved the letters F-U-K right across the passenger door (truancy apparently another of his sins).

Because the letters were so deeply engrained, a quick paint job wouldn't do. And it took a few weeks to arrange for the repairs. So, in the meantime, the Vicar was forced to drive around his parish with an enormous expletive engraved in the passenger door. He would stop at the traffic lights, immaculate in his dog collar, and grin broadly as people stopped and stared, aghast.

After eight years, The Limo was stolen during a family outing to Liverpool.

***

Despite the loss of The Limo – and myriad other possessions in countless burglaries – Dad and Mum were never sentimental. They were completely unmaterialistic. Dad couldn't help but laugh when we returned from one family holiday to find all electrical items stolen – including a prized stereo system which had been stored in the Vicarage for safekeeping over the holidays by one of Madeline's school friends. Madeline was understandably distraught.

As a father, Dad was not particularly sentimental either. It was another side of his inherent, and sometimes unthinking, honesty. He would often point out blemishes on his adolescent daughters' faces, to their utter horror. After yet another serious rugby collision, Thomas was finally jolted into getting an operation when his father looked at him one day and said, "Tom, what IS going on with your nose?"

When Madeline broke ranks and invited a boyfriend to stay for the weekend, an unprecedented event, Dad was sceptical. The poor suitor was treated like some sort of tropical lizard by all of us – a combination of wonder and fascination with this creature, mingled with profound suspicion and distrust. He did his best, attempting to cosy in with everyone's favourite, Lydia, losing comprehensively to the boys at table tennis in the coal cellar, and even purchasing a kitchen appliance for Mum as a thank-you gift (an electric whisk, bizarrely). When the time came for him to depart, we stood as a family in the hallway and waved enthusiastically as he bade us farewell. Dad closed the front door behind him. Silence descended on the tribe as we stood there together, digesting this remarkable experience. After a few moments, Dad finally proclaimed his judgement: "Well, he was a bit of a berk, wasn't he?"

This is not to say that Dad was not affectionate – he was always warm and tactile with us, hugging the boys as well as the girls, and in particular wrapping Lydia in regular, robust cuddles. He would sometimes announce, apropos of nothing, "Dad *loves* his children." On one occasion, when the children were aged 16, 14, 12, 10 and 4, we were together in the living room when there was a brief lull in proceedings. After a short while, Dad said very softly and sincerely, "I just want you all to know, I count you as my friends." It was an incredibly special moment, lifting his offspring to the status of peers and demonstrating love, honour and humility in equal measure.

During familial games of 'Pile On', when we would all jump on top of each other on the sofa and attempt to thrust our socks into one another's faces, the sight of one of Dad's great hooves advancing in your direction was a mixed blessing – it was of course the biggest, and usually the smelliest, of all the socks exploring the couch, and therefore the least desirable; but because it belonged to Dad, it somehow became a great privilege to be on the receiving end, because it meant he was bestowing his attention upon you. It was a particularly conflicting, pungent form of patronage.

The lack of sentimentality translated into a complete blindness to romance. He did refer to his spouse as "Love" and "Sweet"; he would celebrate her cooking; very occasionally, she would snatch him for a quick smooch and he would close the door behind them, with the disgusted cries of their children ringing in their ears. But unfortunately, Dad rarely thought to convert his affection into flowers or gifts, or words of tender affirmation, for his besotted bride. The occasional edition of *Country Life* at the weekend was about as good as it got. To commemorate the birth of their fifth child, Dad bought Mum a microwave.

Dad's lack of sentimentality did provide his beloved with one particularly memorable moment. On a summer's weekend, with the children taken care of, they decided to visit a country estate near Liverpool. It was a wonderfully warm afternoon, and as they wandered around the glorious gardens they consumed a rather merry quantity of alcohol. During the formal tour of the Hall, the guide explained to the group how in the 1950s the aristocratic owner had unfortunately lost the estate and much of the surrounding lands in Lancashire during a vigorous evening of Baccarat at the Clermont Club in London. From the back, the Vicar of Holy Trinity could be heard to mutter audibly, "GOOD RIDDANCE!" before laughing emphatically at his own joke. Nobody else in the tour group found this at all funny, except Mum, who was desperately stifling her giggles behind him.

***

Even as the grip of spiritual depression crept in, the humour continued – indeed, there may well have been a correlation between the two. Chris became part of a group of vicars known as the 'Hippos', including many from the New Wine network, who would go on a weekend away once a year to pastor each other and relax together. Normally this resulted in him returning home with some pretty fruity jokes. On one occasion, at the dinner table with all five children present, he proceeded to recite a limerick he had learned while stalking at Merkland (Georgie Woods' family hunting lodge in Scotland), and had just taught to a room of delighted vicars:

There was a young man from Sprocket,
Who went for a ride on a rocket,
The rocket went bang,
His balls went clang,
And his cock ended up in his pocket.

He roared with laughter, banging the table with clenched fist. His children were thrilled. Kathy, meanwhile, never one for swearing (she would apologise if she so much as uttered the word "Blast!"), yelped "Oh, my goodness!", before dissolving into a cackling heap.

Chris kept a copy of *1001 Best Jokes* in the lectern at Holy Trinity, and he would often start a service simply by reading out a couple of them, just to break the ice and get things moving. They were uniformly terrible, but that was the point. Denise Pennington would respond on behalf of the congregation by shouting, "Shurrup Vicar!", to which Chris would reply "Shut up Denise!" And thus, with this rather unorthodox call and response, the liturgy would begin.

The liturgy itself was not immune to amusing incidents. On one Sunday, an elderly member of the congregation called Eli was receiving the Communion wine with great solemnity, when he suddenly sneezed violently into the chalice. The local lay assistant in charge of the chalice recoiled in horror (as did the person next in line), but – having stopped to dab various bits of residue with the Communion cloth – proceeded dutifully along the altar rail and proffered the wine. The intended recipient was aghast, and hissed loudly, "No chance!" At this, the lay assistant turned to the Vicar and blurted the immortal words, "Eli's snotted in't cup!"

At New Wine in 2005, conducting that day's headline sermon from the main stage in front of 6,000 people, Chris warmed up by recounting some amusing Sunday School tests of children in New Zealand sent to him by his sister Sally:

Jesus was born because Mary had an immaculate contraption.

The Epistles were the wives of the Apostles.

St Paul cavorted to Christianity. He preached Holy Acrimony, which is another name for marriage.

Christians have only one spouse – this is called Monotony.

Lot's wife was a pillar of salt by day, but a ball of fire by night.

***

Back in the cottage on the hilltop in Wales in January 2003, Chris's sense of humour had deserted him, and he was unable to acknowledge any of his myriad achievements and blessings to others. He began to reflect on an idea which he felt God had revealed to him over the previous few years – namely, that he had functioned all of his life in what he called 'Energetic Optimism'. From birth, as a fundamental part of his character, he had functioned as an Energetic Optimist, bringing all of his enthusiasm and positivity to bear on life. Whether it was drinking at Dartmouth, driving Jaguars across the Continent, or driving Reuters' economic sales across Africa, Chris had brought his natural charms and capabilities with him. When he had become a Christian suddenly on the road to Otaki, he now realised that he had just become a Christian Energetic Optimist. He had essentially remained the same as before, but with a new, missional focus for his energy and optimism.

That might not sound like such a bad thing. Surely it demonstrated his integrity, that he stayed true to himself, that he didn't change and adopt a more self-righteous priestly posture? Surely being an Energetic Optimist is preferable to being a Lethargic Pessimist?

Well, yes, and yes – but not quite. A glance at a concordance of the Bible will show that the word 'optimism' does not appear once. Optimism is a human attribute, characteristic of man seeking to shape his own destiny. Optimism does not give God any space to intervene. And so Chris reflected that God had been using the disasters at Holy Trinity to destroy his optimism.

It sounds counter-intuitive, but then Christianity often is. C.S. Lewis summarises this inverted principle beautifully right at the end of *Mere Christianity* (HarperCollins, 2002):

> *The principle runs through all life from top to bottom. Give up your self, and you will find your real self. Lose your life and you will save it. Submit to death, death of your ambitions and favourite wishes every day and death of your whole body in the end: submit with every fibre of your being, and you will find eternal life. Keep back nothing. Nothing that you have not given away will ever be really yours. Nothing in you that has not died will ever be raised from the dead. Look for yourself, and you will find in the long run only hatred, loneliness, despair, rage, ruin, and decay. But look for Christ and you will find Him, and with Him everything else thrown in.*

Lewis also captured brilliantly the process of this death to self in his children's book *The Voyage of the Dawn Treader* (HarperCollins, 2009). In it, young Eustace happens upon a dragon's cave filled with treasure. He is overcome with happiness and glee, as well as thoughts of revenge towards all of those who have ostracised him in the past, and falls asleep on the vast golden horde. When he awakes, he realises to his horror that he has become a dragon himself. After some time, he begins to lose hope that he will ever become a boy again.

Then the lion Aslan appears and takes the dragon Eustace to a shimmering, cleansing pool. He tells him to undress, and jump in.

Eustace is confused by the order to undress, but then recognises that he can use his dragon claws to shed his dragon scales. He is thrilled at the thought of having his own skin back, and scrapes away. But as the first skin peels off beautifully, "as if I was a banana", and he approaches the crystal waters excitedly, he is appalled to see his reflection is still that of a dragon. And so he continues to scratch and scrape, peeling off skin after skin. But no matter how hard he tries, he realises that he cannot undress himself.

Finally, the Lion states that he will have to do it himself. Eustace later recounts this process of painful submission:

> *I was afraid of his claws, I can tell you, but I was pretty nearly desperate now. So I just lay flat down on my back to let him do it.*
>
> *The very first tear he made was so deep that I thought it had gone right into my heart. And when he began pulling the skin off, it hurt worse than anything I've ever felt. The only thing that made me able to bear it was just the pleasure of feeling the stuff peel off. You know – if you've ever picked the scab off a sore place. It hurts like billy-oh but it is such fun to see it coming away.*
>
> *'I know exactly what you mean,' said Edmund.*
>
> *Well, he peeled the beastly stuff right off – just as I thought I'd done it myself the other three times, only they hadn't hurt – and there it was lying on the grass: only ever so much thicker, and darker, and more knobbly-looking than the others had been. And there was I as smooth and soft as a peeled switch and smaller than I had been. Then he caught hold of me – I didn't like that much for I was very tender underneath now that I'd no skin on – and threw me into the water. It smarted like anything but only for a moment. After that it became perfectly delicious and as soon as I started swimming and splashing I found that all the pain had gone from my arm. And then I saw why. I'd turned into a boy again.*

So it was this death – the death of fleshly optimism, the death of his own strength, through the struggles of his ministry at Holy Trinity – that Chris was referring to when he took to the main stage at New Wine in 2005 and announced to 6,000 people, with his usual panache, that "this is a talk about failure and death". He allowed the congregation to stew on that for a bit, grinning broadly, and laughed as somebody stood up pretending to leave, before describing the journey of faith and perseverance that he and Kathy had experienced.

Towards the end of the sermon he reflected on the revelation that God had been stripping him of his earthly skin, and replacing Energetic Optimism with Faith and Hope:

> *Hope is the Bible word for what we call Optimism so often, because you've got to have Hope in somebody, you've got to have Hope in God. If you're an Optimist you can just say, 'Oh, it'll be all right – I'll make sure it is all right'. But God was getting rid of all of that in me, and it was the most painful thing I think I've ever gone through.*
>
> *Now there are issues of that kind when we want to be obedient to God – Kathy and I, we just couldn't understand why we hadn't been called to a nice beach parish in New Zealand, I mean why not? But we weren't – and as the Lord called us to stay where we were we had to go through these kinds of issues.*
>
> *Recently I heard a man called Tommy Tenney talk about 'dismantling your glory', and in 1 Corinthians 11:15 Paul says, 'If a woman has long hair, it is her glory', and in all four gospels we have the story of Mary, who is the sister of Martha and Lazarus, pouring incredibly expensive perfume – think Guerlain, or Chanel, or Christian Dior or something like that – and what does she do, she pours a pint of it, imagine a pint…!*
>
> *When I was a businessman once, I was in Paris on business, I was in publishing, and I met the Director of Librairie Hachette, which is one of the big French publishers, and he took me to lunch at The Traveller's Club and then we walked across the Champs-Élysées and into Guerlain, and he bought a litre of Guerlain*

perfume. And I thought, gosh, he must have got a very nice girlfriend or something – turned out it was for HIMSELF. And we went back to his flat afterwards and I was, you know, making sure I knew where the door was – I wasn't quite sure I knew what was going to happen in there!

But Paul talks about Mary pouring this pint of Guerlain – think of that – on Jesus' head and feet, and then she wipes Jesus' feet with her hair. And we know from one of the descriptions that Simon, the host of the meal, has not offered Jesus the washing of his feet, which was traditional. So here are Jesus' dirty feet being washed by this pint of incredibly expensive perfume, which Mary had bought herself, so it was up to her what she did with it. And then wipes – she cries if you remember, and the tears come and fall on Jesus' feet. And then what does she do, she lets down her hair – her glory – and she presumably has to get down on her knees and wipe his feet with her glory.

And I think that this picture is such a fantastic one – that those of us who are wanting in some way to try and be successful, have a big reputation, these kinds of temptations which sometimes strike us – even in the church – we need to take the example of Mary and lay down our glory, and wipe Jesus' feet with it.

That's all we can offer. The value of the Kingdom is complete, it's total – and if I'm prepared to lay down my life in some degree of a similar nature so that I can serve Jesus and wipe his feet with whatever reputation I think I might have got, then I believe that the Lord will be blessed and the Church will move forward.

Giving his father-of-the-bride speech at Madeline's wedding to James Simpson, May 2004

CHAPTER 9
Faith and Hope
(2003-2007)

"Therefore I will boast all the more gladly of my weakness, so that the power of Christ may rest upon me. For the sake of Christ, then, I am content with weaknesses, insults, hardships, persecutions, and calamities. For when I am weak, then I am strong."

— 2 Corinthians 12:9-10 (NIV)

"Now faith is being sure of what we hope for and certain of what we do not see. This is what the ancients were commended for…All these people [Abel, Enoch, Noah, Abraham] *were still living by faith when they died. They did not receive the things promised; they only saw them and welcomed them from a distance."*

— Hebrews 11:1-2, 13 (NIV)

Following their sabbatical in 2003, Chris and Kathy felt properly rested for the first time in many years. And the physical restoration was accompanied by a spiritual renewal. Clearly the seismic shift out of Energetic Optimism towards Faith and Hope was not a simple, immediate step – in many ways it had been progressing since the start of Chris's ministry in 1979 – but in the summer of 2003 Chris gave his first New Wine seminar on 'Perseverance' and how to move away from human control behaviours and allow the peace and grace of God to replace them.

Leaving behind Energetic Optimism did not mean dropping his sense of humour. As an example of doomed perseverance, Chris opened the session by quoting the joke about the poor builder's insurance claim:

I am writing in response to your request for additional information, for block number 3 of the Accident Reporting Form. I put 'poor planning' as the cause of my accident. You said in your letter that I should explain more fully and I trust the following detail will be sufficient. I am an amateur radio operator and on the day of the accident, I was working alone on the top section of my new 80-foot tower.

When I had completed my work, I discovered that I had, over the course of several trips up the tower, brought up about 300 pounds of tools and spare hardware. Rather than carry the now unneeded tools and material down by hand, I decided to lower the items down in a small barrel by using the pulley attached to the pole at the top of the tower. Securing the rope at ground level, I went to the top of the tower and loaded the tools and material into the barrel. Then I went back to the ground and untied the rope, holding it tightly to ensure a slow descent of the 300 pounds of tools.

You will note in block number 11 of the accident reporting form that I weigh only 155 pounds. Due to my surprise at being jerked off the ground so suddenly, I lost my presence of mind and forgot to let go of the rope. Needless to say, I proceeded at a rather rapid rate of speed up the side of the tower. In the vicinity of the 40-foot level, I met the barrel coming down. This explains my fractured skull and broken collarbone. Slowed only slightly, I continued my rapid ascent, not stopping until the fingers of my right hand were two-knuckles-deep into the pulley. Fortunately, by this time, I had regained my presence of mind and was able to hold on to the rope in spite of my pain. At approximately the same time, however, the barrel of tools hit the ground and the bottom fell out of the barrel.

Devoid of the weight of the tools, the barrel now weighed approximately 20 pounds. I refer you again to my weight in block number 11. As you might imagine, I began a rapid descent down the side of the tower. In the vicinity of the 40-foot level, I met the barrel coming up. This accounts for the two fractured ankles, and the lacerations of my legs and lower body.

The encounter with the barrel slowed me enough to lessen my injuries when I fell onto the pile of tools and, fortunately, only three vertebrae were cracked. I am sorry to report, however, that as I lay there on the tools, in pain, unable to stand and watching the empty barrel 80 feet above me, I again lost my presence of mind. I let go of the rope...

Chris and Kathy's perseverance in the parish of Holy Trinity was ended in rather a more civilised fashion than the poor radio operator. In 2004, while enjoying a regular one-to-one meeting with the Bishop of Liverpool, the Rt Rev James Jones, they were discussing the retirement of Rev Chris Byworth – a good friend – from St Helens Parish Church, when the Bishop abruptly stopped and said, "I don't know if this is just me, or the Lord, but I think you should take over". Immediately, Chris knew he was right.

A short time later, when he and Kathy were discussing the move further, they recalled that on arriving in Fingerpost back in 1979, Kathy had suggested that they would need to stay in the parish for a generation in order to have a real impact. The biblical definition of a generation is 25 years. And they realised to their astonishment that Bishop James' suggestion had come 25 years, to the month, after they had arrived at Holy Trinity.

Chris became Rector of the Parish Church in July 2005. In doing so, he added the honorary role of Canon of Liverpool Cathedral to his existing one as Area Dean of St Helens, which he had been performing for two years already. As Area Dean, Rector and Canon, he now had every opportunity to energise and optimise the town with his usual gusto. However, he deliberately decided not to surge into new plans and activities, but to have faith and hope in the Lord's plans instead.

This is not to say that he stopped ministering – far from it. Chris was always a great upholder of the Parable of the Sheep and the Goats in Matthew 25, where Jesus explains in no uncertain terms that failing to support the least and the lost – whether providing food for the hungry, water for the thirsty, shelter for the stranger, clothes for the naked, care for the sick, company for the imprisoned – will result in banishment from the Lord's presence and eternal damnation.

Chris often referred to Jackie Pullinger's concept of 'Soft Hearts and Hard Feet': the importance of being moved by compassion to come alongside people in their pain and suffering, and to suffer with them. He warned the middle-classes at New Wine and large wealthy churches like HTB that they risked having Hard Hearts and Soft Feet, too comfortable in their way of life and their introspective, occasionally elite and exclusive, cultures, to bother leaving the church to come alongside the least and the lost out in the community. He would quote a favourite poem by Amy Carmichael:

Hast thou no scar, no hidden scar on foot or side or hand?
I hear thee sung as mighty in the land
I hear them hail their bright ascendant star
Hast thou no scar?

Hast thou no wound?
Yet I was wounded by the archers, spent
Leaned me against the tree to die, and rend
By ravening beasts that compass me I swooned
Hast thou no wound?

No wound, no scar?
Yet as the master shall the servant be,
And pierced are the feet that follow me
But thine are whole
Can he have followed far who has no wound, no scar?

For his part, aside from the total immersion into the brokenness of Fingerpost life which he and Kathy had committed to, Chris had ensured that the SHINE network was running a food bank; he was Chaplain at Risley Prison (known as 'Grisly' for good reason), where – with Paul Cowley, a former inmate – he had established the Alpha Course for offenders; and he had also begun to consider how the Parish Church could be opened up, physically and spiritually, to the town centre around it – it seemed such a waste to have the large wooden doors closed to so many shoppers.

Indeed, it is important when we look at Chris's Energetic Optimism and see it being peeled away, that we do not allow all of his other remarkable gifts and successes to be invalidated. As we have seen, his vision, faith and inspirational leadership were great strengths throughout his ministry, which bore great fruit. In particular, his notable characteristic of releasing others into their ministries and taking little or no credit was a mark of his humility. This was often the gist of family conversation at the dinner table in later years, when talk turned to his legacy in St Helens: he just could not see how many lives and causes he had impacted, and this exacerbated his feeling of failure. This was precisely the nature of the wonderful, visionary 'door opening' quality that he had.

***

As Chris and Kathy established their ministry at the Parish Church from 2005, and with all the children now either away at school, university or work, Kathy began to get more directly involved in ministry herself. She used her Catholic connections to set up and lead a SHINE prayer group, accepted a number of invitations to speak at women's conferences about her experience of life and ministry in St Helens, and supported her husband in his popular New Wine seminars on perseverance.

Whatever the situation, Chris always had a tenacity and steadfast belief to expect that God had good things and big things planned for St Helens. His faith and hope was to see lives rescued and restored, communities transformed, and the Church renewed.

He continued to hope that his big vision for the town would come to fruition now that he was Rector. The idea was that an enormous blue warehouse in an industrial estate would be converted into a church. He called it the "Blue Cathedral". This fed directly into his vision for a spiritual revival in St Helens, with thousands of people coming to faith and coming to church from all over the town. He had faith that God would provide the resources – and the spiritual upheaval – to realise it. And yet, like the Old Testament leaders cited by the author of the Epistle to the Hebrews, he did not receive the things promised, and was still living by faith when he died just two years later.

Dietrich Bonhoeffer, in *The Cost of Discipleship* (SCM Press, 2009), explains that when Jesus invites the rich young man to give away all of his possessions and follow him, he does it so that the man has an opportunity to have faith in him. The point is the faith itself, the hope that lies in fellowship with Jesus, not the dogmatic adherence to giving everything away. "In the last resort what matters is not what a man *does,* but only his faith in Jesus…everything depends on faith alone."

In his address to the thousands gathered in the conference hall at New Wine in 2005, Chris reflected that the key to his ministry was his obedience to, and faith in, God's call on his life:

> *I don't know what's going to happen after our 26 years in that place. We've seen blessing, disaster, blessing again, more disasters. I don't know what the final thing is going to be – but all I know is that I do believe that it has washed the Lord's feet, and it has*

> *blessed Him, whatever it might have done to the people around us and ourselves, and in fact we have felt blessed, we have felt fulfilled in doing it.*

Despite all of the ups and downs, it had been, as his grandfather Edward once wrote, a life worth living.

Canon Christopher Samuel Woods
Died December 10th 2007
Beloved husband and father
of five devoted children
Faithful Servant of the
Liverpool Diocese

EPILOGUE

Dad was buried on Saturday 22nd December 2007 – the day after the funeral at Liverpool Cathedral – in the snow-flecked cemetery of St James's church, at Hutton-in-the-Forest in Cumbria. It was a short walk from the small cottage that he and Mum had been renting for a few years from friends Richard and Cressida Vane (Lord and Lady Inglewood), thanks to generous financial support from various family members. Only a few months earlier, while walking through the cemetery on a stroll, Dad had remarked to Mum and Lydia that it would be a lovely place to be buried. With characteristic kindness, the Inglewoods provided a beautiful spot for him at the foot of a mighty Scots pine tree.

His gravestone, made of pink Cumbrian sandstone, bears the epitaph: 'Messiah's Handle'. This derives from a conference he had attended with Bob Hopkins, where they were seated at the back of the auditorium. Towards the end of the evening, the speaker – a man they had never met – announced, "There's a man here with a handlebar moustache..." (that's Bob, who proceeded to stand a little nervously). The speaker continued:

> *This has never happened to me before. I have had a vision and I saw trees, forest...woods, woods...no, not woods, it's a man. Is there a man here by the name of Woods? Christopher Woods?* [The two of them were now standing nervously together.] *You two are connected somehow, something to do with the Trinity, is that right?*
>
> *This is what I believe the Lord is saying to you, Christopher: 'Because you would rather be Messiah's handle than Handel's Messiah, I will richly bless you.'*

***

The alternative epitaph could well have been 'Mr Wonderful' – Dad was quite fond of this 1955 Peggy Lee tune, which includes lyrics such as 'Why this feeling? Why this glow? / Why the thrill when you say hello? / It's a strange and tender magic you do / Mister Wonderful, that's you.' Except in Dad's version, he just sang "Mr Wonderful, THAT'S ME" at the top of his voice, to a chorus of disapproval from around the Vicarage. It was particularly infuriating when he sang it during our epic games of Trivial Pursuit, which he always won, deploying his vast general knowledge to ruthless effect against wife and children, right index finger raised in salute whenever fiendishly obscure questions were answered.

Sadly, Mr Wonderful never got to meet any of his grandchildren. Madeline's children refer to him in absentia as "Grandpa Kik". Now I have a child of my own (a son, Josiah Christopher John), born halfway through the writing of this memoir, it has reawakened some of the grief lain dormant with time over the last decade – a grief at the loss of my own father and mentor, a heroic figure made all the stronger for his weakness, a man who did so much good with so little worldly reward and yet still felt as though he should have done more. He would have been an inspirational example to his grandson. And although I began researching and writing this book a long time before Emma and I started a family, I can now see that much of its value will be in providing Josiah with a picture of who my father was – and, perhaps more importantly, what he lived for.

It is inevitable that one day Josiah will ask me about Grandpa Kik, and I will attempt to explain his legacy – it will probably be a few years before I can say, "Just read the book". From a family perspective, his legacy was immense. Together with Mum, he created an incredibly close-knit, affectionate, boisterous and relatively functional ensemble of children. We can of course be dysfunctional with the best of them, and it is a miracle none of our prospective spouses ran a mile at the first rumblings of a dinner debate: these are marked by a series of circular, unsubstantiated arguments being added to each other in ascending volume and pitch, like a Shepard Tone, until finally a wine glass shatters or somebody cries. Five minutes later, everyone is laughing uproariously. Our father's DNA is clear in these moments.

His DNA is also clear in the career paths we chose: Isabella as a singer and editor; Madeline training for ordination; my work in Africa and elsewhere; Thomas working in politics and journalism; and Lydia's vocation as a music tutor – including running singing workshops at Her Majesty's Prison in Northumberland.

At the funeral, cousin Robert Woods read an excerpt from *The Pilgrim's Progress* – a Woods staple – which, in the character of Mr Valiant-for-Truth, we felt reflected the manner in which Dad would have faced his own death and legacy as he lay dying in his hospital bed:

> *Then said he, 'I am going to my Father's; and though with great difficulty I have got hither, yet now I do not repent me of all the trouble I have been at to arrive where I am. My sword I give to him that shall succeed me in my pilgrimage, and my courage and skill to him that can get it. My marks and scars I carry with me, to be a witness for me that I have fought His battles who will now be my rewarder.' When the day that he must go hence was come, many accompanied him to the river-side, into which as he went, he said, 'Death, where is thy sting?' And as he went down deeper, he said, 'Grave, where is thy victory?' So he passed over, and all the trumpets sounded for him on the other side.* [Wordsworth Editions, 1996]

***

The legacy of a clergyman's ministry is much more complex, as we have seen. Do we even know what a truly Christian view of success looks like?

Take the eight Beatitudes which Jesus proclaimed in his Sermon on the Mount overlooking the Sea of Galilee – blessed are: the poor in spirit; those who mourn; the meek; those who hunger and thirst for righteousness; the merciful; the pure of heart; the peacemakers; and the persecuted. None of these things is easily quantifiable.

Take the Prayer of St Francis, where he asks the Lord to help him sow love, pardon, faith, hope, light, joy, consolation, understanding, and love. How does one measure that?

Take the Fruits of the Spirit that St Paul lists in his letter to the church in Galatia: love, joy, peace, forbearance, kindness, goodness, faithfulness, gentleness and self-control. If these are Christian Key Performance Indicators, then it remains almost impossible to predict how any of us is scoring on the great heavenly leader board.

And so we return to the heart of the message of the Prodigal Son: calling, obedience, humility, and faith. And on these KPIs, Dad scored very highly indeed. He heeded the call on the road to Otaki, he remained true to that calling until the day he died, and he remained true to himself throughout.

There is a poem, often read out at funerals, entitled 'The Measure of a Man'. In this, the anonymous author seeks to define a man's legacy beyond the usual human metrics:

Not how did he die, but how did he live?
Not what did he gain, but what did he give?
These are the units to measure the worth
Of a man as a man, regardless of birth.

Not what was his church, nor what was his creed?
But had he befriended those really in need?
Was he ever ready, with word of good cheer,
To bring back a smile, to banish a tear?

Not what did the words in the newspapers say
But how many were sad when he passed away.
This was a man, a father, a friend,
A man who loved life and is loved without end.

I was reminded of this when speaking with Rev Mark Melluish, Vicar of St Mark's, Ealing, who had worked with Dad at New Wine and provided strong competition for naughty limericks at Hippos gatherings. I bumped into Mark at New Wine in 2014, and he began to get rather teary at the memory of his old friend. He explained that when the Hippos convened in 2008, for the first time after Dad passed away, they sat around talking about him and comparing stories – and it was only then that they realised they all had tales of turning to him for help and support. He was the one they all went to when they needed advice and guidance, ever ready with words of good cheer, bringing back smiles and banishing tears.

The fact that he never really understood or acknowledged his own importance to the network of clergy he encouraged over the years was noted by Rev Tom Gillum in his funeral tribute:

> *Kik found it difficult to accept how much he had inspired the many green young ordinands who, during training, spent time with him in Gasworks View Vicarage at Fingerpost. His and Kathy's example of living and staying put through thick and thin in what was most evidently not their natural métier opened my and many other eyes to a way of ministry which breaks down human divides and which shines as a beacon of hope in our inner cities.*
>
> *He taught me more than anyone else has about the paradox which lies at the heart of the Christian faith – divine strength in human weakness. He identified himself as an 'energetic optimist' who, if not trained in the ways of 'faith and hope' would stand in the way of the much more creative life of God.*
>
> *One hallmark was laughter, flowing from a deep joy, inspiring a confidence in Jesus Christ's dynamic working today, however unpromising the outward circumstances might appear. Another was patient listening...And perhaps above all, it was his vulnerability and openness which allowed us to come close, as he laid himself open and laid bare his heart, to taste something of the power of the Christ-like way of self-giving love.*

Tom touched on one of the key aspects of Dad's legacy: strength in weakness. As Bob Hopkins has said, "It is not that he was some sort of faultless superhero, but it's precisely because he was so human and real that his strengths were so powerful." It was this humanity which allowed him to break down human divides and connect with people from all backgrounds.

Another clergyman, Rev Paul Cowley, who led Alpha in prisons with Dad, has said that he "smelled of the sheep". It is a wonderful symbol of the devoted, down-to-earth service that Dad – and Mum – gave to the people of Merseyside, and beyond, for thirty years. They were shepherd and shepherdess together. Justin Welby captured the importance of this partnership in his sermon at the funeral:

> *I am sure that there would be a hundred other tributes here, from individuals touched by his concern and pastoral care and patience, to friends mourning the passing of such a source of fun and laughter, to fellow clergy inspired by his vision and direction and faith, and by his capacity to see the absurd and laugh, his lack of pomposity – it's hard to imagine a less pompous man – and so on and so on. The Maori saying, 'A mighty tree has fallen', sums up many of the things that we feel, and that bring us here with such a torturing mixture of thanks and loss.*
>
> *And then everyone has spoken of your wonderful ministry together. Those of us who had the privilege of staying with you on placement from training saw that very clearly. Family was real, welcome was unstinting, there was a bit to drink, well quite a bit, the pace was measured, especially when Wimbledon was on, but the commitment and dedication and openness to God were contagious. That wonderful teamwork was from both of you, equally.*

Clearly Dad's gift of enabling and encouraging was a fundamental part of his legacy. He was the unwitting inspiration and support for so many who got to know him, people who were blessed through a combination of vision, joy, and releasing into their full potential. An individual's legacy is normally attached to themselves in some way – the number of goals scored by a footballer, the rulings passed by a judge, the books written by an author – but Dad's legacy was attached to other people, who got to know him throughout his ministry and who he helped to flourish through his leadership and guidance. He didn't even realise he was doing it, and this unconscious empowering of those around him almost certainly contributed to his own lack of appreciation for the extraordinary impact of his life's ministry.

He was an opener of doors, standing in the narthex alone and wondering what he had achieved in life – when his legacy was all the people standing in the sanctuary on the other side.

His legacy may not have been a big, successful church, but there are many who, like Cath Kirkham, can say, "We would never be where we are today without him". Even locals in Fingerpost have been overheard saying that the church is not the same as when Chris Woods was there. Bob says, "His focus on the local has affected the global. Already, things have gone way beyond what Chris had seen, way beyond what any of us will see, and they continue to go on beyond." Twenty-five years of a life and ministry laid down at Fingerpost, a place that is unknown outside St Helens, have resulted in his very own Butterfly Effect, the ripples of which are as profound as any of those generated by his more famous clergy forebears.

***

Perhaps the best summary of Dad's legacy I can give to Josiah is that which Dad himself gave to Madeline in 2006 when, with her father's directness, she asked him what he thought his life's work was all about. He paused, sighed, and said, "Mad, I'm just washing Jesus' feet."

He was not ministering for an audience of hundreds, but for an audience of one. Despite all of his abilities, achievements and larger-than-life character, he laid down his glory like Mary and her perfume – and as with her, his service was costly and humbling. But as Madeline says, "Perhaps Dad spent most of his time looking down at the floor, at Jesus' feet, but all the time Jesus was looking directly at him."

He was an inspirational husband, father and friend, a devoted servant, a selfless opener of doors – Messiah's Handle.